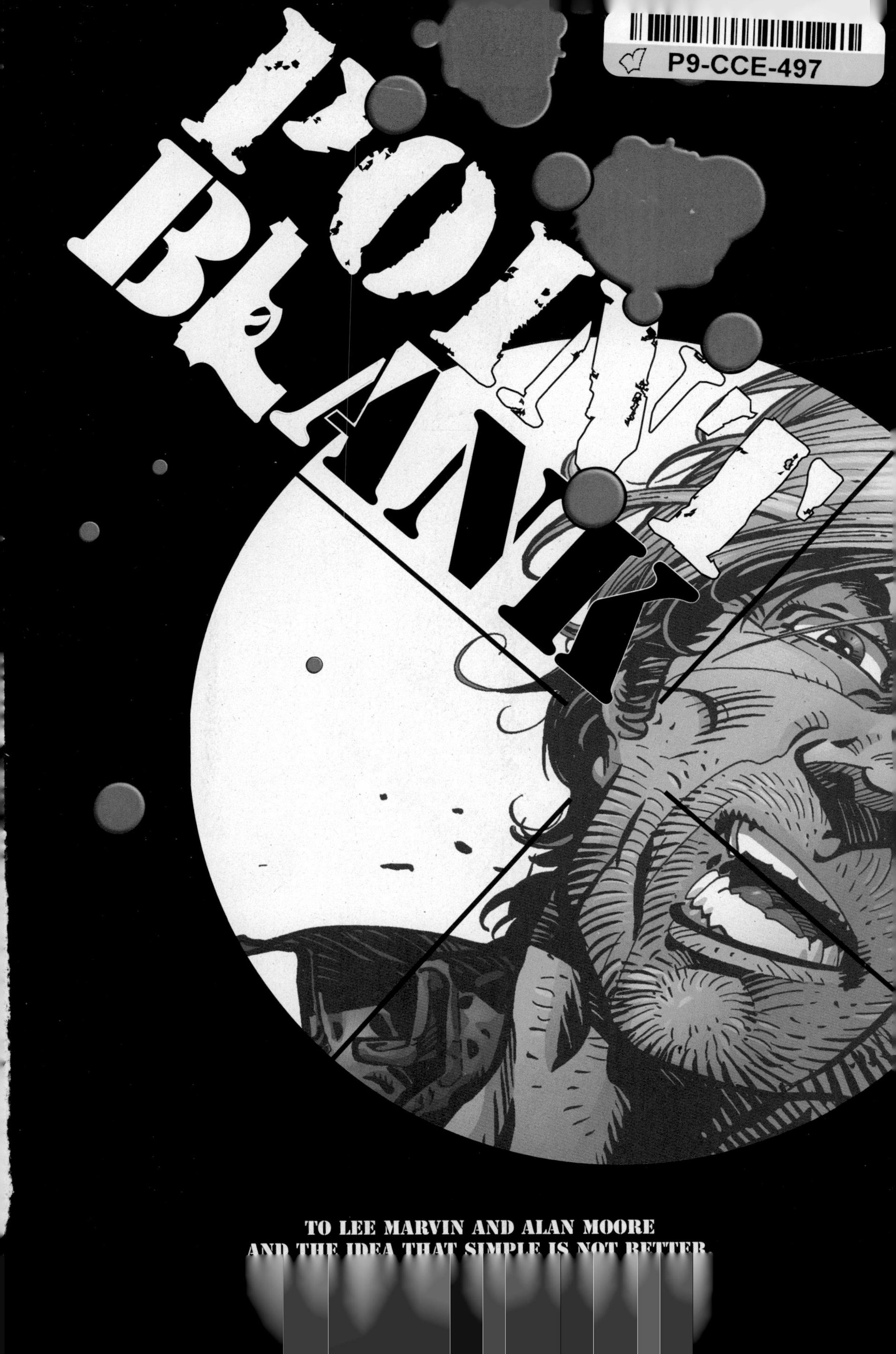
POINT
BLANK

TO LEE MARVIN AND ALAN MOORE
AND THE IDEA THAT SIMPLE IS NOT BETTER.

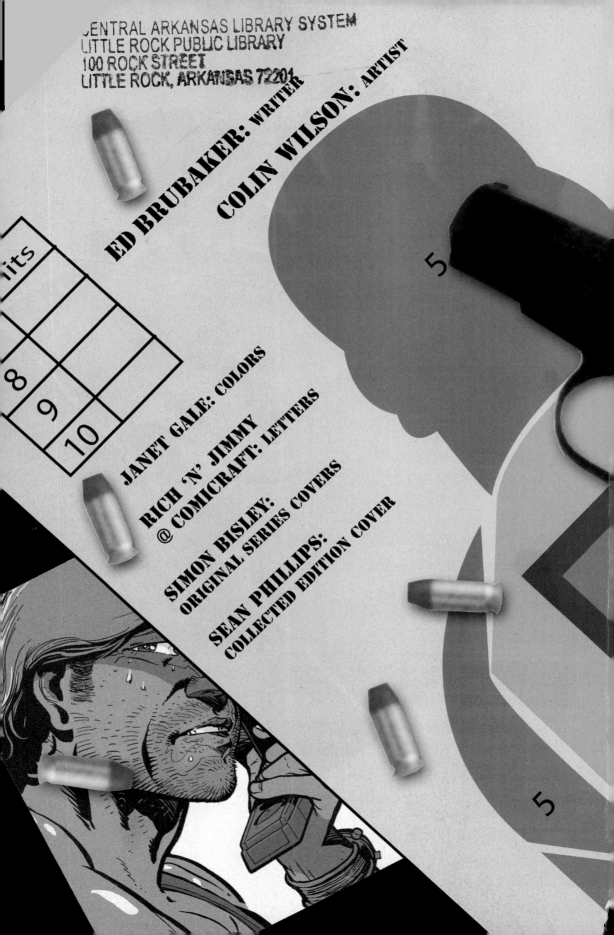

ED BRUBAKER: WRITER

COLIN WILSON: ARTIST

JANET GALE: COLORS

RICH 'N' JIMMY @ COMICRAFT: LETTERS

SIMON BISLEY: ORIGINAL SERIES COVERS

SEAN PHILLIPS: COLLECTED EDITION COVER

LARRY BERRY: DESIGN

COLIN WILSON:
TITLE PAGE ART

Jim Lee, Editorial Director • John Nee, VP & General Manager • Scott Dunbier, Group Editor
Scott Dunbier Editor—Original Series • Kristy Quinn, Editor—Collected Edition • Robbin Brosterman, Senior Art Director
Ed Roeder, Art Director • Paul Levitz, President & Publisher • Georg Brewer, VP—Design & Retail Product Development
Richard Bruning, Senior VP—Creative Director • Patrick Caldon, Senior VP—Finance & Operations
Chris Caramalis, VP—Finance • Terri Cunningham, VP—Managing Editor • Dan DiDio, VP—Editorial
Alison Gill, VP—Manufacturing • Rich Johnson, VP—Book Trade Sales • Hank Kanalz, VP—General Manager, WildStorm
Lillian Laserson, Senior VP & General Counsel
David McKillips, VP—Advertising & Custom Publishing
Cheryl Rubin, VP—Brand Management • Bob Wayne, VP—Sales & Marketing

POINT BLANK published by WildStorm Productions, 888 Prospect St.
#240, La Jolla, CA 92037. Compilation Copyright © 2009.
Copyright © 2009 WildStorm Productions, an imprint of DC Comics,
Rights Reserved. WildStorm and logo, POINT BLANK, all characters, the
distinctive likenesses thereof and all related elements are trademarks of
DC Comics. Originally published in single magazine form as POINT
BLANK #1-5. © 2002, 2003 DC Comics. The stories, characters, and
incidents mentioned in this magazine are entirely fictional. Printed on
recyclable paper. WildStorm does not read or accept unsolicited
submissions of ideas, stories or artwork. Printed in Canada. Second Printing
DC Comics, a Warner Bros. Entertainment Company.
ISBN: 978-1-4012-0116-6

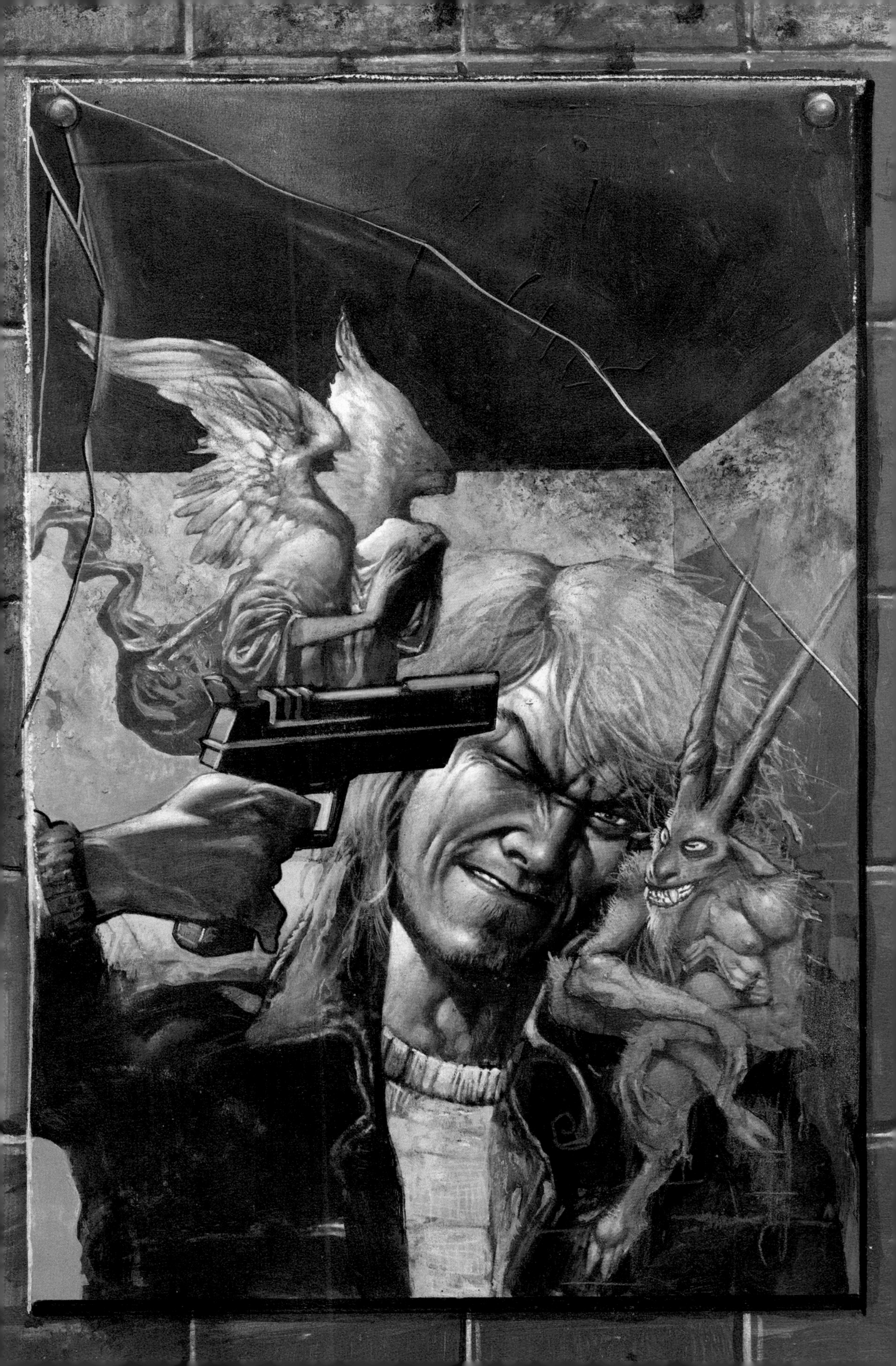

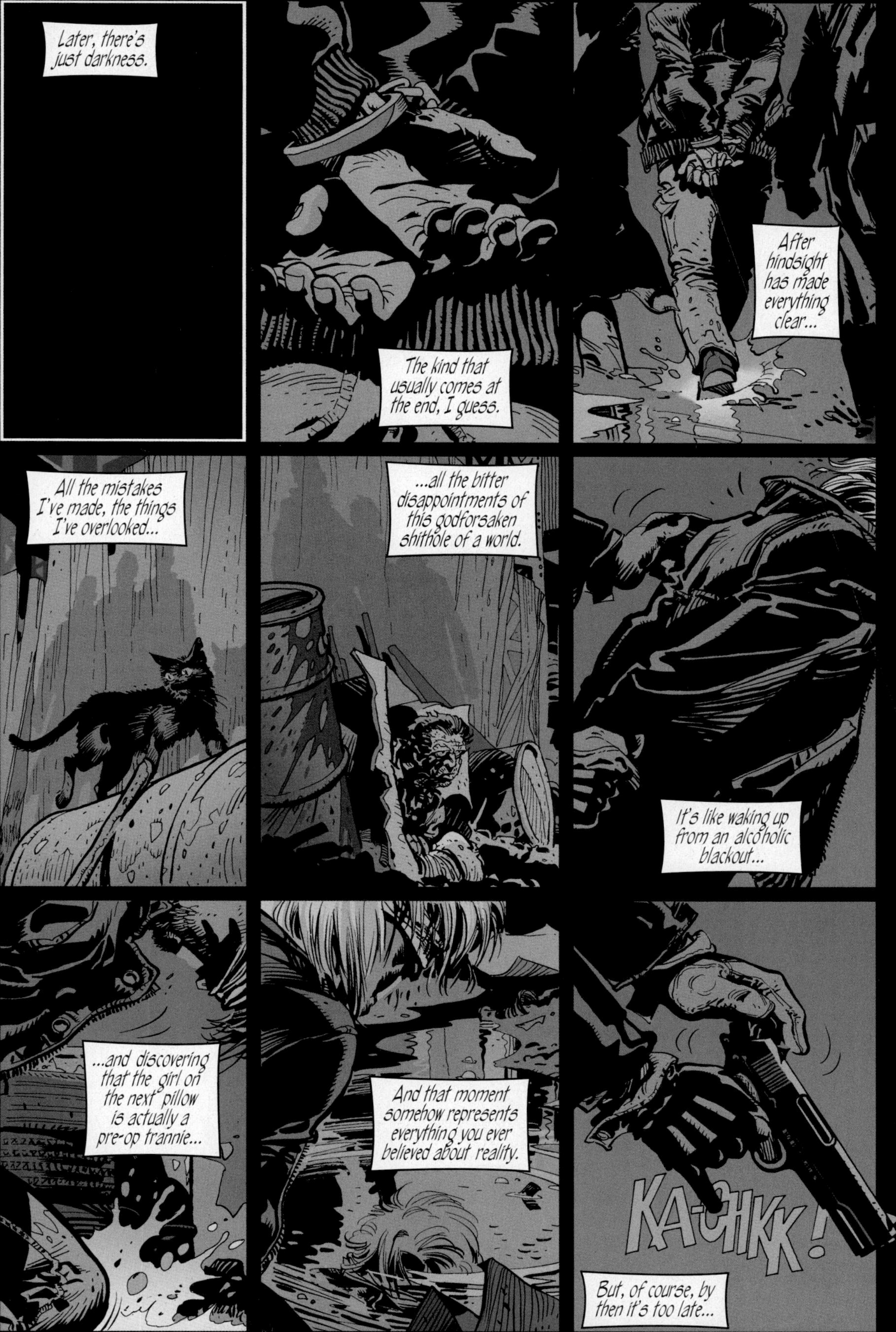
Later, there's just darkness.
The kind that usually comes at the end, I guess.
After hindsight has made everything clear...
All the mistakes I've made, the things I've overlooked...
...all the bitter disappointments of this godforsaken shithole of a world.
It's like waking up from an alcoholic blackout...
...and discovering that the girl on the next pillow is actually a pre-op trannie...
And that moment somehow represents everything you ever believed about reality.
KA-CHKK!
But, of course, by then it's too late...

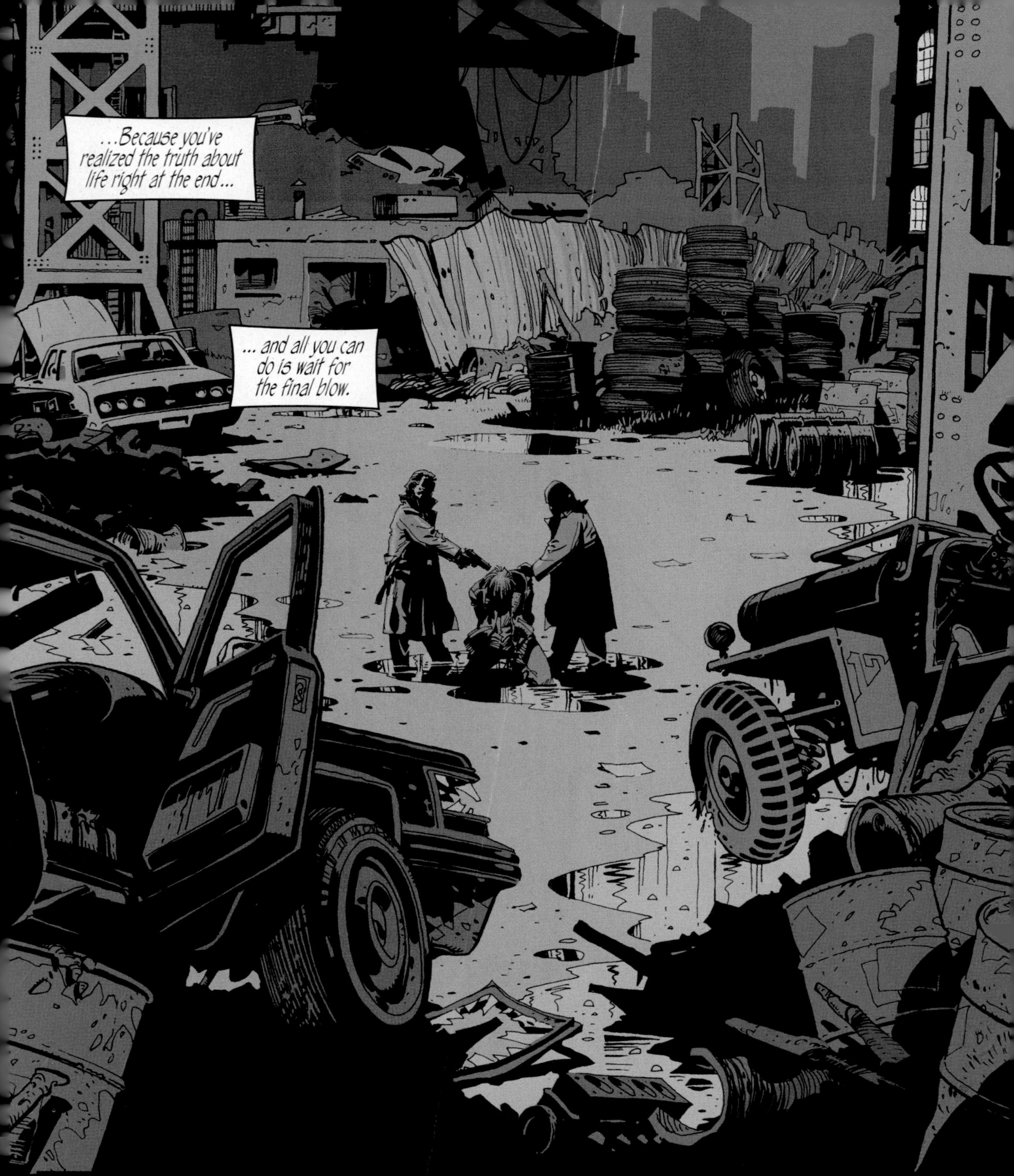
...Because you've realized the truth about life right at the end...
... and all you can do is wait for the final blow.
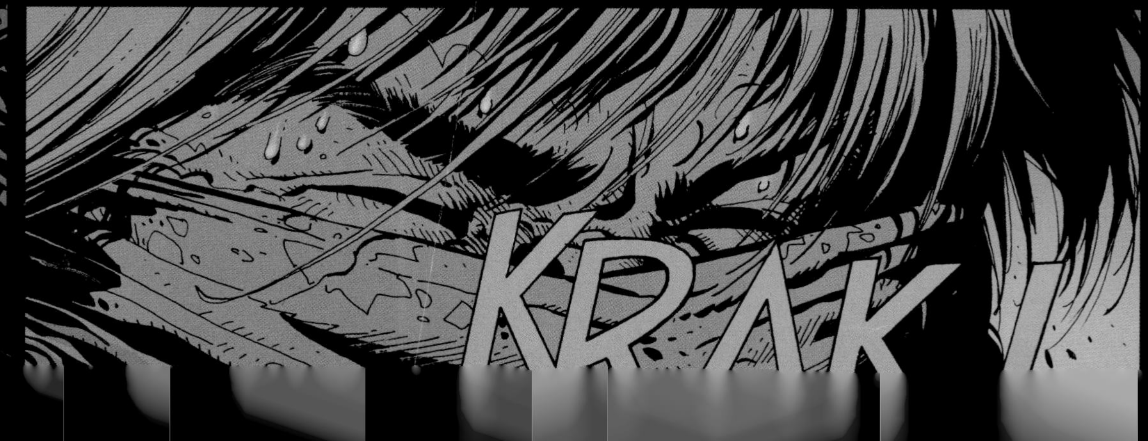
KRAK

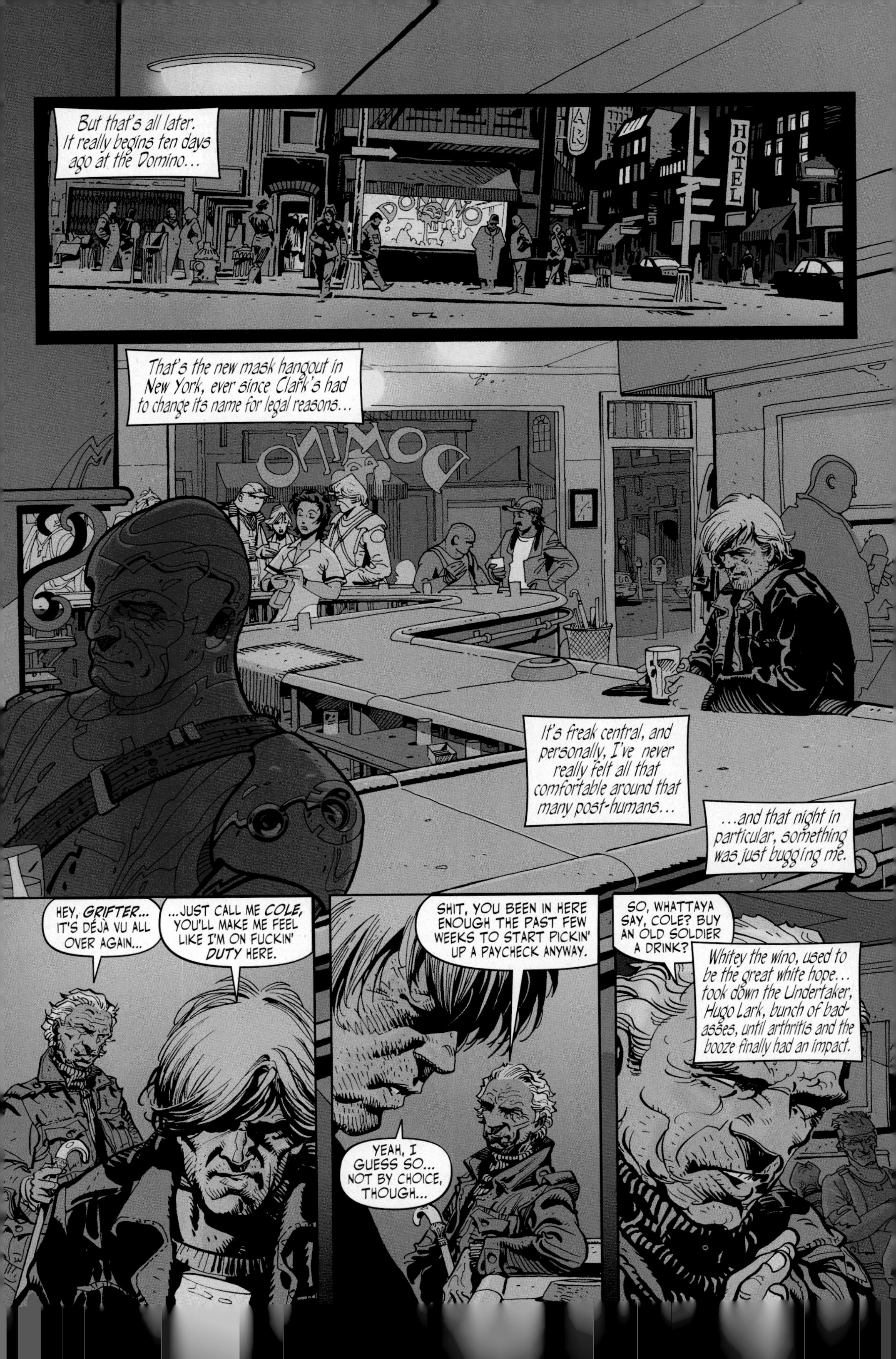

But that's all later. It really begins ten days ago at the Domino...
HOTEL
DOMINO
That's the new mask hangout in New York, ever since Clark's had to change its name for legal reasons...
It's freak central, and personally, I've never really felt all that comfortable around that many post-humans...
...and that night in particular, something was just bugging me.
HEY, GRIFTER... IT'S DÉJÀ VU ALL OVER AGAIN...
...JUST CALL ME COLE, YOU'LL MAKE ME FEEL LIKE I'M ON FUCKIN' DUTY HERE.
SHIT, YOU BEEN IN HERE ENOUGH THE PAST FEW WEEKS TO START PICKIN' UP A PAYCHECK ANYWAY.
YEAH, I GUESS SO... NOT BY CHOICE, THOUGH...
SO, WHATTAYA SAY, COLE? BUY AN OLD SOLDIER A DRINK?
Whitey the wino, used to be the great white hope... took down the Undertaker, Hugo Lark, bunch of bad-asses, until arthritis and the booze finally had an impact.

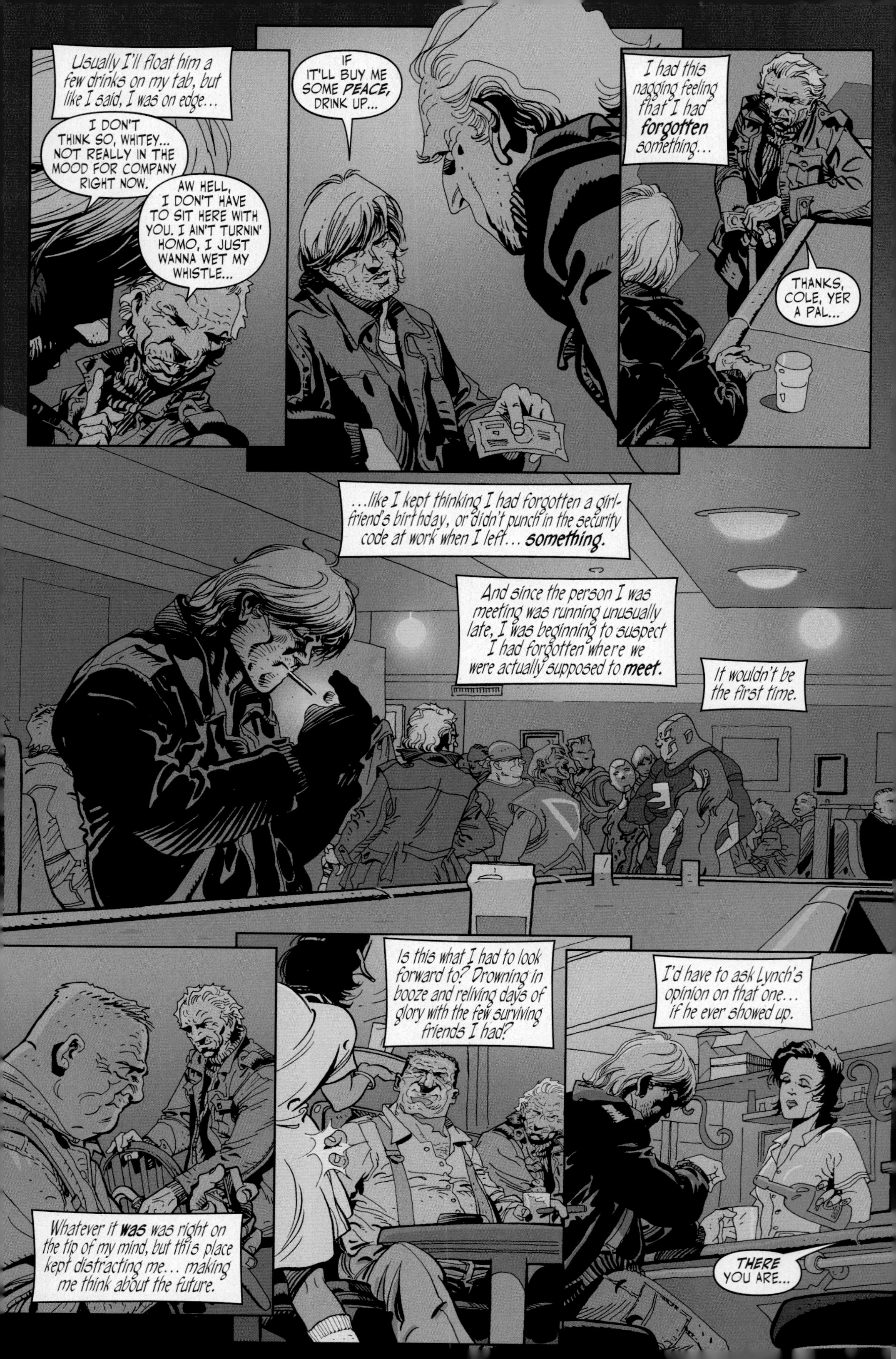

Usually I'll float him a few drinks on my tab, but like I said, I was on edge...
I DON'T THINK SO, WHITEY... NOT REALLY IN THE MOOD FOR COMPANY RIGHT NOW.
AW HELL, I DON'T HAVE TO SIT HERE WITH YOU. I AIN'T TURNIN' HOMO, I JUST WANNA WET MY WHISTLE...
IF IT'LL BUY ME SOME PEACE, DRINK UP...
I had this nagging feeling that I had forgotten something...
THANKS, COLE, YER A PAL...
...like I kept thinking I had forgotten a girl-friend's birthday, or didn't punch in the security code at work when I left... something.
And since the person I was meeting was running unusually late, I was beginning to suspect I had forgotten where we were actually supposed to meet.
It wouldn't be the first time.
Whatever it was was right on the tip of my mind, but this place kept distracting me... making me think about the future.
Is this what I had to look forward to? Drowning in booze and reliving days of glory with the few surviving friends I had?
I'd have to ask Lynch's opinion on that one... if he ever showed up.
THERE YOU ARE...

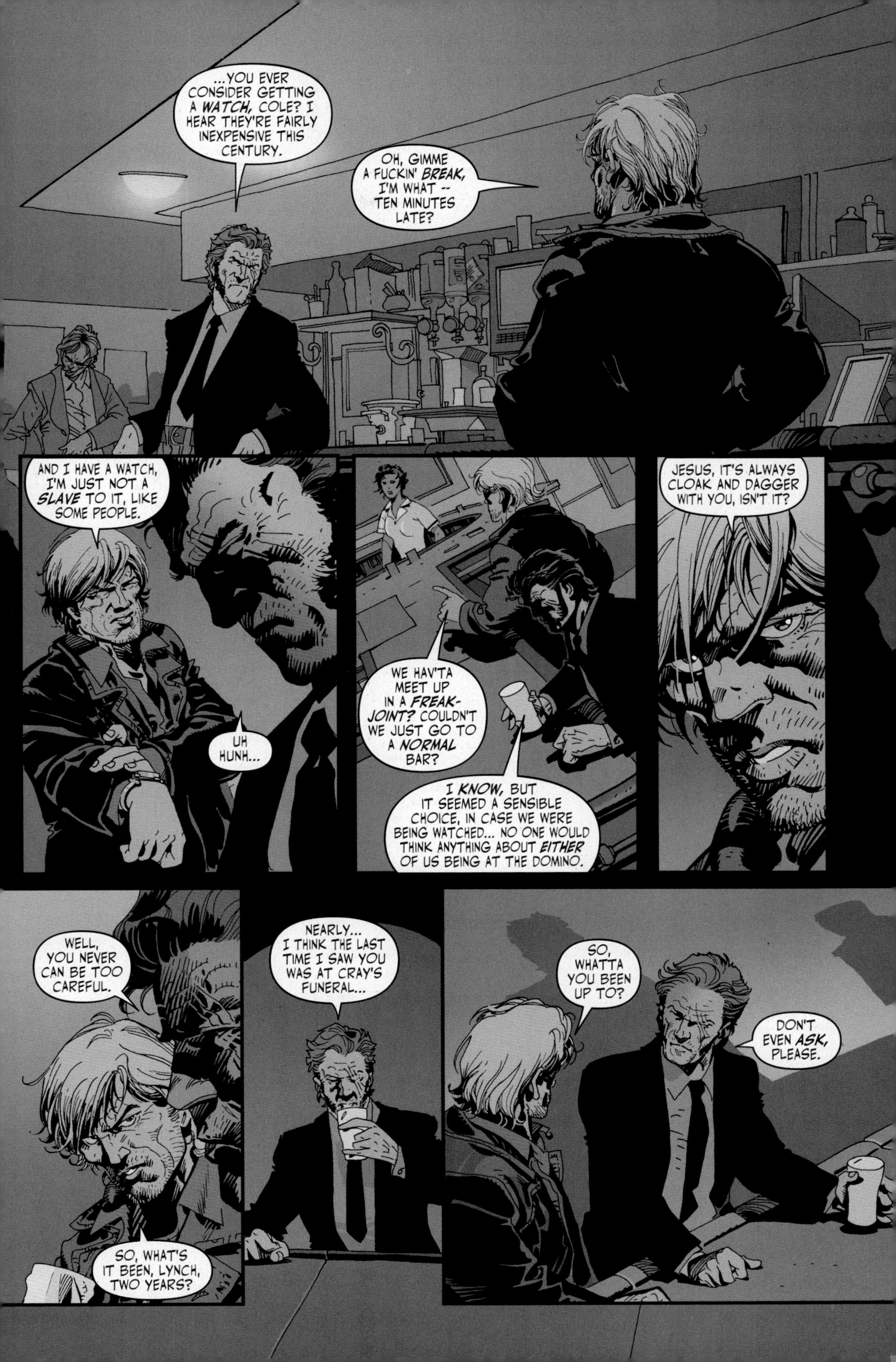
...YOU EVER CONSIDER GETTING A WATCH, COLE? I HEAR THEY'RE FAIRLY INEXPENSIVE THIS CENTURY.
OH, GIMME A FUCKIN' BREAK, I'M WHAT -- TEN MINUTES LATE?
AND I HAVE A WATCH, I'M JUST NOT A SLAVE TO IT, LIKE SOME PEOPLE.
UH HUNH...
WE HAV'TA MEET UP IN A FREAK-JOINT? COULDN'T WE JUST GO TO A NORMAL BAR?
I KNOW, BUT IT SEEMED A SENSIBLE CHOICE, IN CASE WE WERE BEING WATCHED... NO ONE WOULD THINK ANYTHING ABOUT EITHER OF US BEING AT THE DOMINO.
JESUS, IT'S ALWAYS CLOAK AND DAGGER WITH YOU, ISN'T IT?
WELL, YOU NEVER CAN BE TOO CAREFUL.
SO, WHAT'S IT BEEN, LYNCH, TWO YEARS?
NEARLY... I THINK THE LAST TIME I SAW YOU WAS AT CRAY'S FUNERAL...
SO, WHATTA YOU BEEN UP TO?
DON'T EVEN ASK, PLEASE.

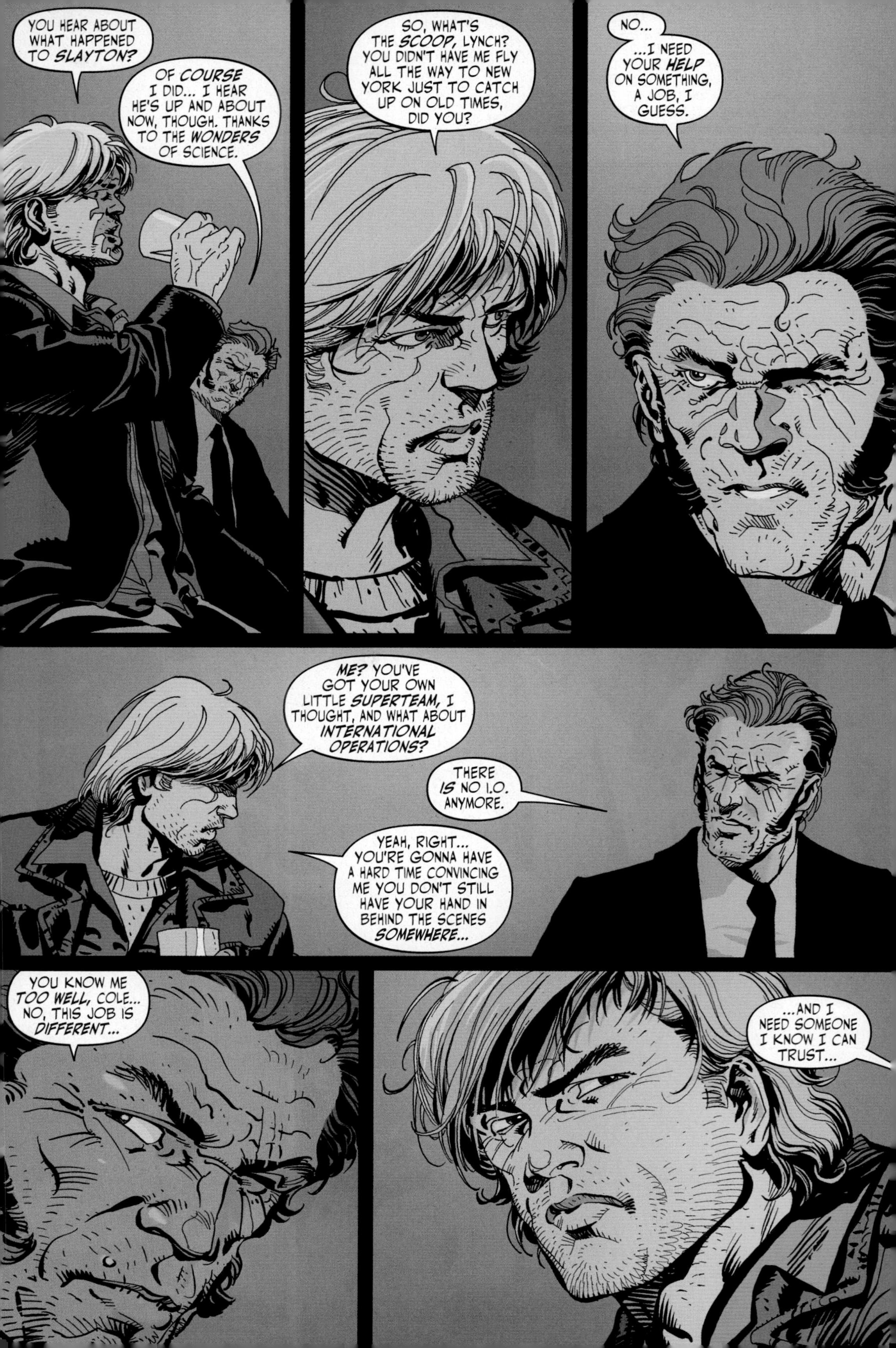
YOU HEAR ABOUT WHAT HAPPENED TO SLAYTON?
OF COURSE I DID... I HEAR HE'S UP AND ABOUT NOW, THOUGH. THANKS TO THE WONDERS OF SCIENCE.
SO, WHAT'S THE SCOOP, LYNCH? YOU DIDN'T HAVE ME FLY ALL THE WAY TO NEW YORK JUST TO CATCH UP ON OLD TIMES, DID YOU?
NO...
...I NEED YOUR HELP ON SOMETHING, A JOB, I GUESS.
ME? YOU'VE GOT YOUR OWN LITTLE SUPERTEAM, I THOUGHT, AND WHAT ABOUT INTERNATIONAL OPERATIONS?
THERE IS NO I.O. ANYMORE.
YEAH, RIGHT... YOU'RE GONNA HAVE A HARD TIME CONVINCING ME YOU DON'T STILL HAVE YOUR HAND IN BEHIND THE SCENES SOMEWHERE...
YOU KNOW ME TOO WELL, COLE... NO, THIS JOB IS DIFFERENT...
...AND I NEED SOMEONE I KNOW I CAN TRUST...

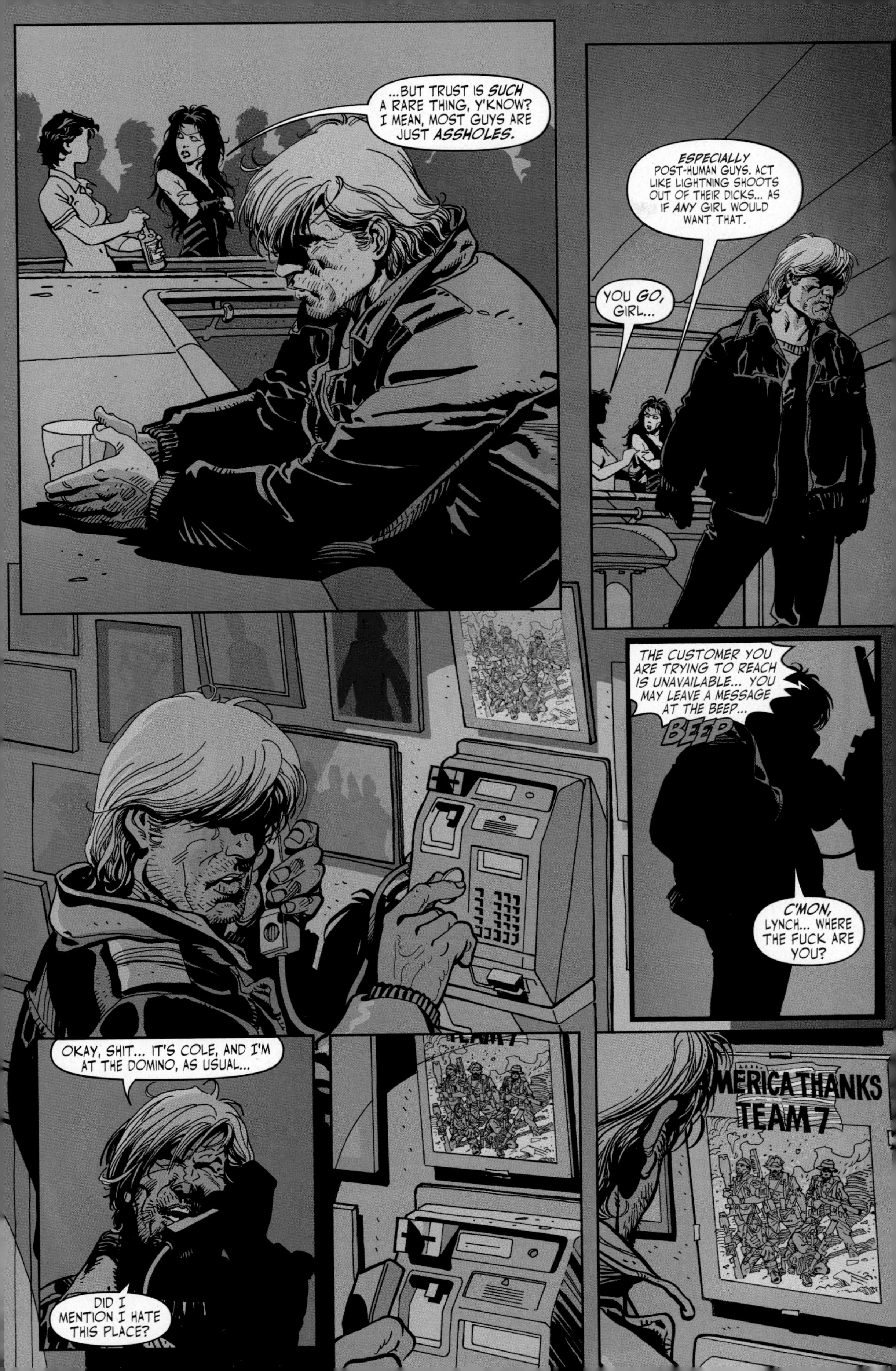
...BUT TRUST IS SUCH A RARE THING, Y'KNOW? I MEAN, MOST GUYS ARE JUST ASSHOLES.
ESPECIALLY POST-HUMAN GUYS. ACT LIKE LIGHTNING SHOOTS OUT OF THEIR DICKS... AS IF ANY GIRL WOULD WANT THAT.
YOU GO, GIRL...
THE CUSTOMER YOU ARE TRYING TO REACH IS UNAVAILABLE... YOU MAY LEAVE A MESSAGE AT THE BEEP...
BEEP
C'MON, LYNCH... WHERE THE FUCK ARE YOU?
OKAY, SHIT... IT'S COLE, AND I'M AT THE DOMINO, AS USUAL...
DID I MENTION I HATE THIS PLACE?
AMERICA THANKS TEAM 7

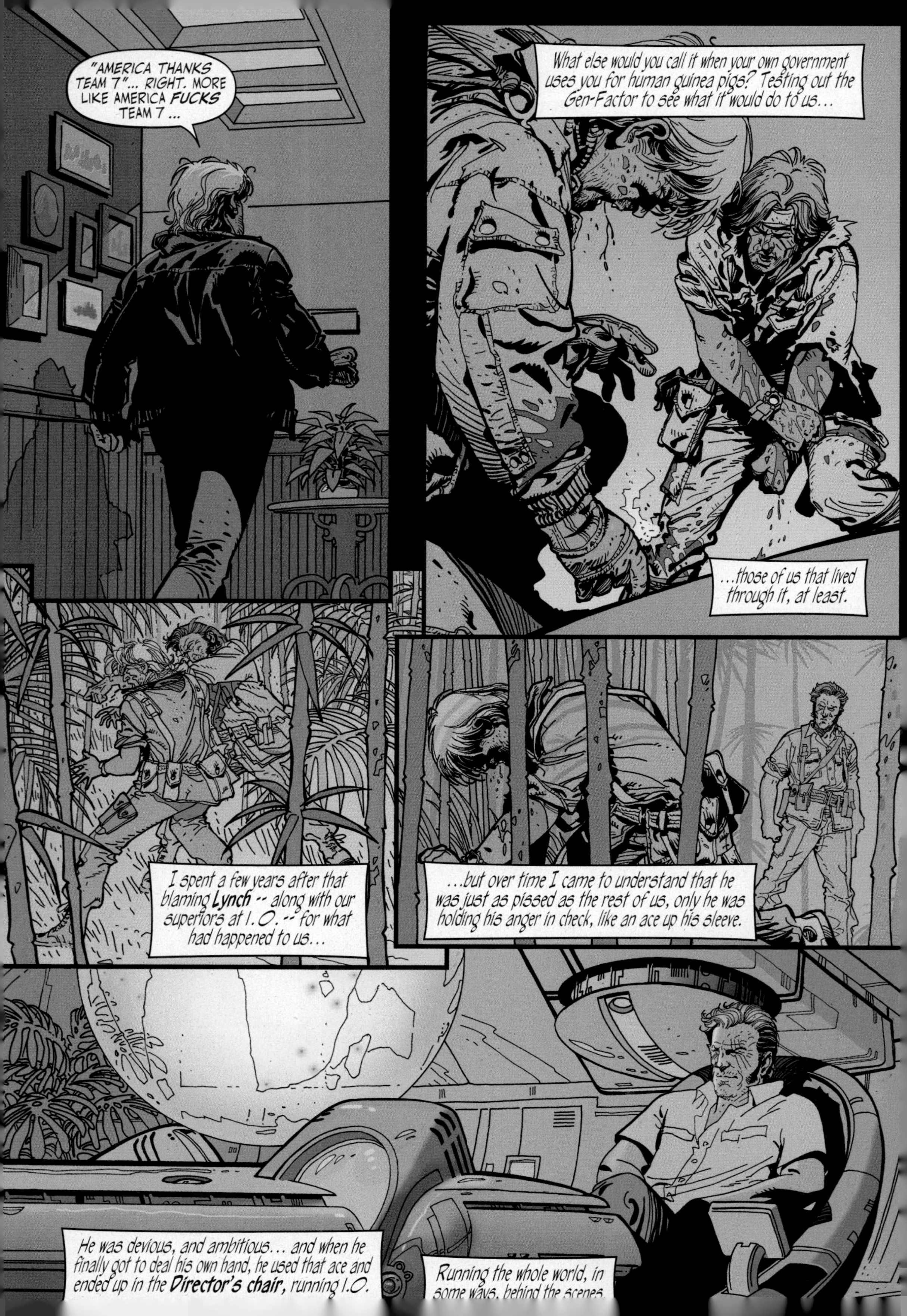
"AMERICA THANKS TEAM 7"... RIGHT. MORE LIKE AMERICA FUCKS TEAM 7 ...
What else would you call it when your own government uses you for human guinea pigs? Testing out the Gen-Factor to see what it would do to us...
...those of us that lived through it, at least.
I spent a few years after that blaming Lynch -- along with our superiors at I.O. -- for what had happened to us...
...but over time I came to understand that he was just as pissed as the rest of us, only he was holding his anger in check, like an ace up his sleeve.
He was devious, and ambitious... and when he finally got to deal his own hand, he used that ace and ended up in the Director's chair, running I.O.
Running the whole world, in some ways, behind the scenes.

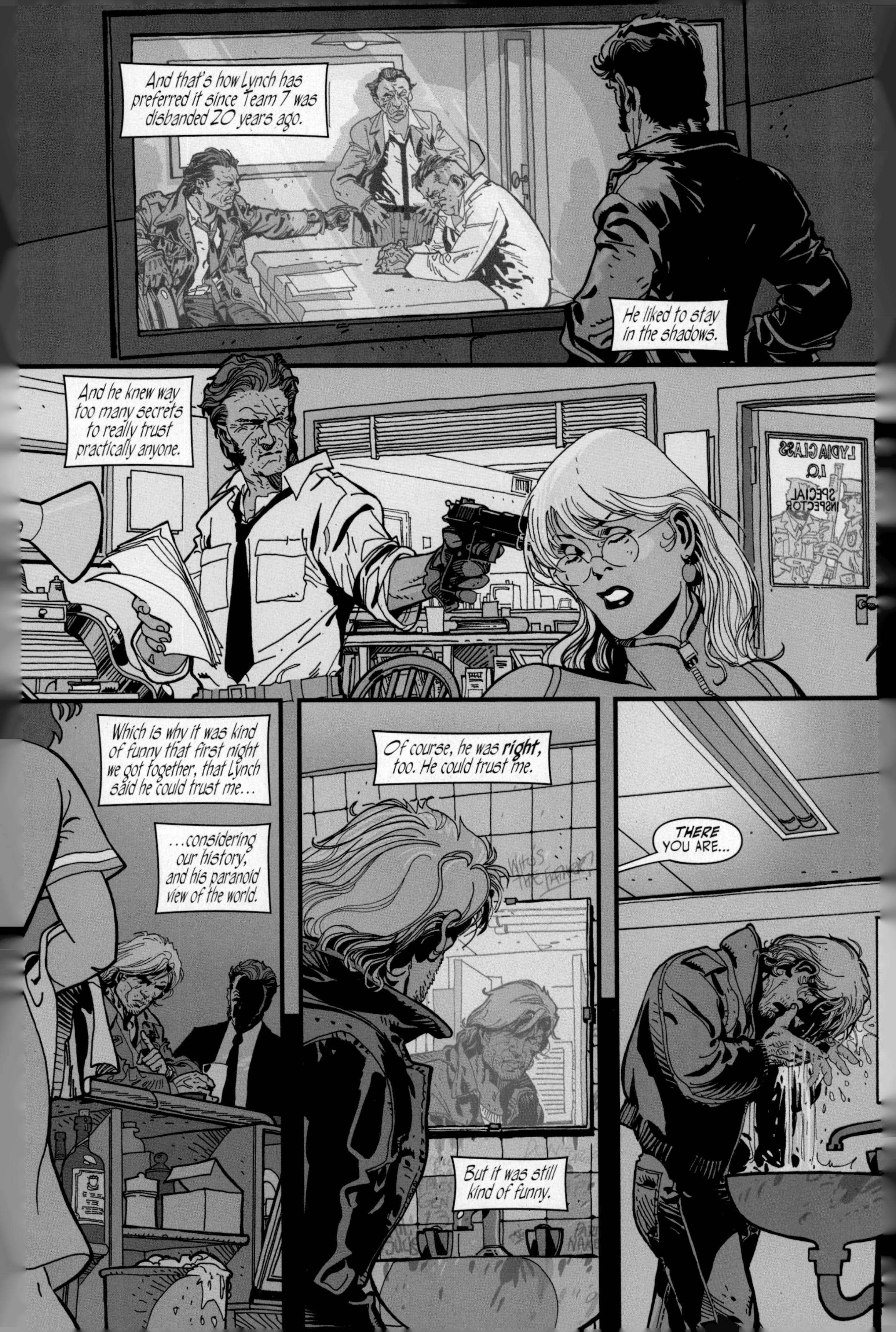

And that's how Lynch has preferred it since Team 7 was disbanded 20 years ago.
He liked to stay in the shadows.
And he knew way too many secrets to really trust practically anyone.
LYDIA GLASS
I.Q.
SPECIAL INSPECTOR
Which is why it was kind of funny that first night we got together, that Lynch said he could trust me...
...considering our history, and his paranoid view of the world.
Of course, he was **right**, too. He could trust me.
But it was still kind of funny.
THERE YOU ARE...

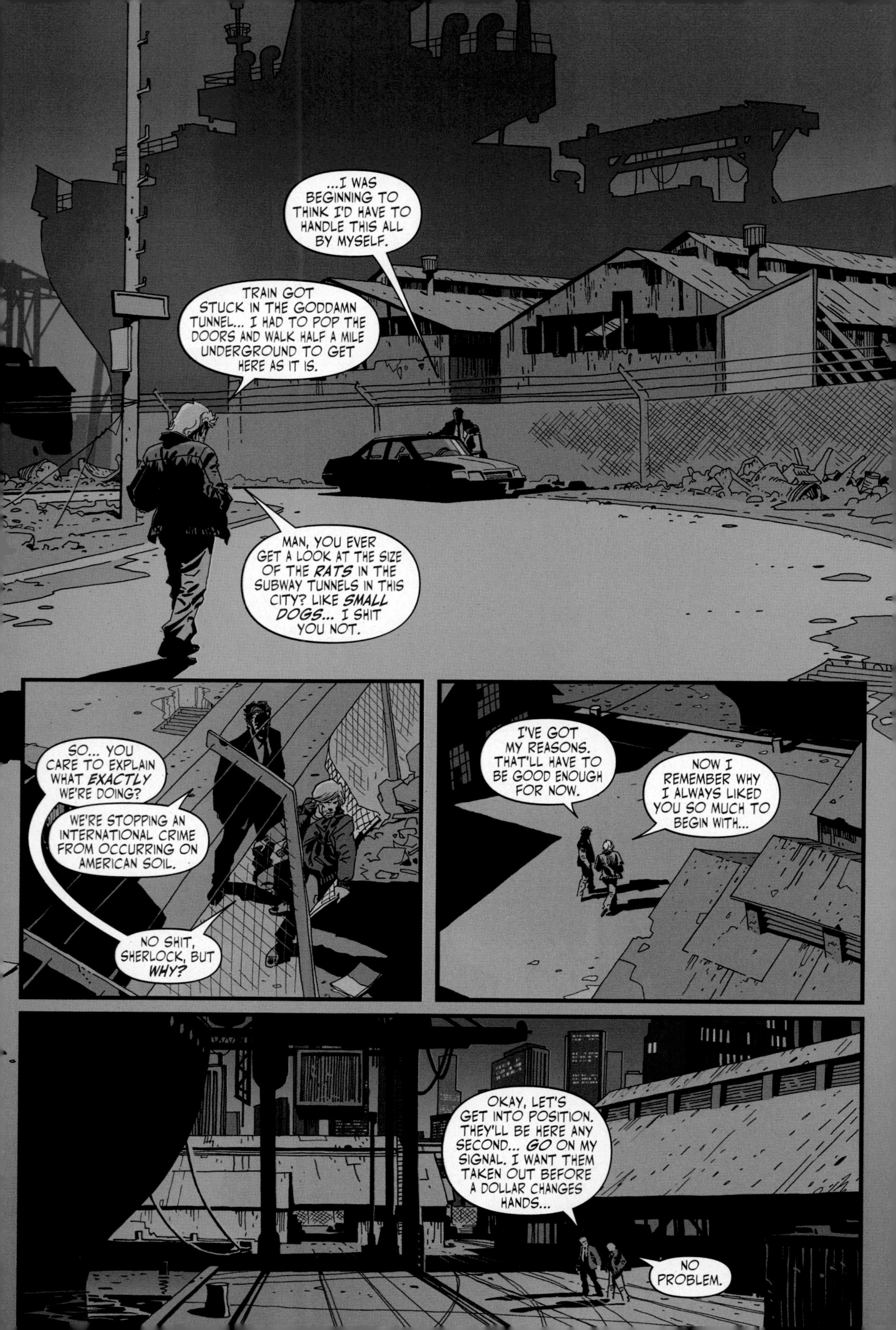
...I WAS BEGINNING TO THINK I'D HAVE TO HANDLE THIS ALL BY MYSELF.
TRAIN GOT STUCK IN THE GODDAMN TUNNEL... I HAD TO POP THE DOORS AND WALK HALF A MILE UNDERGROUND TO GET HERE AS IT IS.
MAN, YOU EVER GET A LOOK AT THE SIZE OF THE *RATS* IN THE SUBWAY TUNNELS IN THIS CITY? LIKE *SMALL DOGS*... I SHIT YOU NOT.
SO... YOU CARE TO EXPLAIN WHAT *EXACTLY* WE'RE DOING?
WE'RE STOPPING AN INTERNATIONAL CRIME FROM OCCURRING ON AMERICAN SOIL.
NO SHIT, SHERLOCK, BUT *WHY?*
I'VE GOT MY REASONS. THAT'LL HAVE TO BE GOOD ENOUGH FOR NOW.
NOW I REMEMBER WHY I ALWAYS LIKED YOU SO MUCH TO BEGIN WITH...
OKAY, LET'S GET INTO POSITION. THEY'LL BE HERE ANY SECOND... *GO* ON MY SIGNAL. I WANT THEM TAKEN OUT BEFORE A DOLLAR CHANGES HANDS...
NO PROBLEM.

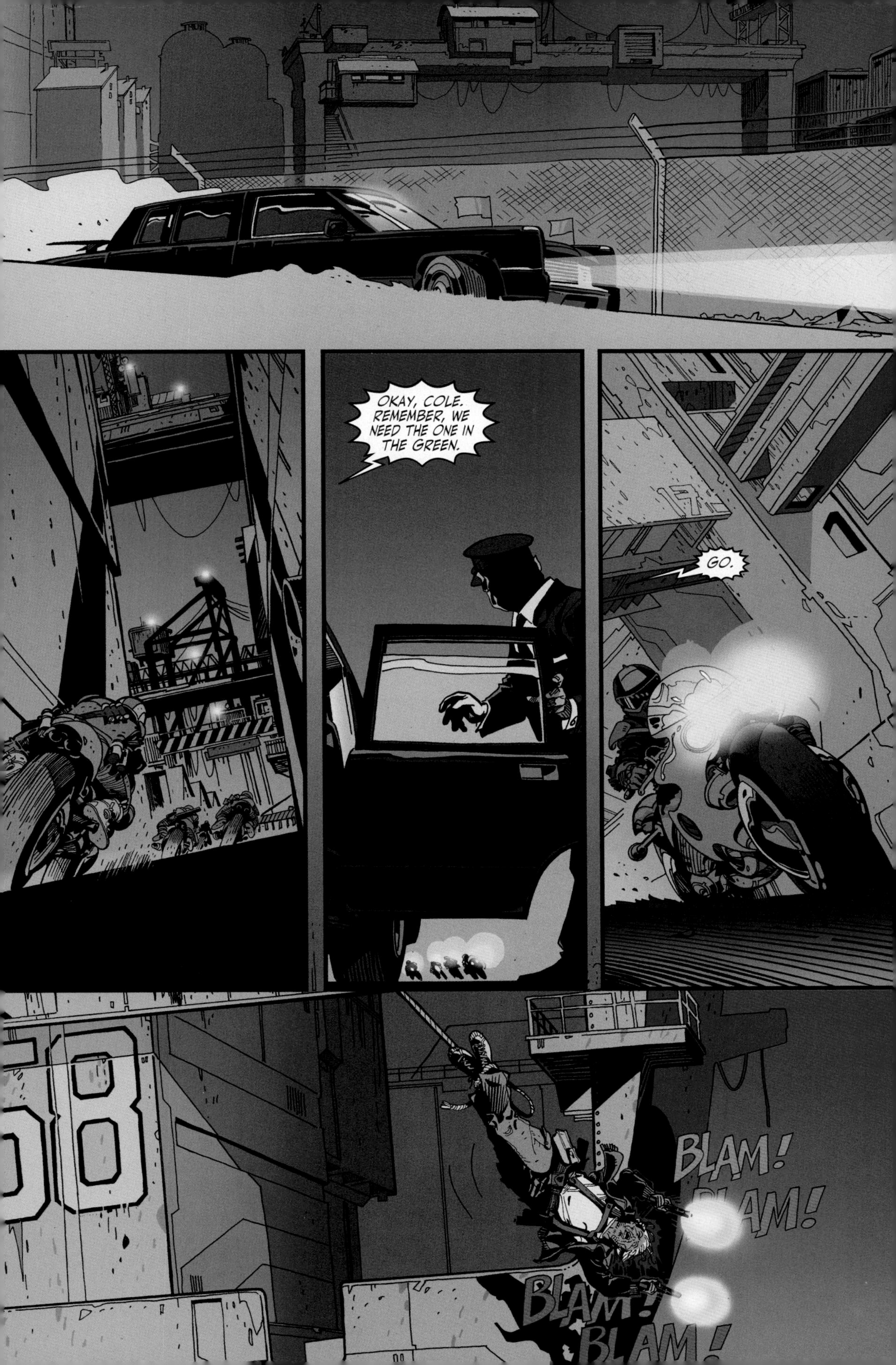
OKAY, COLE. REMEMBER, WE NEED THE ONE IN THE GREEN.
GO.
BLAM!
BLAM!
BLAM!
BLAM!

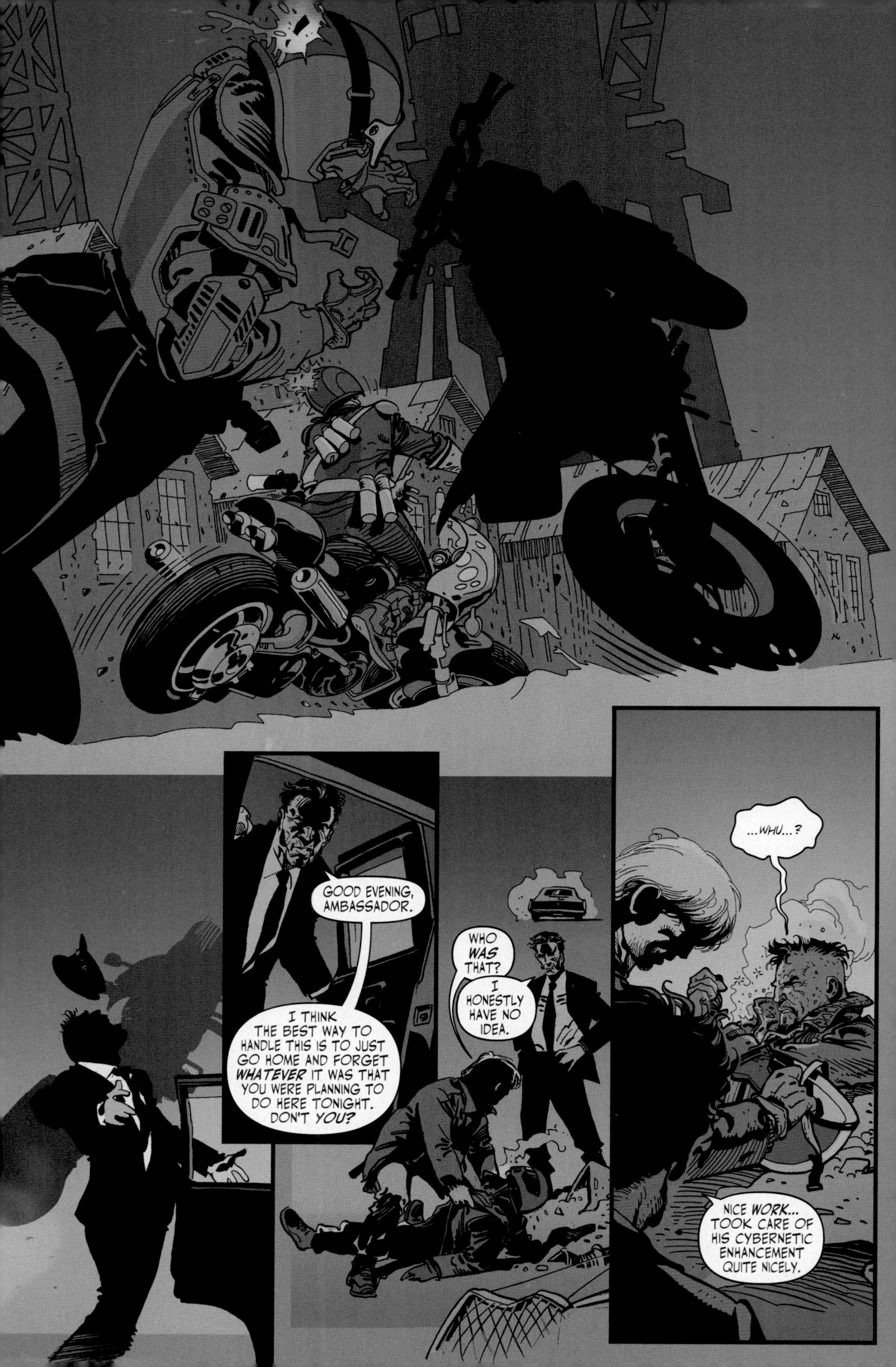
GOOD EVENING, AMBASSADOR.
I THINK THE BEST WAY TO HANDLE THIS IS TO JUST GO HOME AND FORGET WHATEVER IT WAS THAT YOU WERE PLANNING TO DO HERE TONIGHT. DON'T YOU?
WHO WAS THAT?
I HONESTLY HAVE NO IDEA.
...WHU...?
NICE WORK... TOOK CARE OF HIS CYBERNETIC ENHANCEMENT QUITE NICELY.

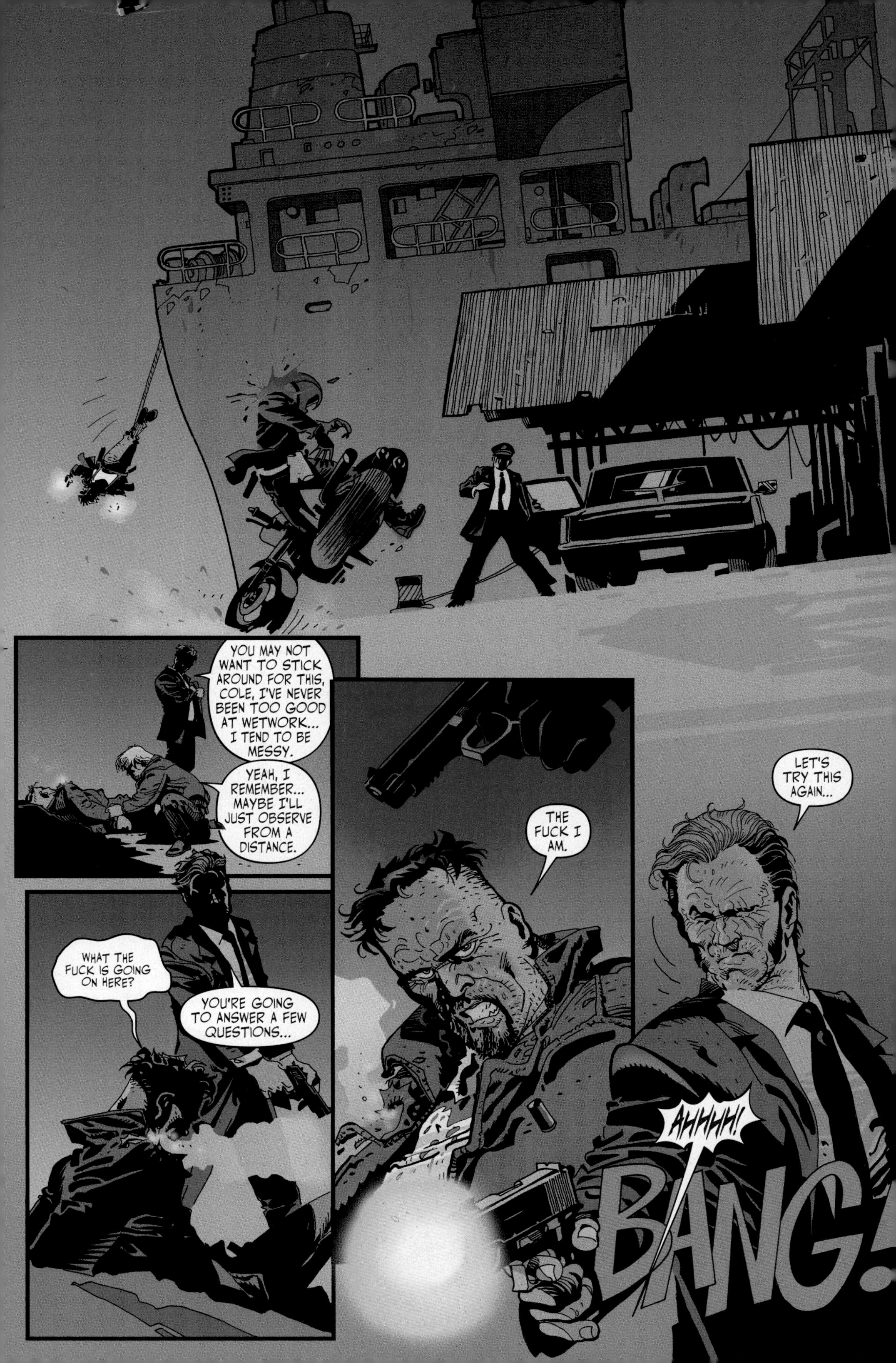
YOU MAY NOT WANT TO STICK AROUND FOR THIS, COLE, I'VE NEVER BEEN TOO GOOD AT WETWORK... I TEND TO BE MESSY.
YEAH, I REMEMBER... MAYBE I'LL JUST OBSERVE FROM A DISTANCE.
WHAT THE FUCK IS GOING ON HERE?
YOU'RE GOING TO ANSWER A FEW QUESTIONS...
THE FUCK I AM.
LET'S TRY THIS AGAIN...
AHHHH!
BANG!

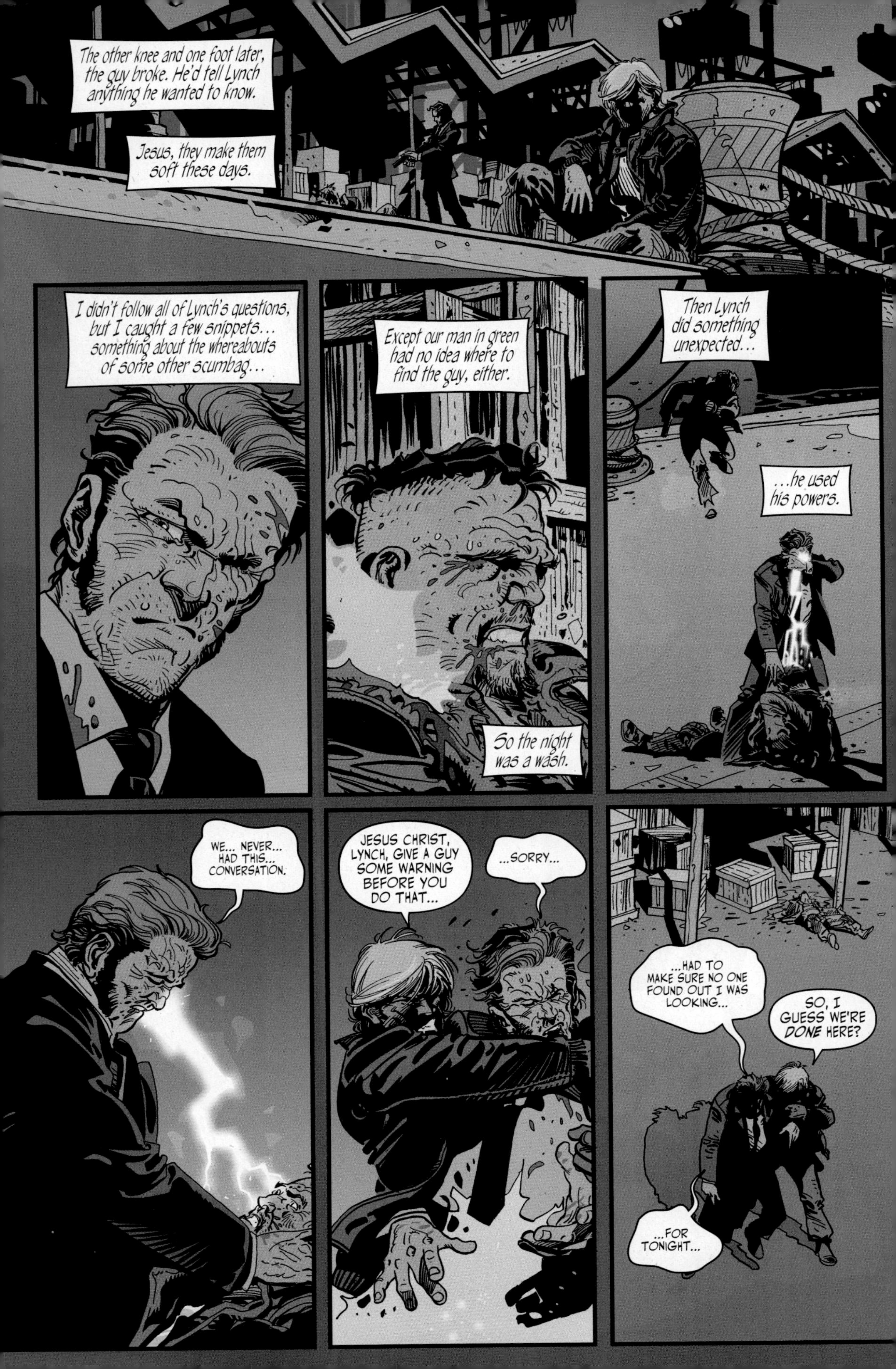
The other knee and one foot later, the guy broke. He'd tell Lynch anything he wanted to know.
Jesus, they make them soft these days.
I didn't follow all of Lynch's questions, but I caught a few snippets... something about the whereabouts of some other scumbag...
Except our man in green had no idea where to find the guy, either.
So the night was a wash.
Then Lynch did something unexpected...
...he used his powers.
WE... NEVER... HAD THIS... CONVERSATION.
JESUS CHRIST, LYNCH, GIVE A GUY SOME WARNING BEFORE YOU DO THAT...
...SORRY...
...HAD TO MAKE SURE NO ONE FOUND OUT I WAS LOOKING...
SO, I GUESS WE'RE *DONE* HERE?
...FOR TONIGHT...

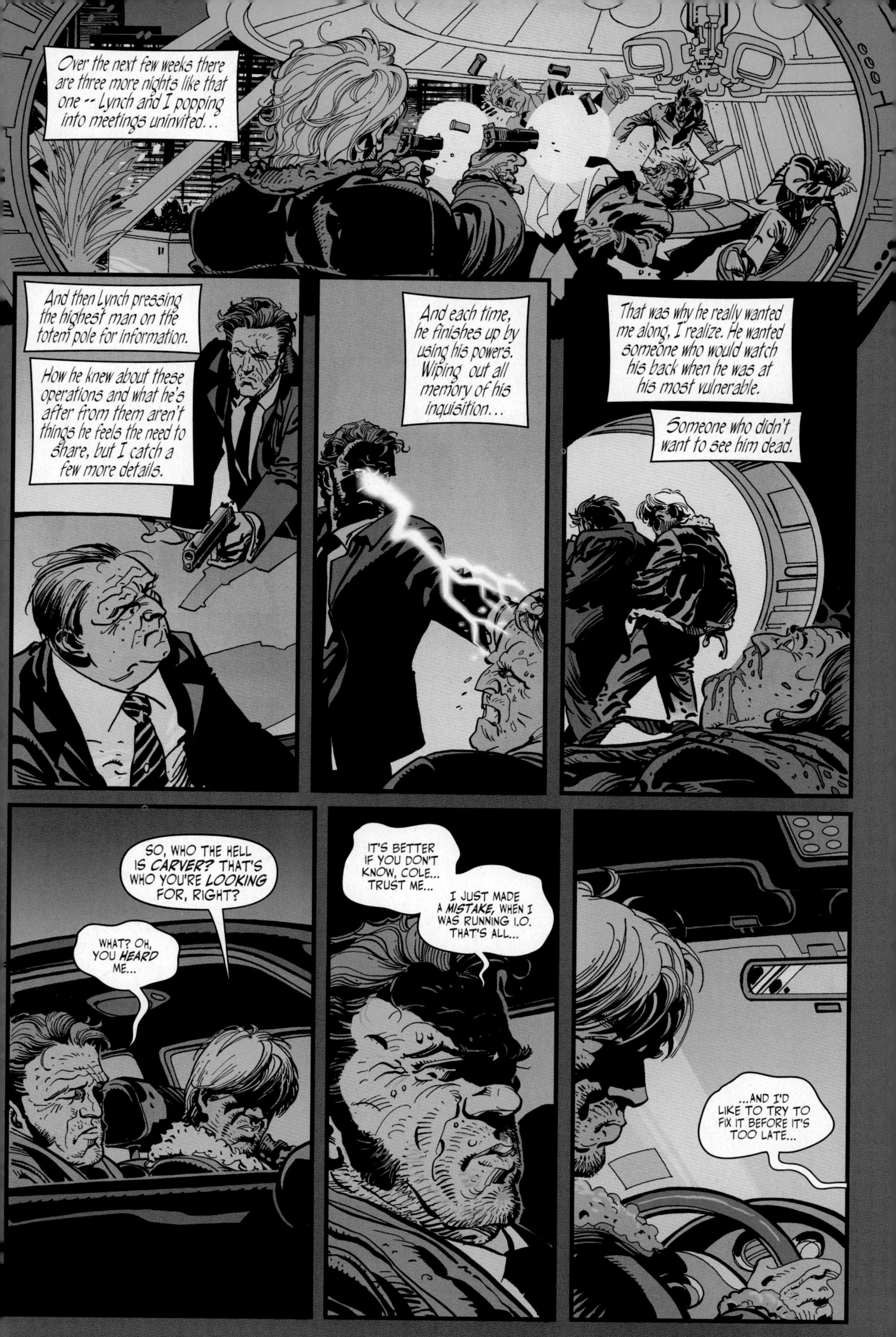
Over the next few weeks there are three more nights like that one -- Lynch and I popping into meetings uninvited...
And then Lynch pressing the highest man on the totem pole for information.
How he knew about these operations and what he's after from them aren't things he feels the need to share, but I catch a few more details.
And each time, he finishes up by using his powers. Wiping out all memory of his inquisition...
That was why he really wanted me along, I realize. He wanted someone who would watch his back when he was at his most vulnerable.
Someone who didn't want to see him dead.
SO, WHO THE HELL IS CARVER? THAT'S WHO YOU'RE LOOKING FOR, RIGHT?
WHAT? OH, YOU HEARD ME...
IT'S BETTER IF YOU DON'T KNOW, COLE... TRUST ME...
I JUST MADE A MISTAKE, WHEN I WAS RUNNING I.O. THAT'S ALL...
...AND I'D LIKE TO TRY TO FIX IT BEFORE IT'S TOO LATE...

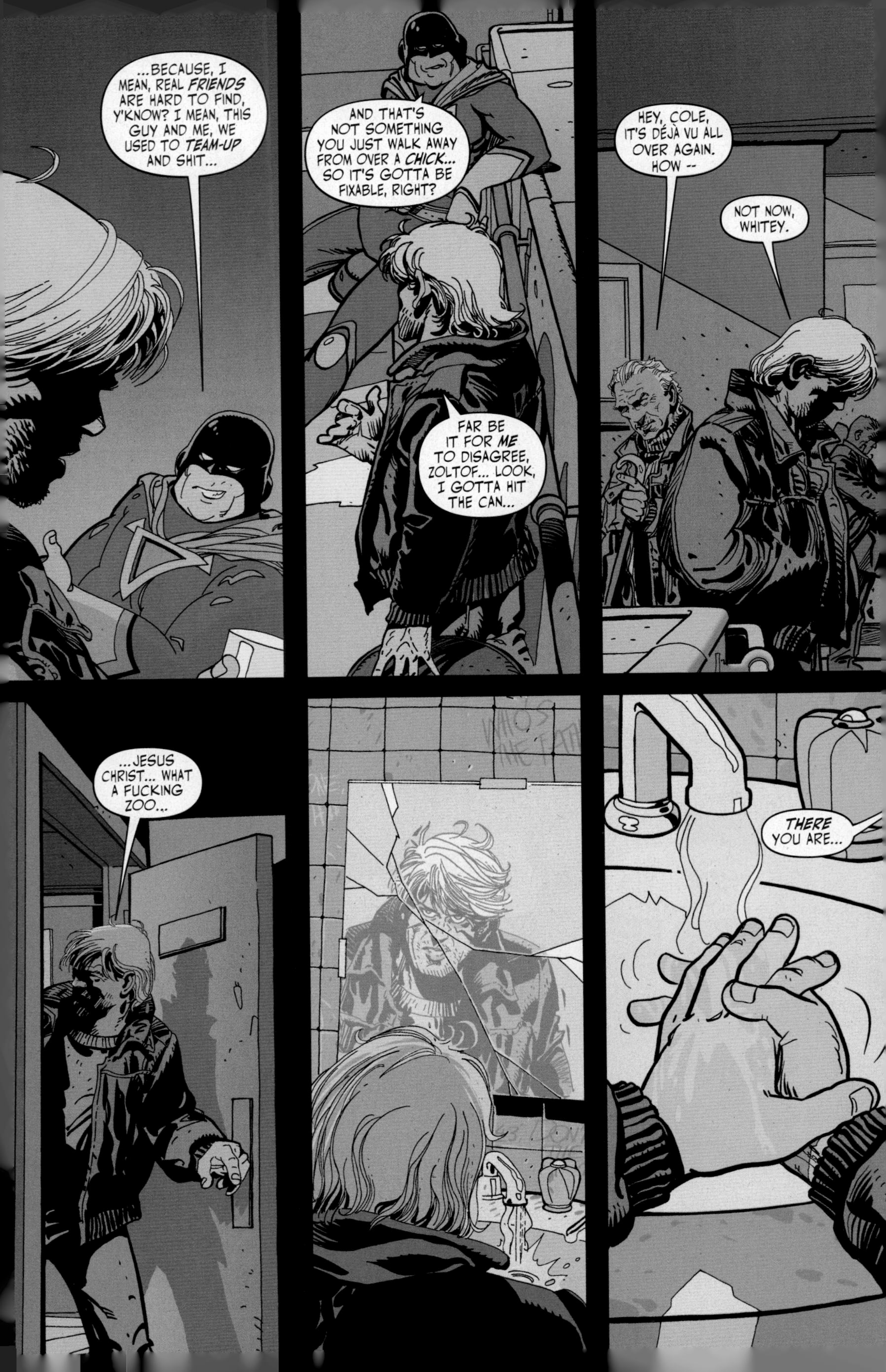
...BECAUSE, I MEAN, REAL FRIENDS ARE HARD TO FIND, Y'KNOW? I MEAN, THIS GUY AND ME, WE USED TO TEAM-UP AND SHIT...
AND THAT'S NOT SOMETHING YOU JUST WALK AWAY FROM OVER A CHICK... SO IT'S GOTTA BE FIXABLE, RIGHT?
FAR BE IT FOR ME TO DISAGREE, ZOLTOF... LOOK, I GOTTA HIT THE CAN...
HEY, COLE, IT'S DÉJÀ VU ALL OVER AGAIN. HOW --
NOT NOW, WHITEY.
...JESUS CHRIST... WHAT A FUCKING ZOO...
THERE YOU ARE...

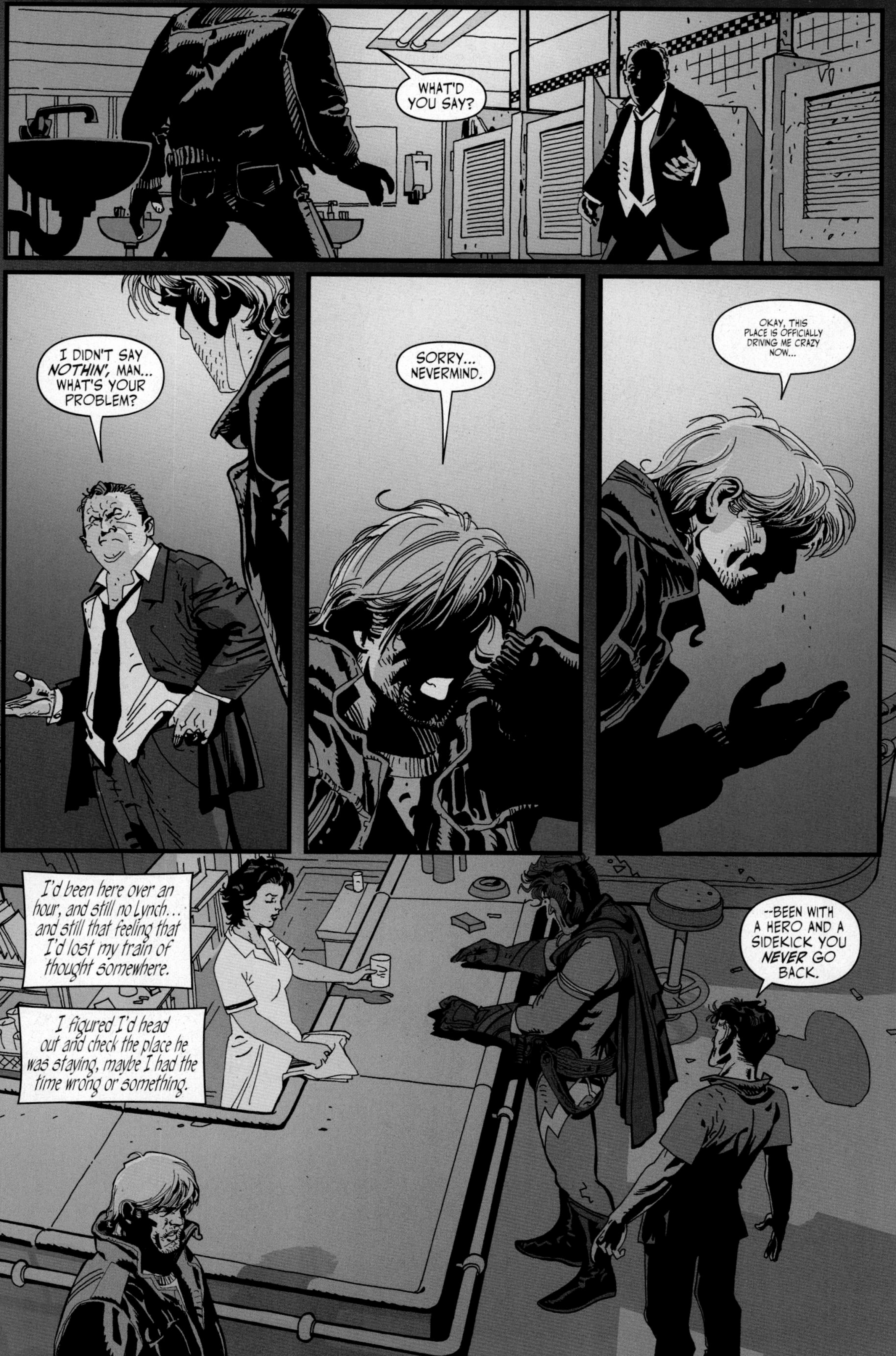
WHAT'D YOU SAY?
I DIDN'T SAY *NOTHIN'*, MAN... WHAT'S YOUR PROBLEM?
SORRY... NEVERMIND.
OKAY, THIS PLACE IS OFFICIALLY DRIVING ME CRAZY NOW...
I'd been here over an hour, and still no Lynch... and still that feeling that I'd lost my train of thought somewhere.
I figured I'd head out and check the place he was staying, maybe I had the time wrong or something.
--BEEN WITH A HERO AND A SIDEKICK YOU *NEVER* GO BACK.

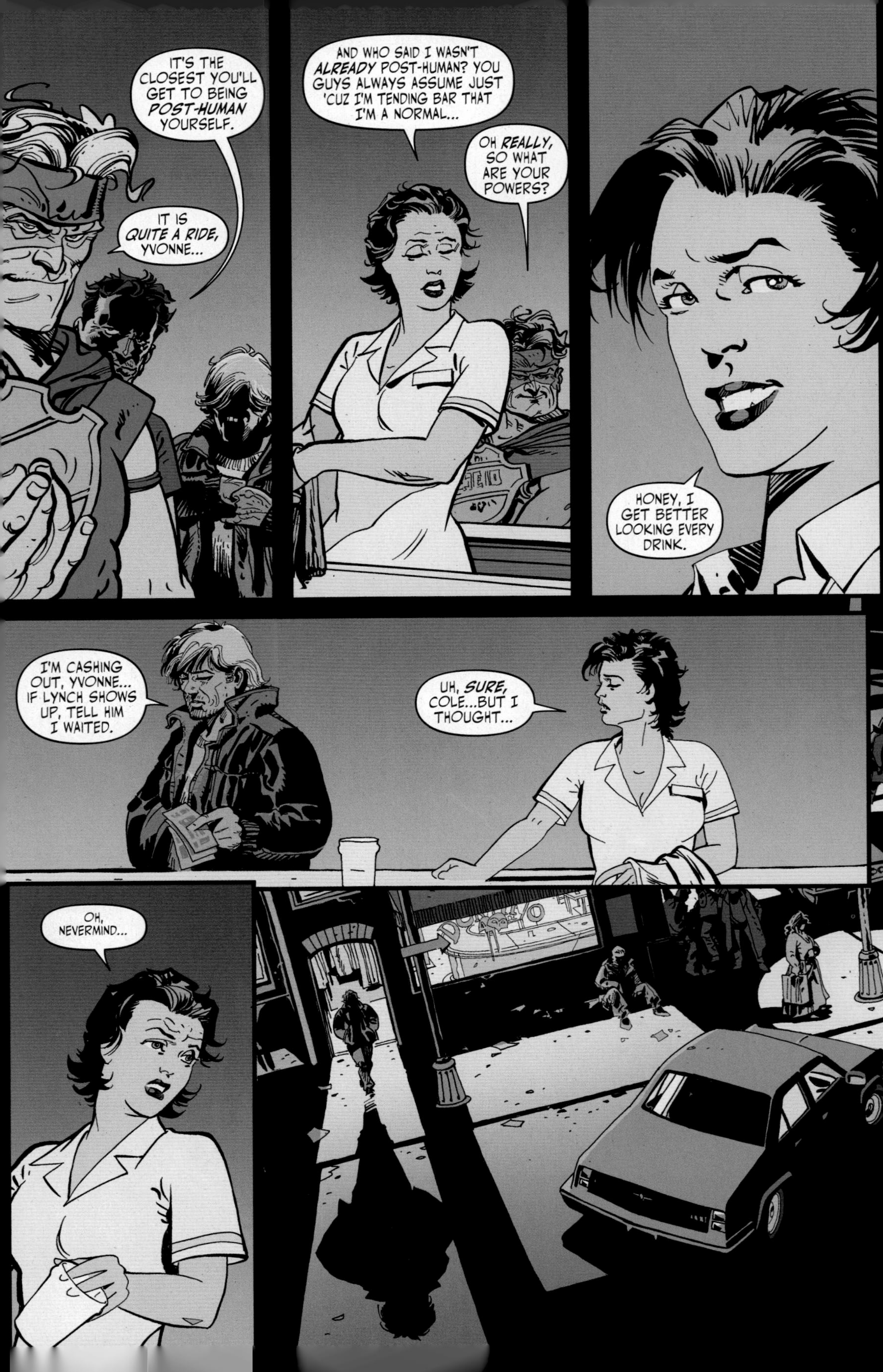
IT'S THE CLOSEST YOU'LL GET TO BEING POST-HUMAN YOURSELF.
IT IS QUITE A RIDE, YVONNE...
AND WHO SAID I WASN'T ALREADY POST-HUMAN? YOU GUYS ALWAYS ASSUME JUST 'CUZ I'M TENDING BAR THAT I'M A NORMAL...
OH REALLY, SO WHAT ARE YOUR POWERS?
HONEY, I GET BETTER LOOKING EVERY DRINK.
I'M CASHING OUT, YVONNE... IF LYNCH SHOWS UP, TELL HIM I WAITED.
UH, SURE, COLE...BUT I THOUGHT...
OH, NEVERMIND...

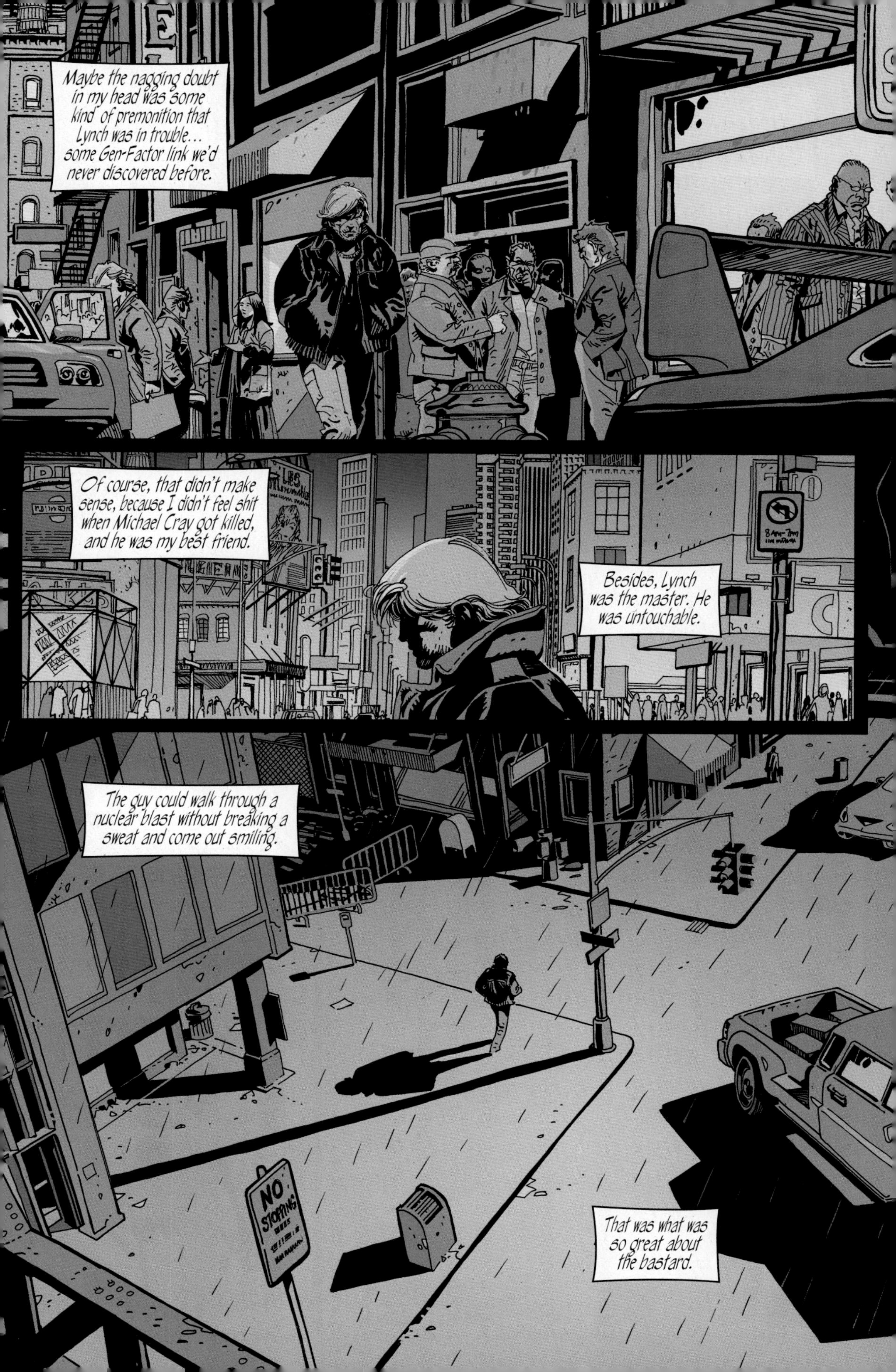

Maybe the nagging doubt in my head was some kind of premonition that Lynch was in trouble... some Gen-Factor link we'd never discovered before.
Of course, that didn't make sense, because I didn't feel shit when Michael Cray got killed, and he was my best friend.
Besides, Lynch was the master. He was untouchable.
The guy could walk through a nuclear blast without breaking a sweat and come out smiling.
NO STOPPING
That was what was so great about the bastard.

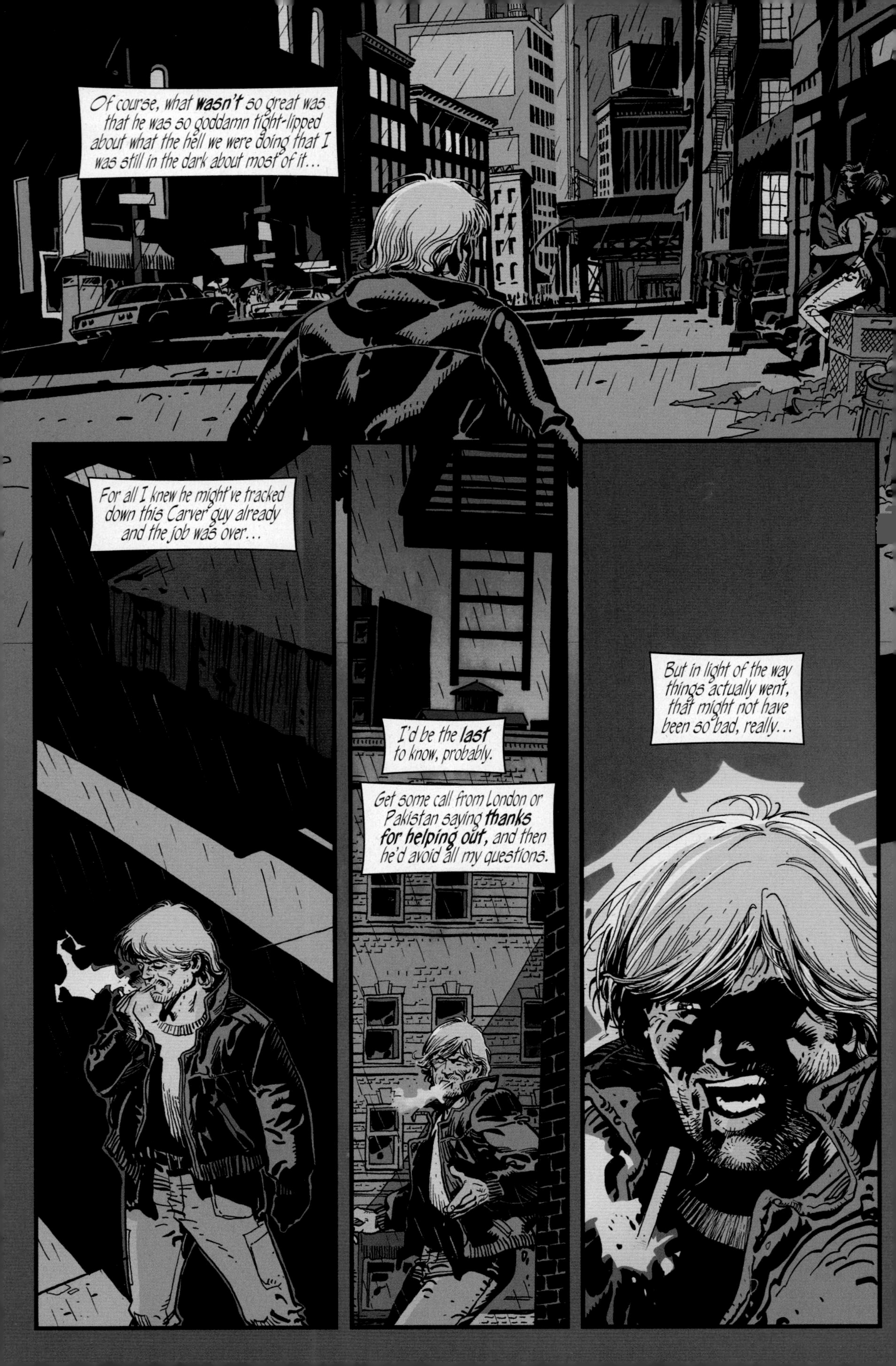
Of course, what **wasn't** so great was that he was so goddamn tight-lipped about what the hell we were doing that I was still in the dark about most of it...
For all I knew he might've tracked down this Carver guy already and the job was over...
I'd be the **last** to know, probably.
Get some call from London or Pakistan saying **thanks for helping out**, and then he'd avoid all my questions.
But in light of the way things actually went, that might not have been so bad, really...

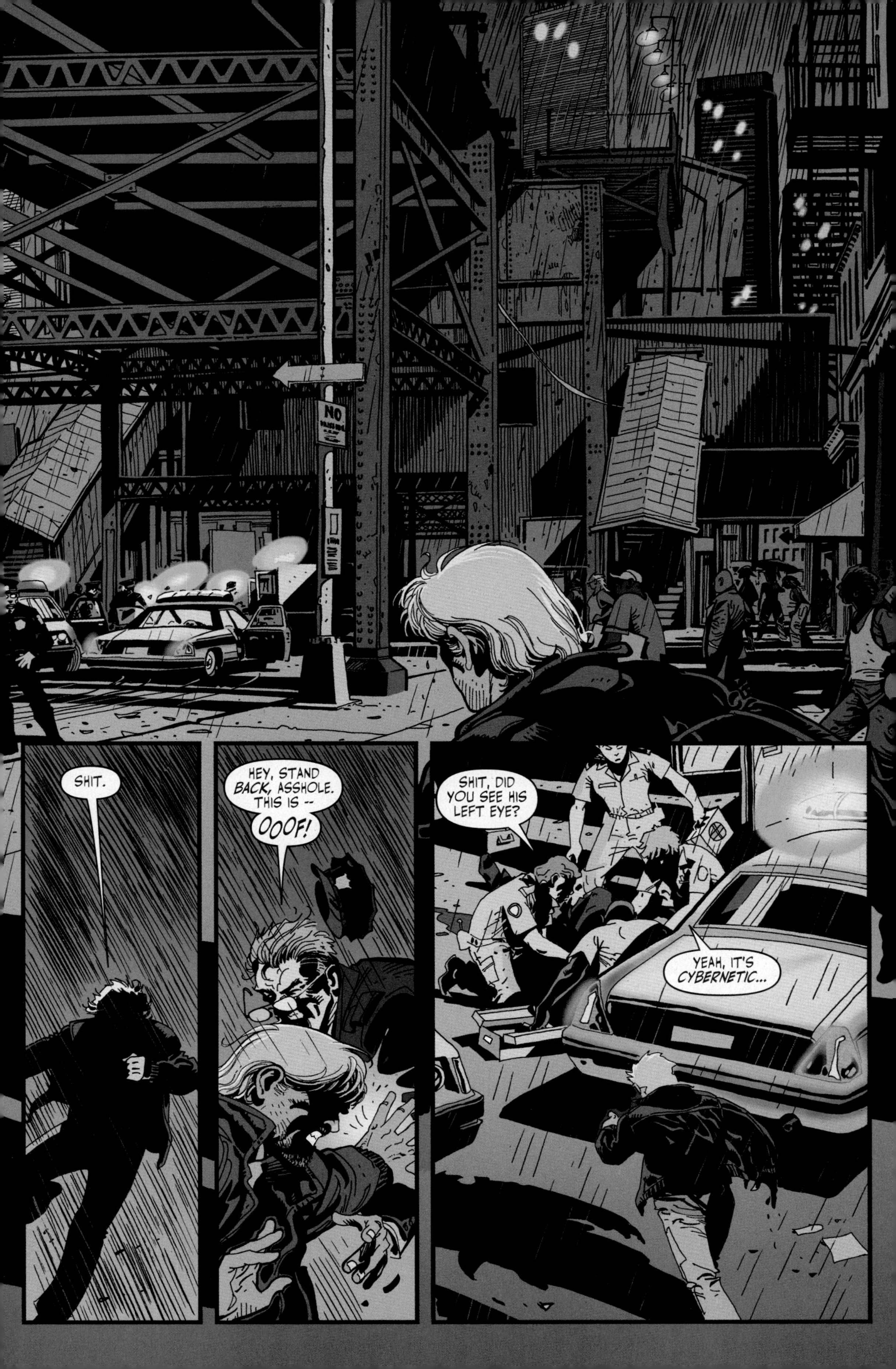
NO
SHIT.
HEY, STAND BACK, ASSHOLE. THIS IS --
OOOF!
SHIT, DID YOU SEE HIS LEFT EYE?
YEAH, IT'S CYBERNETIC...

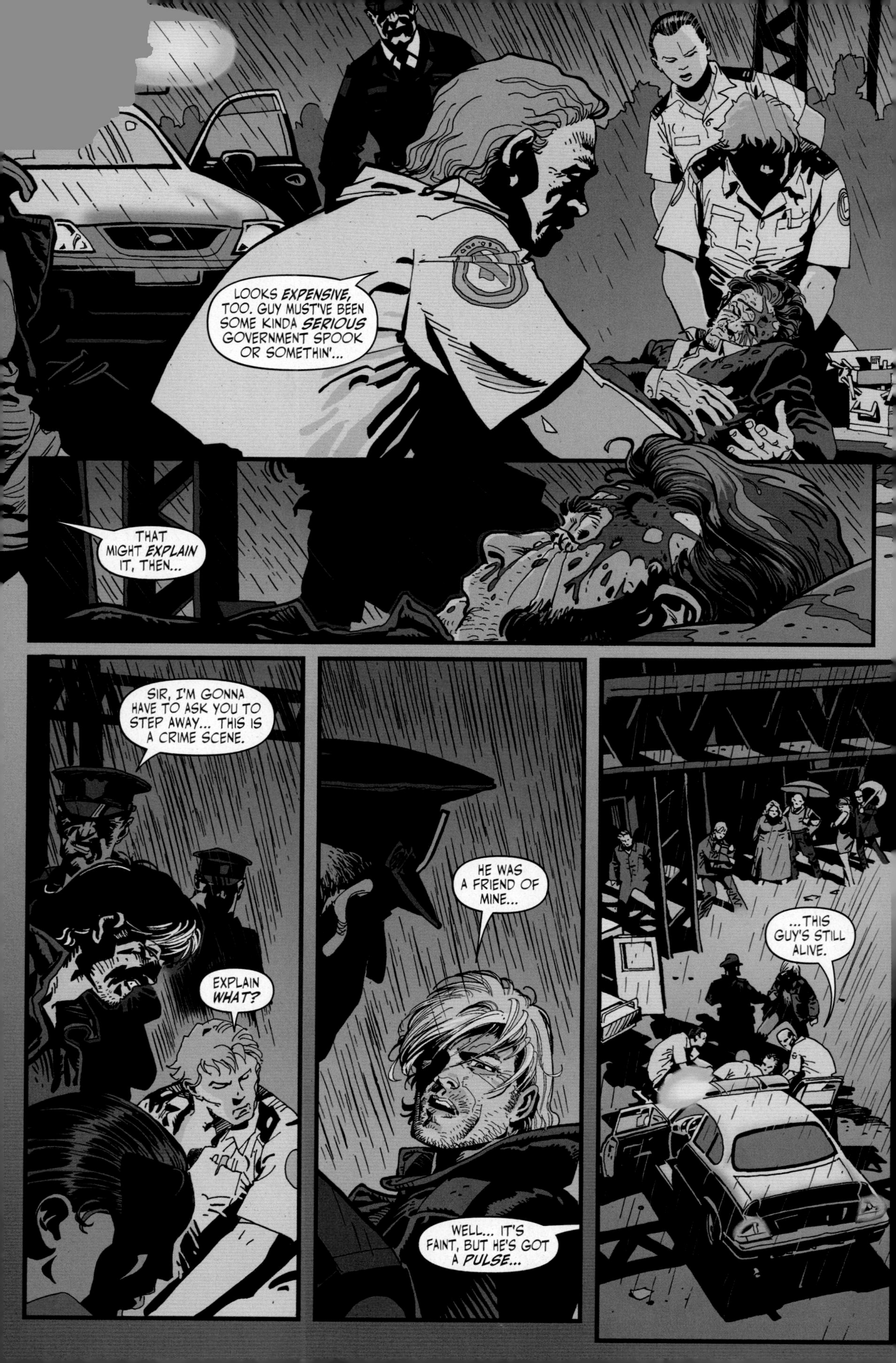

LOOKS EXPENSIVE, TOO. GUY MUST'VE BEEN SOME KINDA SERIOUS GOVERNMENT SPOOK OR SOMETHIN'...
THAT MIGHT EXPLAIN IT, THEN...
SIR, I'M GONNA HAVE TO ASK YOU TO STEP AWAY... THIS IS A CRIME SCENE.
EXPLAIN WHAT?
HE WAS A FRIEND OF MINE...
WELL... IT'S FAINT, BUT HE'S GOT A PULSE...
...THIS GUY'S STILL ALIVE.

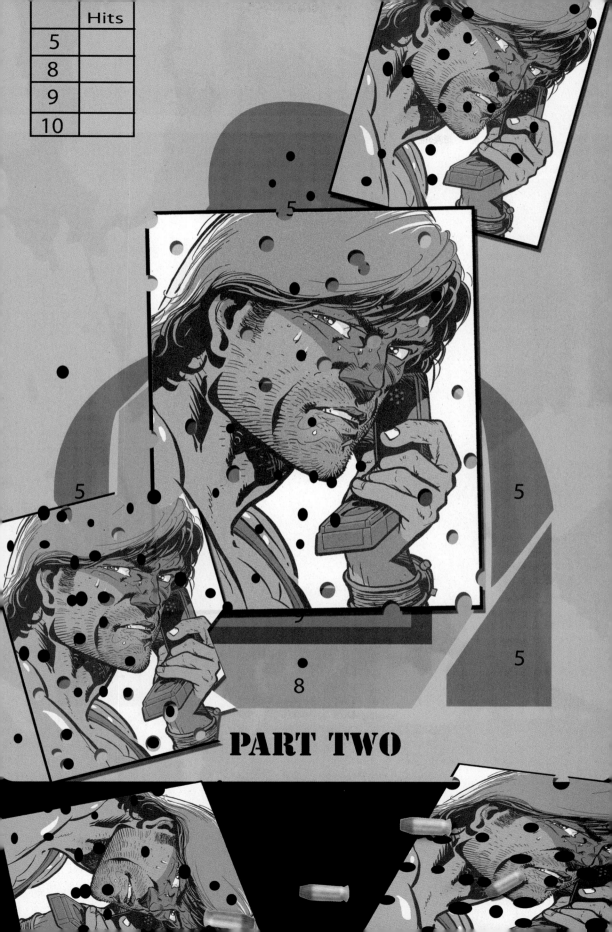

	Hits
5	
8	
9	
10	

PART TWO

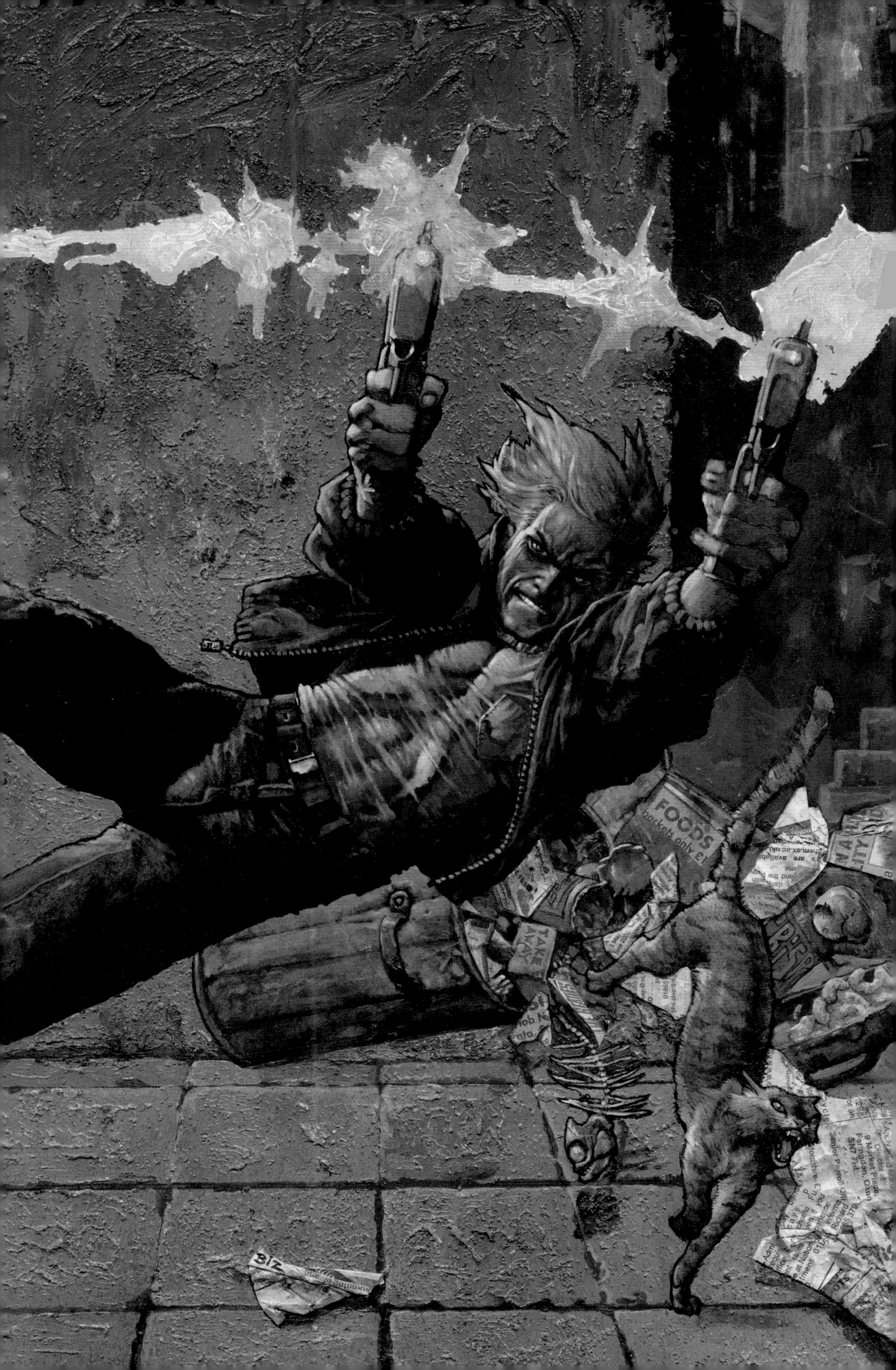
FOODS

When we were kids, my brother Max was always trying to come up with **get-rich-quick** schemes...

...he figured since our last name was **Cash**, we should be loaded.

Of course, he didn't realize that we **would be** loaded someday... loaded with ammunition and death...

But I remember Max's last great idea... something he came up with the night our mother died...

We'd been at the hospital for days... Max was too young to really understand what was happening, and Dad seemed a million miles away.

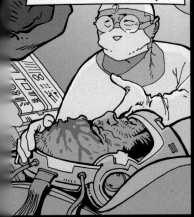

When the doctor finally came out and told us she was gone, we followed Dad as he wandered aimlessly down the halls of the building, trying to find the exit...

And the only thing that he said was "God, I need a drink..."

Then Max had his brilliant idea. There should be **bars** in hospitals.

He said all the sad people would have places to go, then, besides the chapels, where we had seen

Bars were so much more fun than churches, anyway, and think of the **money** you could make...

The stupid kid couldn't shut up about it, he was so excited... and so oblivious to Dad's pain.

Dad beat the shit out of him in the parking lot...

...and Max never talked about get-rich-quick schemes again.

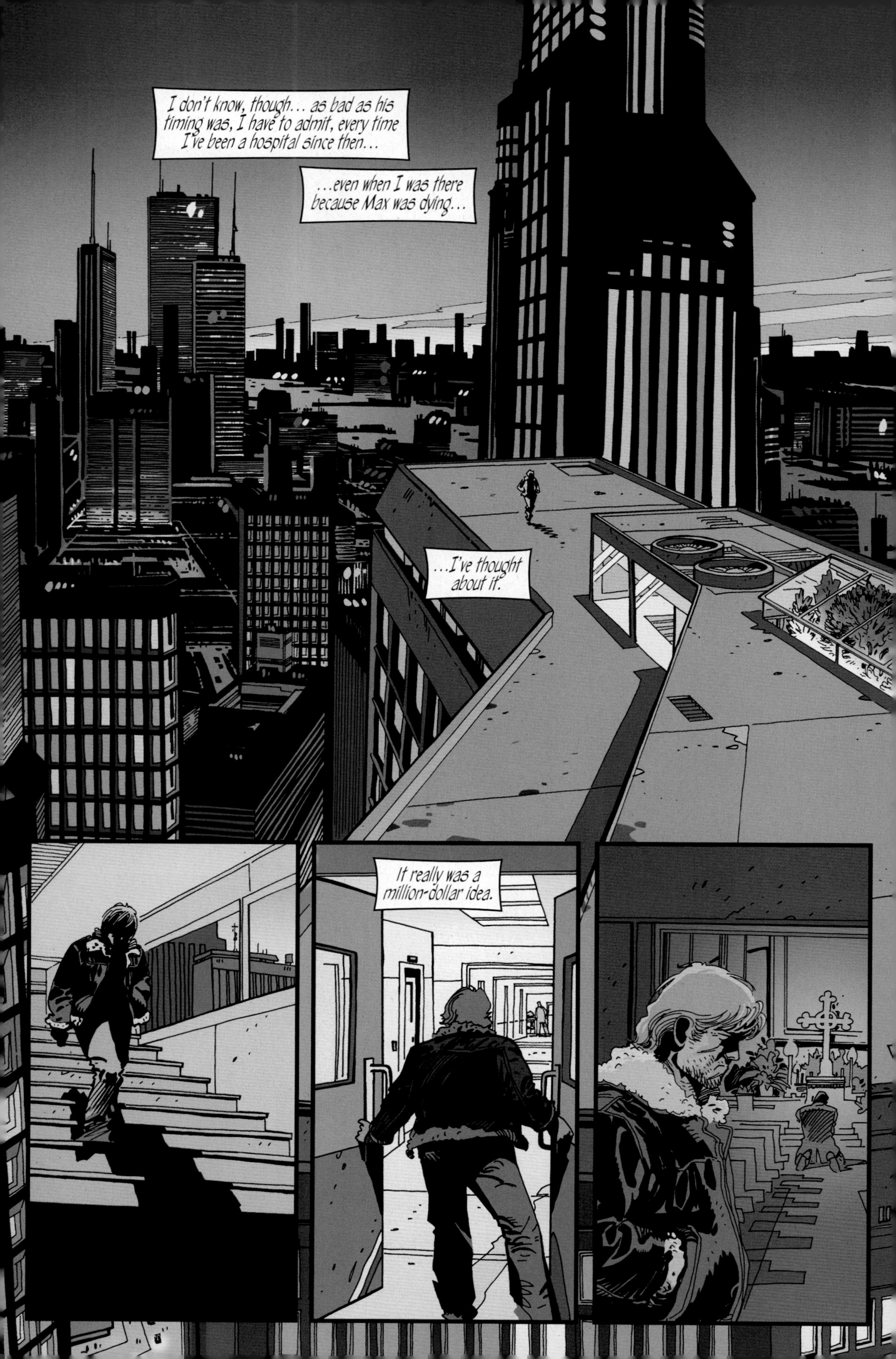
I don't know, though… as bad as his timing was, I have to admit, every time I've been a hospital since then…
…even when I was there because Max was dying…
…I've thought about it.
It really was a million-dollar idea.

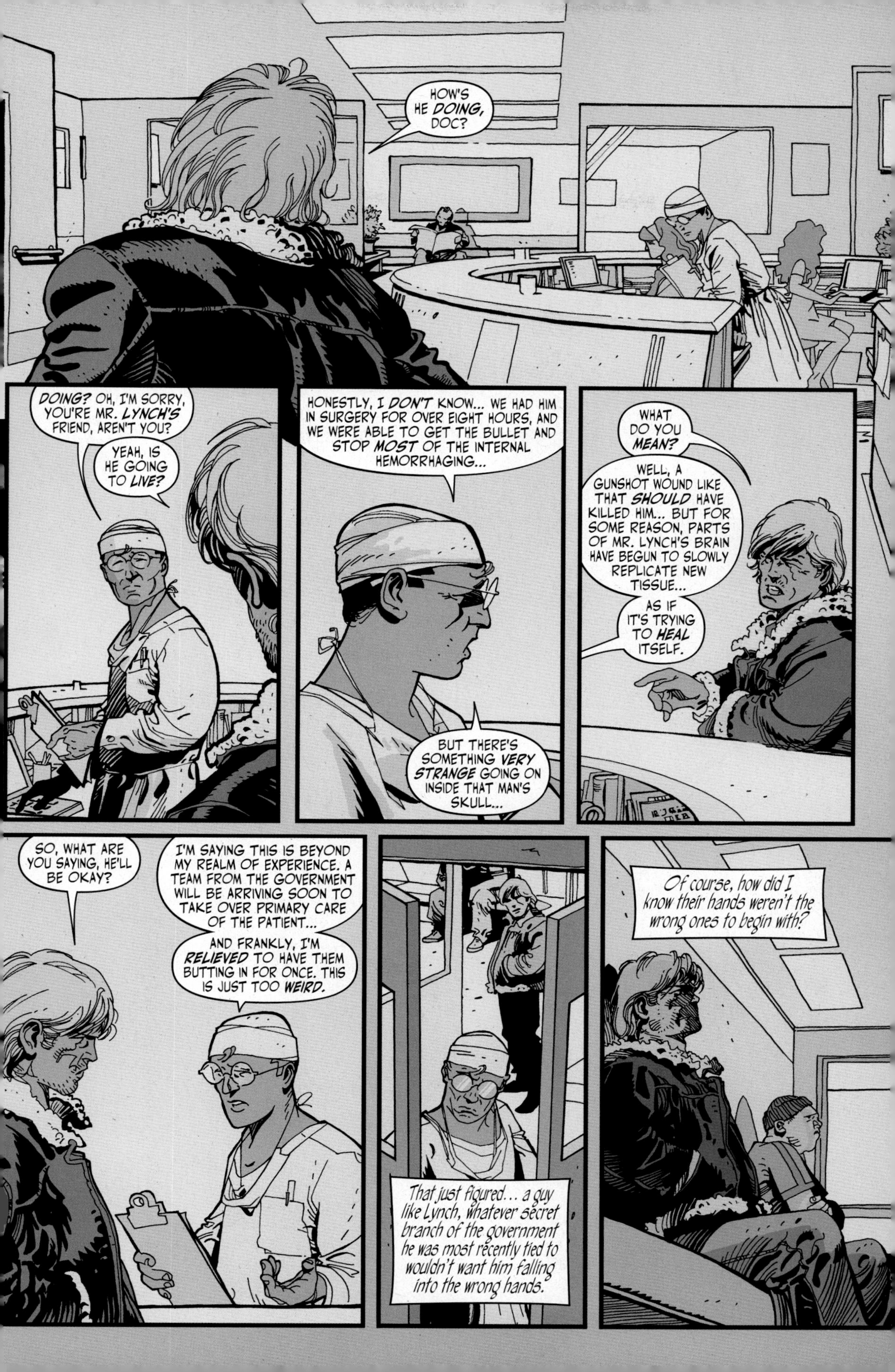
HOW'S HE DOING, DOC?
DOING? OH, I'M SORRY, YOU'RE MR. LYNCH'S FRIEND, AREN'T YOU?
YEAH, IS HE GOING TO LIVE?
HONESTLY, I DON'T KNOW... WE HAD HIM IN SURGERY FOR OVER EIGHT HOURS, AND WE WERE ABLE TO GET THE BULLET AND STOP MOST OF THE INTERNAL HEMORRHAGING...
BUT THERE'S SOMETHING VERY STRANGE GOING ON INSIDE THAT MAN'S SKULL...
WHAT DO YOU MEAN?
WELL, A GUNSHOT WOUND LIKE THAT SHOULD HAVE KILLED HIM... BUT FOR SOME REASON, PARTS OF MR. LYNCH'S BRAIN HAVE BEGUN TO SLOWLY REPLICATE NEW TISSUE...
AS IF IT'S TRYING TO HEAL ITSELF.
SO, WHAT ARE YOU SAYING, HE'LL BE OKAY?
I'M SAYING THIS IS BEYOND MY REALM OF EXPERIENCE. A TEAM FROM THE GOVERNMENT WILL BE ARRIVING SOON TO TAKE OVER PRIMARY CARE OF THE PATIENT...
AND FRANKLY, I'M RELIEVED TO HAVE THEM BUTTING IN FOR ONCE. THIS IS JUST TOO WEIRD.
That just figured... a guy like Lynch, whatever secret branch of the government he was most recently tied to wouldn't want him falling into the wrong hands.
Of course, how did I know their hands weren't the wrong ones to begin with?

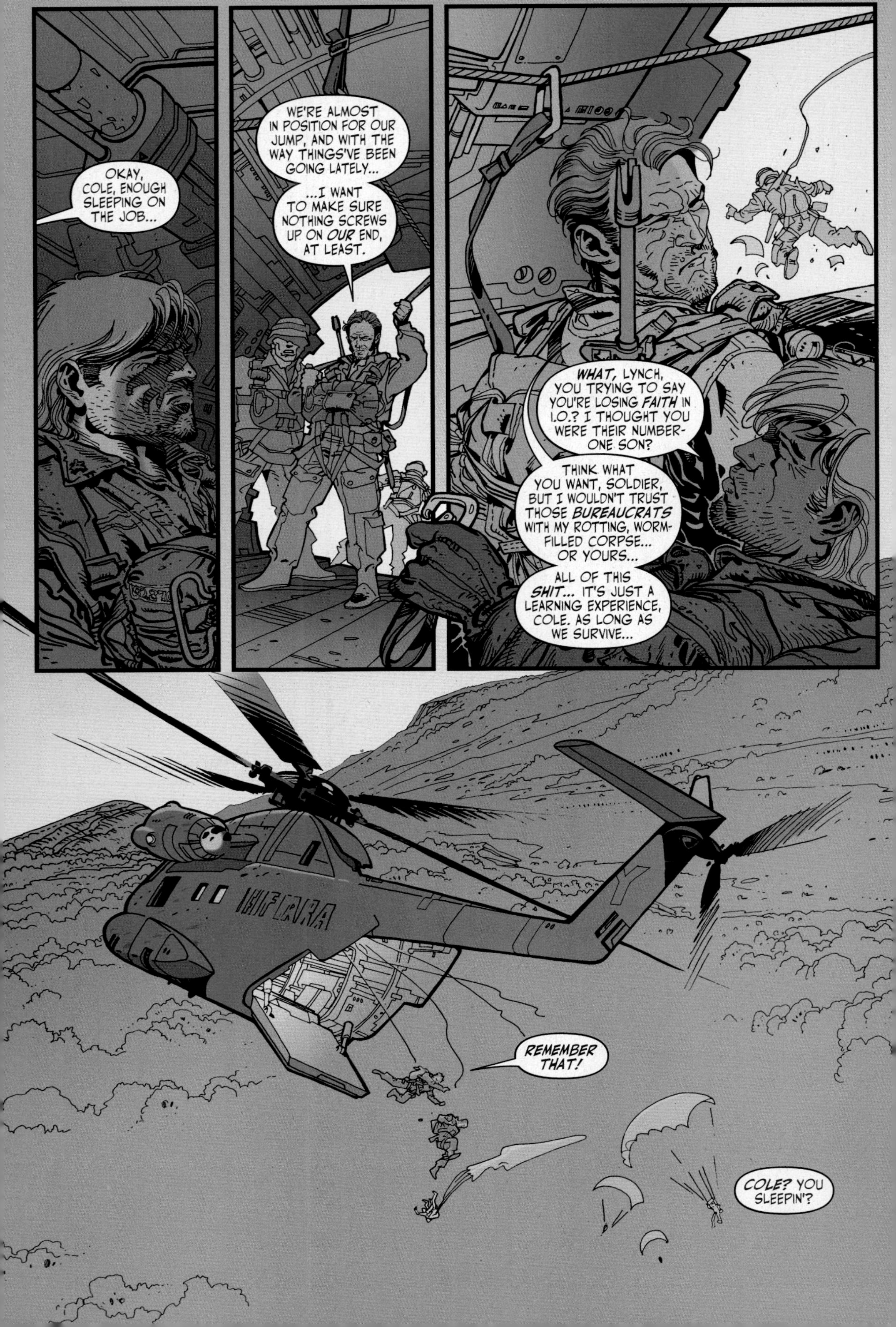

OKAY, COLE, ENOUGH SLEEPING ON THE JOB...
WE'RE ALMOST IN POSITION FOR OUR JUMP, AND WITH THE WAY THINGS'VE BEEN GOING LATELY...
...I WANT TO MAKE SURE NOTHING SCREWS UP ON *OUR* END, AT LEAST.
WHAT, LYNCH, YOU TRYING TO SAY YOU'RE LOSING *FAITH* IN I.O.? I THOUGHT YOU WERE THEIR NUMBER-ONE SON?
THINK WHAT YOU WANT, SOLDIER, BUT I WOULDN'T TRUST THOSE *BUREAUCRATS* WITH MY ROTTING, WORM-FILLED CORPSE... OR YOURS...
ALL OF THIS *SHIT...* IT'S JUST A LEARNING EXPERIENCE, COLE. AS LONG AS WE SURVIVE...
REMEMBER THAT!
COLE? YOU SLEEPIN'?

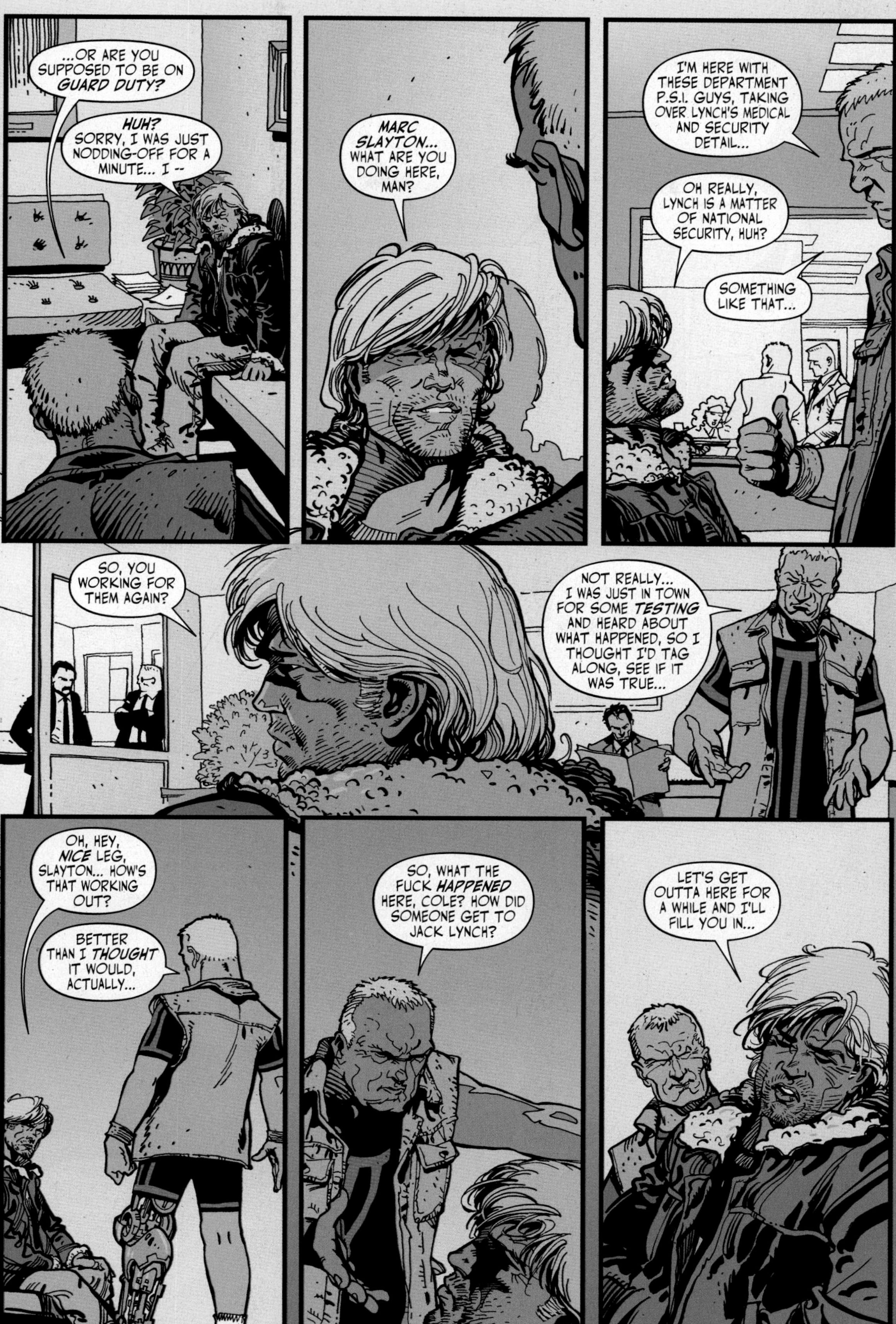
...OR ARE YOU SUPPOSED TO BE ON GUARD DUTY?
HUH? SORRY, I WAS JUST NODDING-OFF FOR A MINUTE... I --
MARC SLAYTON... WHAT ARE YOU DOING HERE, MAN?
I'M HERE WITH THESE DEPARTMENT P.S.I. GUYS, TAKING OVER LYNCH'S MEDICAL AND SECURITY DETAIL...
OH REALLY, LYNCH IS A MATTER OF NATIONAL SECURITY, HUH?
SOMETHING LIKE THAT...
SO, YOU WORKING FOR THEM AGAIN?
NOT REALLY... I WAS JUST IN TOWN FOR SOME TESTING AND HEARD ABOUT WHAT HAPPENED, SO I THOUGHT I'D TAG ALONG, SEE IF IT WAS TRUE...
OH, HEY, NICE LEG, SLAYTON... HOW'S THAT WORKING OUT?
BETTER THAN I THOUGHT IT WOULD, ACTUALLY...
SO, WHAT THE FUCK HAPPENED HERE, COLE? HOW DID SOMEONE GET TO JACK LYNCH?
LET'S GET OUTTA HERE FOR A WHILE AND I'LL FILL YOU IN...

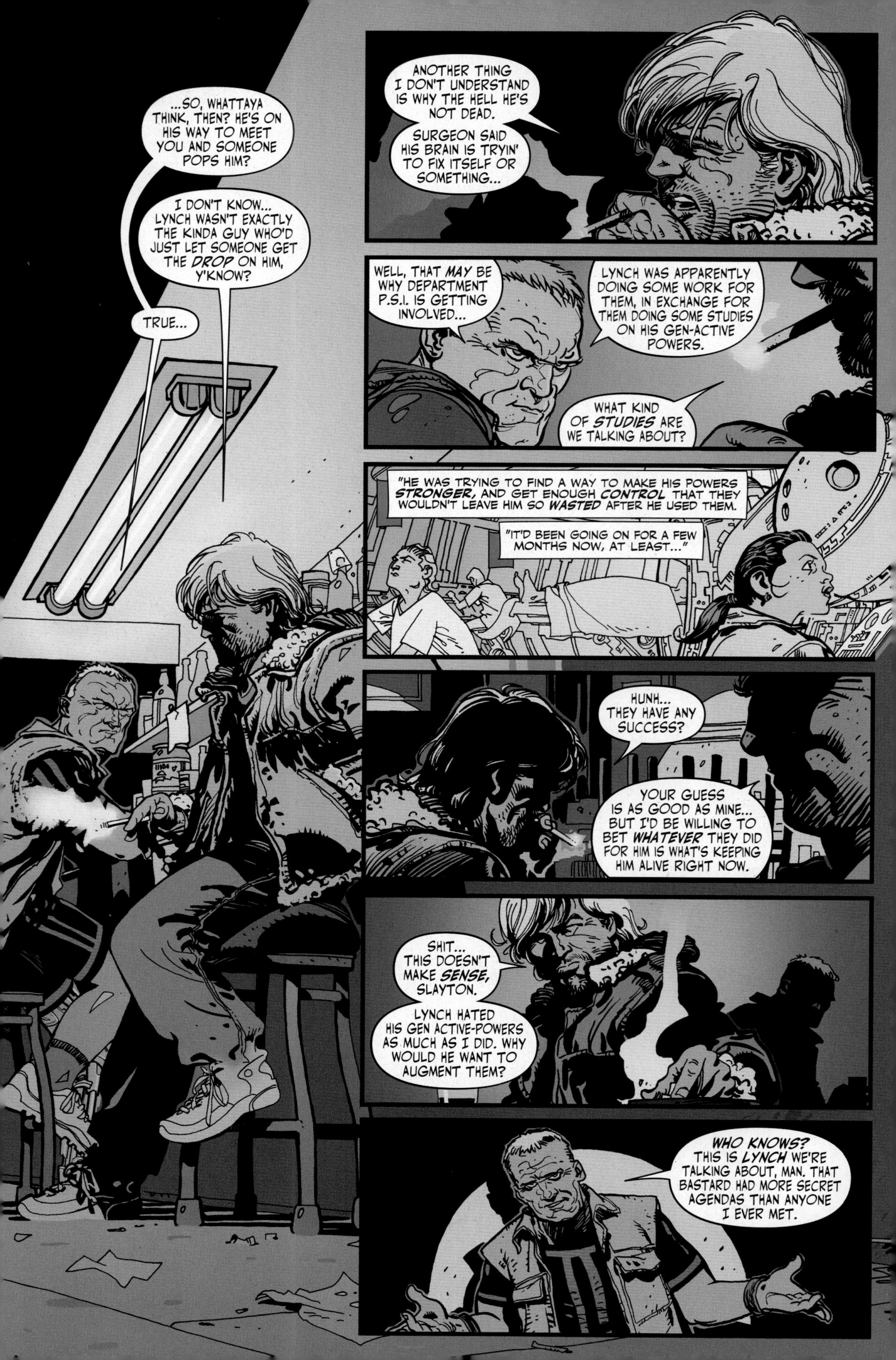
...SO, WHATTAYA THINK, THEN? HE'S ON HIS WAY TO MEET YOU AND SOMEONE POPS HIM?
I DON'T KNOW... LYNCH WASN'T EXACTLY THE KINDA GUY WHO'D JUST LET SOMEONE GET THE DROP ON HIM, Y'KNOW?
TRUE...
ANOTHER THING I DON'T UNDERSTAND IS WHY THE HELL HE'S NOT DEAD.
SURGEON SAID HIS BRAIN IS TRYIN' TO FIX ITSELF OR SOMETHING...
WELL, THAT MAY BE WHY DEPARTMENT P.S.I. IS GETTING INVOLVED...
LYNCH WAS APPARENTLY DOING SOME WORK FOR THEM, IN EXCHANGE FOR THEM DOING SOME STUDIES ON HIS GEN-ACTIVE POWERS.
WHAT KIND OF STUDIES ARE WE TALKING ABOUT?
"HE WAS TRYING TO FIND A WAY TO MAKE HIS POWERS STRONGER, AND GET ENOUGH CONTROL THAT THEY WOULDN'T LEAVE HIM SO WASTED AFTER HE USED THEM.
"IT'D BEEN GOING ON FOR A FEW MONTHS NOW, AT LEAST..."
HUNH... THEY HAVE ANY SUCCESS?
YOUR GUESS IS AS GOOD AS MINE... BUT I'D BE WILLING TO BET WHATEVER THEY DID FOR HIM IS WHAT'S KEEPING HIM ALIVE RIGHT NOW.
SHIT... THIS DOESN'T MAKE SENSE, SLAYTON.
LYNCH HATED HIS GEN ACTIVE-POWERS AS MUCH AS I DID. WHY WOULD HE WANT TO AUGMENT THEM?
WHO KNOWS? THIS IS LYNCH WE'RE TALKING ABOUT, MAN. THAT BASTARD HAD MORE SECRET AGENDAS THAN ANYONE I EVER MET.

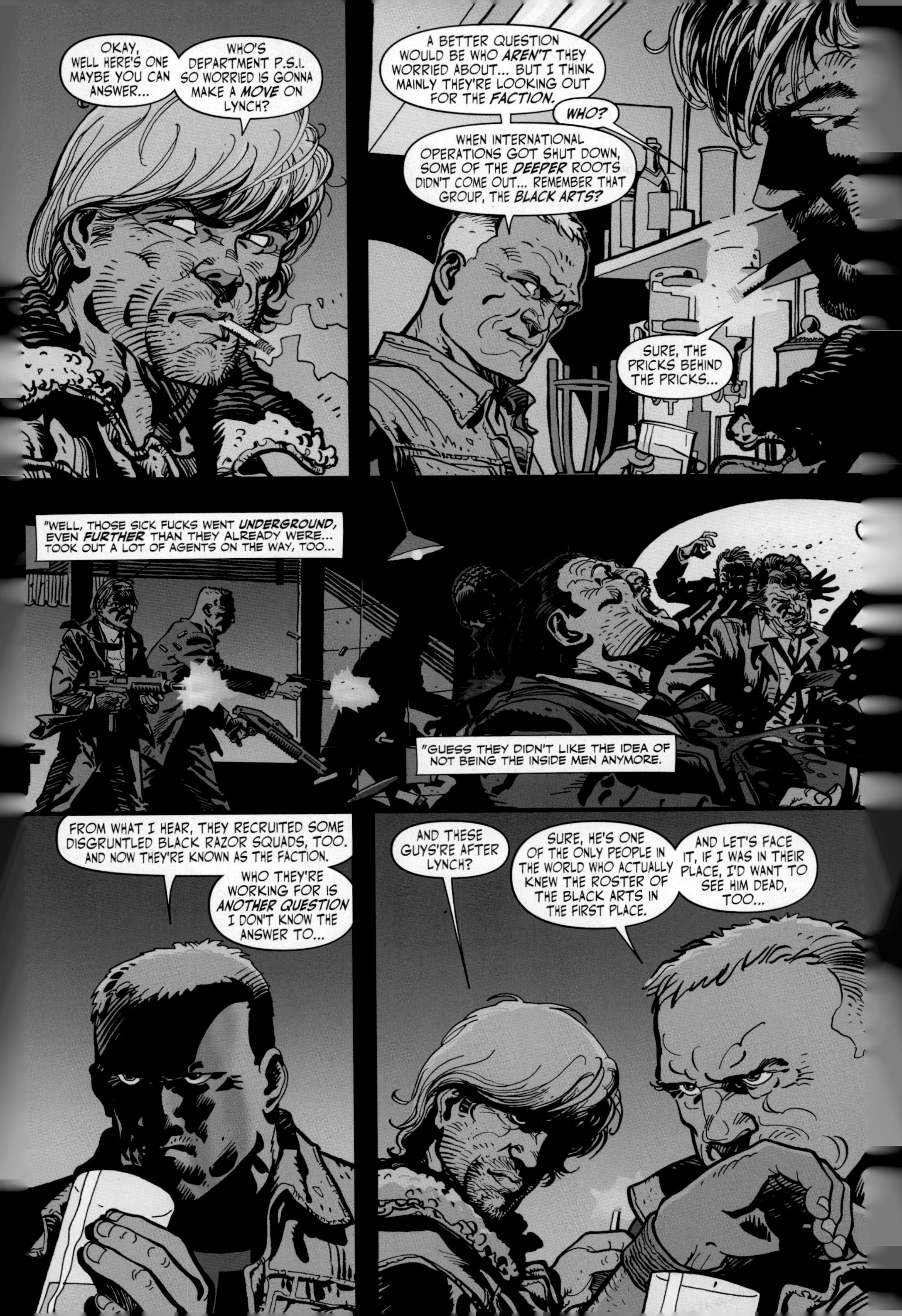
OKAY, WELL HERE'S ONE MAYBE YOU CAN ANSWER...
WHO'S DEPARTMENT P.S.I. SO WORRIED IS GONNA MAKE A *MOVE* ON LYNCH?
A BETTER QUESTION WOULD BE WHO *AREN'T* THEY WORRIED ABOUT... BUT I THINK MAINLY THEY'RE LOOKING OUT FOR THE *FACTION.*
WHO?
WHEN INTERNATIONAL OPERATIONS GOT SHUT DOWN, SOME OF THE *DEEPER* ROOTS DIDN'T COME OUT... REMEMBER THAT GROUP, THE *BLACK ARTS?*
SURE, THE PRICKS BEHIND THE PRICKS...
"WELL, THOSE SICK FUCKS WENT *UNDERGROUND,* EVEN *FURTHER* THAN THEY ALREADY WERE... TOOK OUT A LOT OF AGENTS ON THE WAY, TOO...
"GUESS THEY DIDN'T LIKE THE IDEA OF NOT BEING THE INSIDE MEN ANYMORE.
FROM WHAT I HEAR, THEY RECRUITED SOME DISGRUNTLED BLACK RAZOR SQUADS, TOO. AND NOW THEY'RE KNOWN AS THE FACTION.
WHO THEY'RE WORKING FOR IS *ANOTHER QUESTION* I DON'T KNOW THE ANSWER TO...
AND THESE GUYS'RE AFTER LYNCH?
SURE, HE'S ONE OF THE ONLY PEOPLE IN THE WORLD WHO ACTUALLY KNEW THE ROSTER OF THE BLACK ARTS IN THE FIRST PLACE.
AND LET'S FACE IT, IF I WAS IN THEIR PLACE, I'D WANT TO SEE HIM DEAD, TOO...

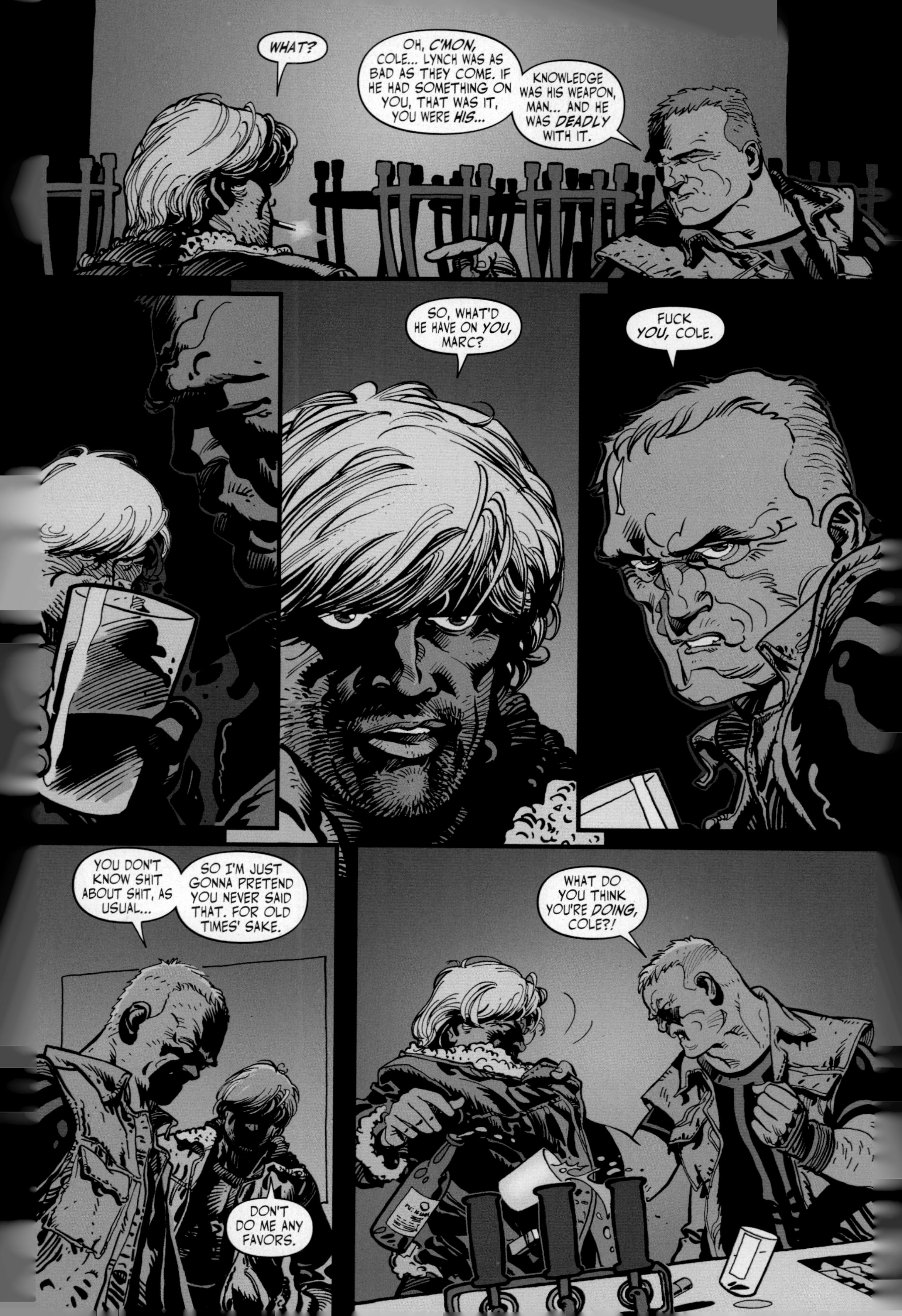
WHAT?
OH, C'MON, COLE... LYNCH WAS AS BAD AS THEY COME. IF HE HAD SOMETHING ON YOU, THAT WAS IT, YOU WERE HIS...
KNOWLEDGE WAS HIS WEAPON, MAN... AND HE WAS DEADLY WITH IT.
SO, WHAT'D HE HAVE ON YOU, MARC?
FUCK YOU, COLE.
YOU DON'T KNOW SHIT ABOUT SHIT, AS USUAL...
SO I'M JUST GONNA PRETEND YOU NEVER SAID THAT. FOR OLD TIMES' SAKE.
DON'T DO ME ANY FAVORS.
WHAT DO YOU THINK YOU'RE DOING, COLE?!

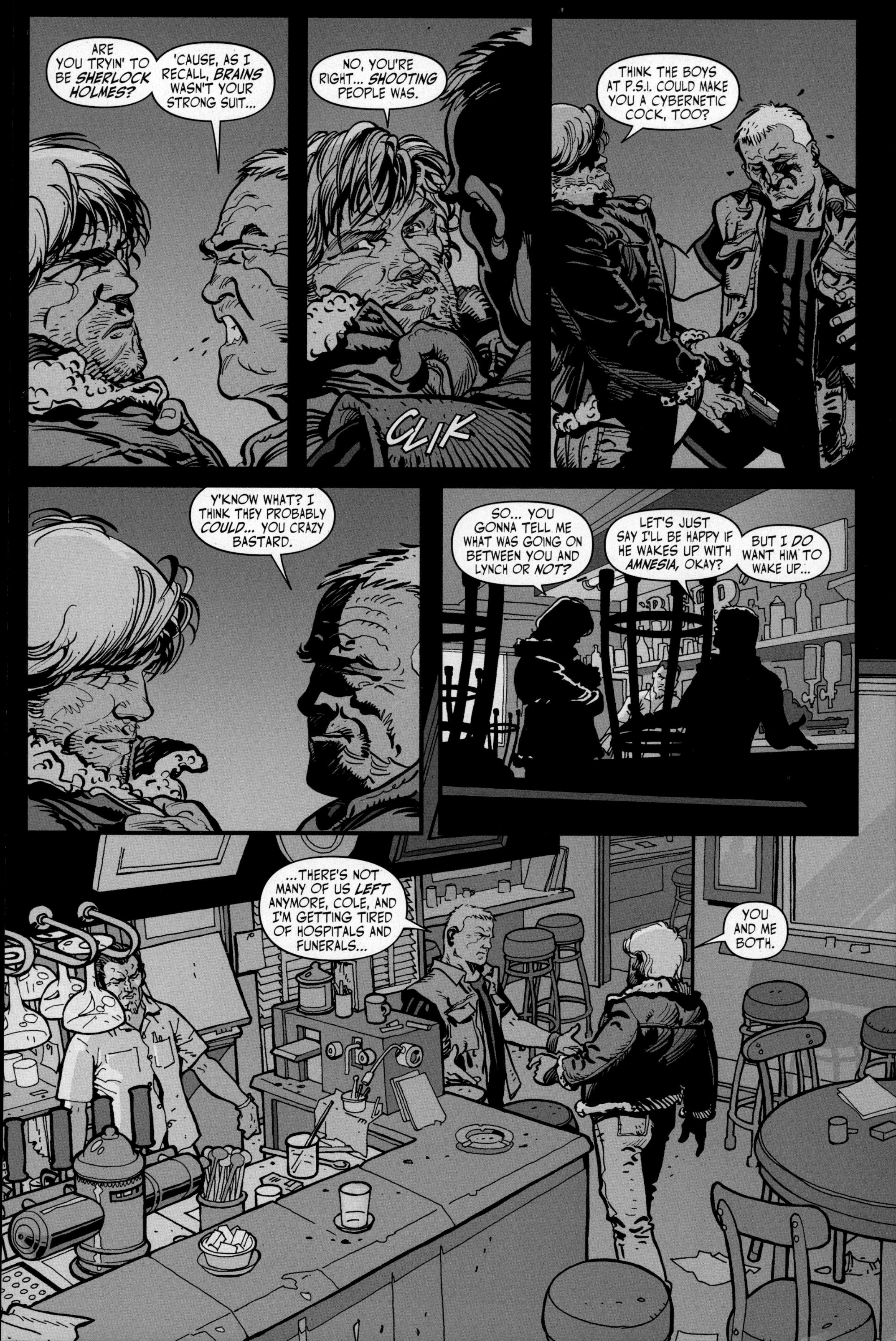
ARE YOU TRYIN' TO BE SHERLOCK HOLMES?
'CAUSE, AS I RECALL, BRAINS WASN'T YOUR STRONG SUIT...
NO, YOU'RE RIGHT... SHOOTING PEOPLE WAS.
CLIK
THINK THE BOYS AT P.S.I. COULD MAKE YOU A CYBERNETIC COCK, TOO?
Y'KNOW WHAT? I THINK THEY PROBABLY COULD... YOU CRAZY BASTARD.
SO... YOU GONNA TELL ME WHAT WAS GOING ON BETWEEN YOU AND LYNCH OR NOT?
LET'S JUST SAY I'LL BE HAPPY IF HE WAKES UP WITH AMNESIA, OKAY?
BUT I DO WANT HIM TO WAKE UP...
...THERE'S NOT MANY OF US LEFT ANYMORE, COLE, AND I'M GETTING TIRED OF HOSPITALS AND FUNERALS...
YOU AND ME BOTH.

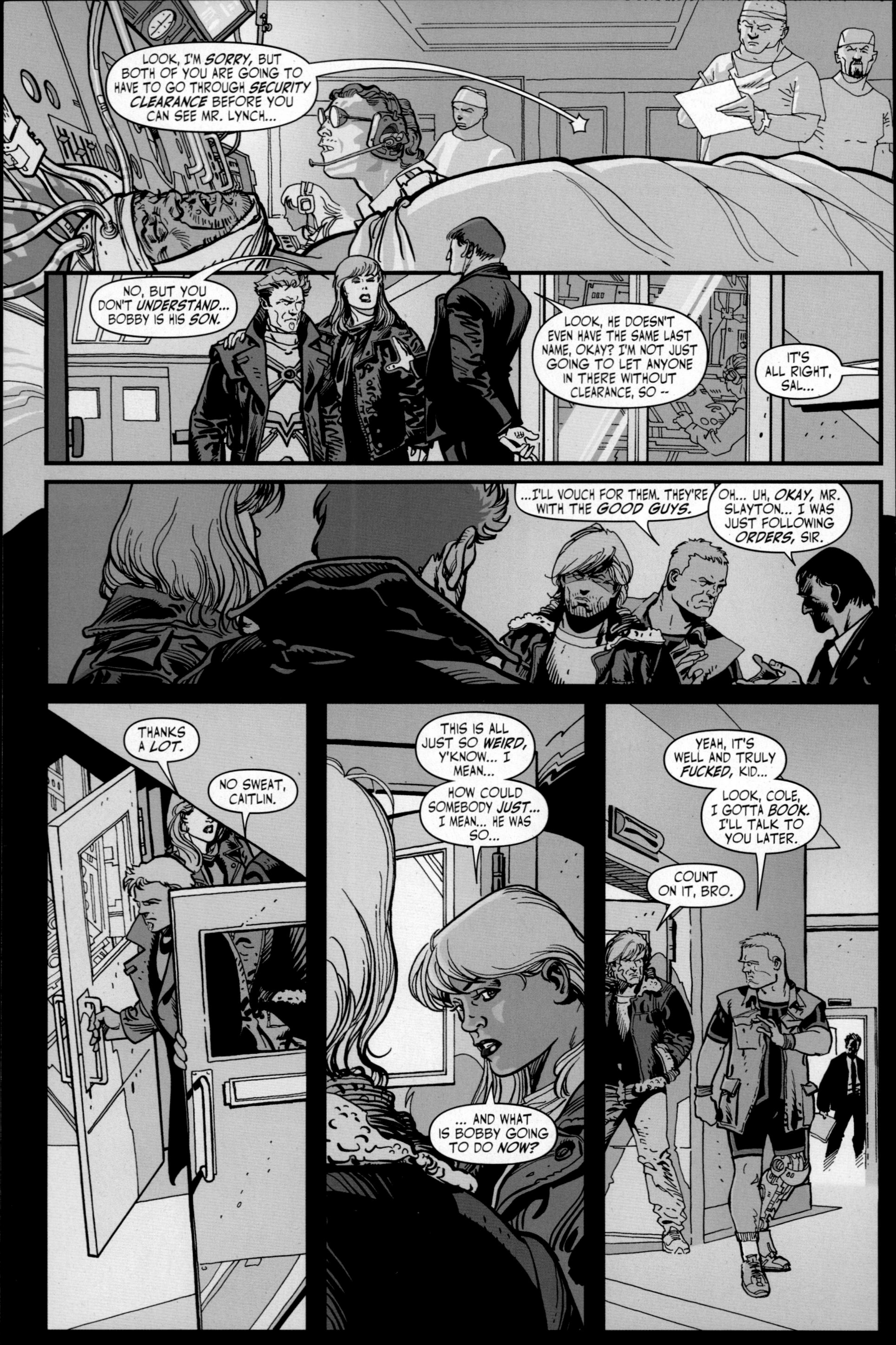
LOOK, I'M SORRY, BUT BOTH OF YOU ARE GOING TO HAVE TO GO THROUGH SECURITY CLEARANCE BEFORE YOU CAN SEE MR. LYNCH...
NO, BUT YOU DON'T UNDERSTAND... BOBBY IS HIS SON.
LOOK, HE DOESN'T EVEN HAVE THE SAME LAST NAME, OKAY? I'M NOT JUST GOING TO LET ANYONE IN THERE WITHOUT CLEARANCE, SO --
IT'S ALL RIGHT, SAL...
...I'LL VOUCH FOR THEM. THEY'RE WITH THE GOOD GUYS.
OH... UH, OKAY, MR. SLAYTON... I WAS JUST FOLLOWING ORDERS, SIR.
THANKS A LOT.
NO SWEAT, CAITLIN.
THIS IS ALL JUST SO WEIRD, Y'KNOW... I MEAN...
HOW COULD SOMEBODY JUST... I MEAN... HE WAS SO...
... AND WHAT IS BOBBY GOING TO DO NOW?
YEAH, IT'S WELL AND TRULY FUCKED, KID...
LOOK, COLE, I GOTTA BOOK. I'LL TALK TO YOU LATER.
COUNT ON IT, BRO.

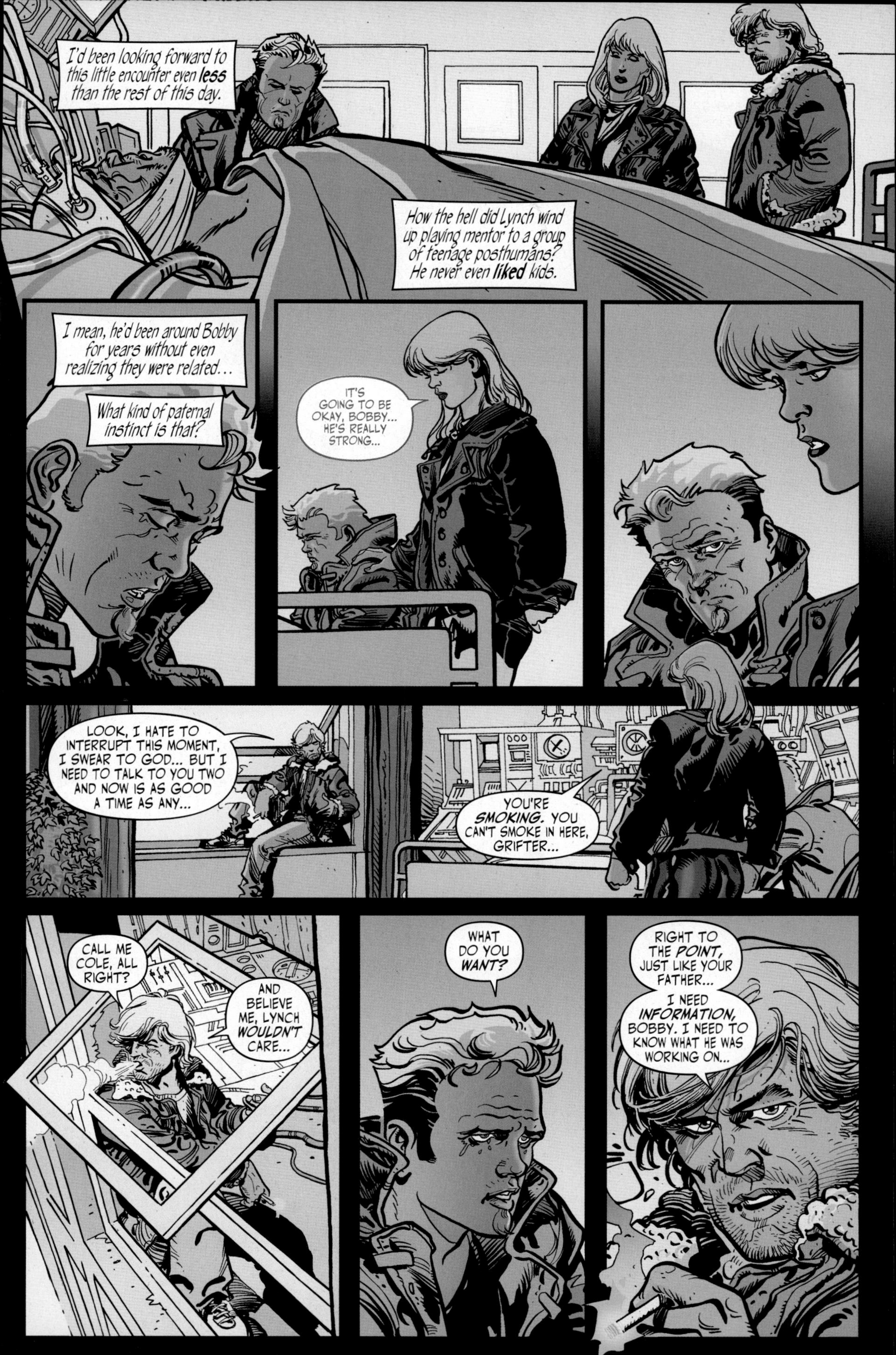
I'd been looking forward to this little encounter even **less** than the rest of this day.
How the hell did Lynch wind up playing mentor to a group of teenage posthumans? He never even **liked** kids.
I mean, he'd been around Bobby for years without even realizing they were related...
What kind of paternal instinct is that?
IT'S GOING TO BE OKAY, BOBBY... HE'S REALLY STRONG...
LOOK, I HATE TO INTERRUPT THIS MOMENT, I SWEAR TO GOD... BUT I NEED TO TALK TO YOU TWO AND NOW IS AS GOOD A TIME AS ANY...
YOU'RE ***SMOKING.*** YOU CAN'T SMOKE IN HERE, GRIFTER...
CALL ME COLE, ALL RIGHT?
AND BELIEVE ME, LYNCH ***WOULDN'T*** CARE...
WHAT DO YOU ***WANT?***
RIGHT TO THE ***POINT,*** JUST LIKE YOUR FATHER...
I NEED ***INFORMATION,*** BOBBY. I NEED TO KNOW WHAT HE WAS WORKING ON...

HAS HE EVER MENTIONED ANYONE NAMED *CARVER* THAT YOU CAN REMEMBER? PROBABLY IN THE LAST FEW MONTHS...

IT *MIGHT* HAVE SOMETHING TO DO WITH THIS SHOOTING...

DID YOU EVEN *KNOW* MY DAD? DO YOU REALLY THINK HE'D BE *CONFIDING* IN ME?

I HAVEN'T EVEN *SEEN* HIM FOR MOST OF THE LAST *YEAR*...

SHIT... I'M SORRY, BOBBY. I'M NO GOOD AT THIS SHIT...

BUT LISTEN, I'M GONNA FIND OUT WHAT HAPPENED TO HIM, AND MAKE WHOEVER DID IT *PAY*...

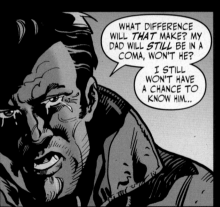

WHAT DIFFERENCE WILL *THAT* MAKE? MY DAD WILL *STILL* BE IN A COMA, WON'T HE?

I STILL WON'T HAVE A CHANCE TO KNOW HIM...

I JUST MEANT --

AND YOU'RE *WRONG*, COLE... I'M NOT LIKE HIM AT ALL. BUT YOU *ARE*...

YOU THINK ALL YOUR MILITARY BULLSHIT AND SECRET WARS CAN SOLVE EVERYTHING...

WELL, I DON'T WANT *REVENGE*. I JUST WANTED A FATHER.

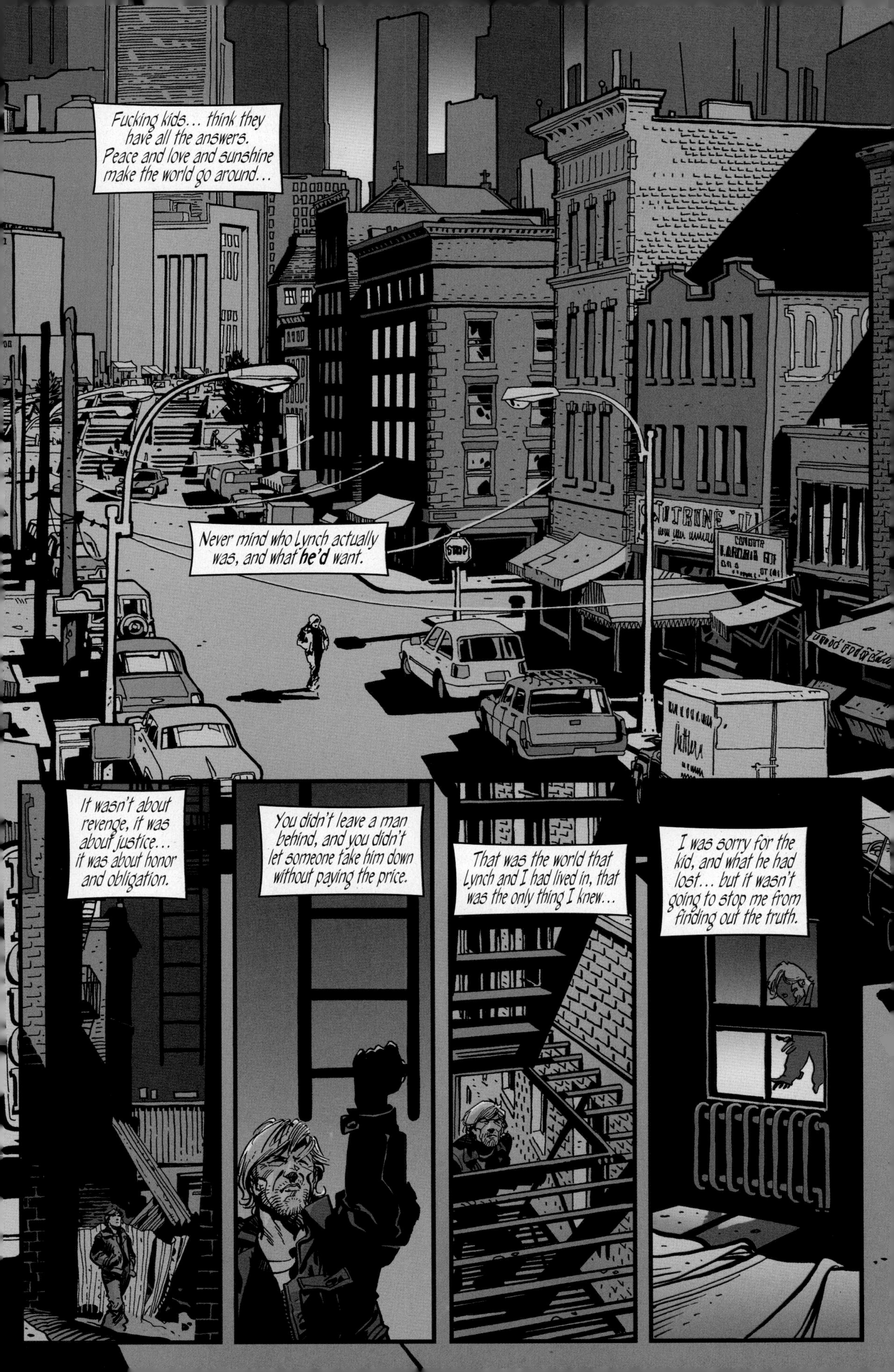
Fucking kids... think they have all the answers. Peace and love and sunshine make the world go around...
Never mind who Lynch actually was, and what **he'd** want.
STOP
It wasn't about revenge, it was about justice... it was about honor and obligation.
You didn't leave a man behind, and you didn't let someone take him down without paying the price.
That was the world that Lynch and I had lived in, that was the only thing I knew...
I was sorry for the kid, and what he had lost... but it wasn't going to stop me from finding out the truth.

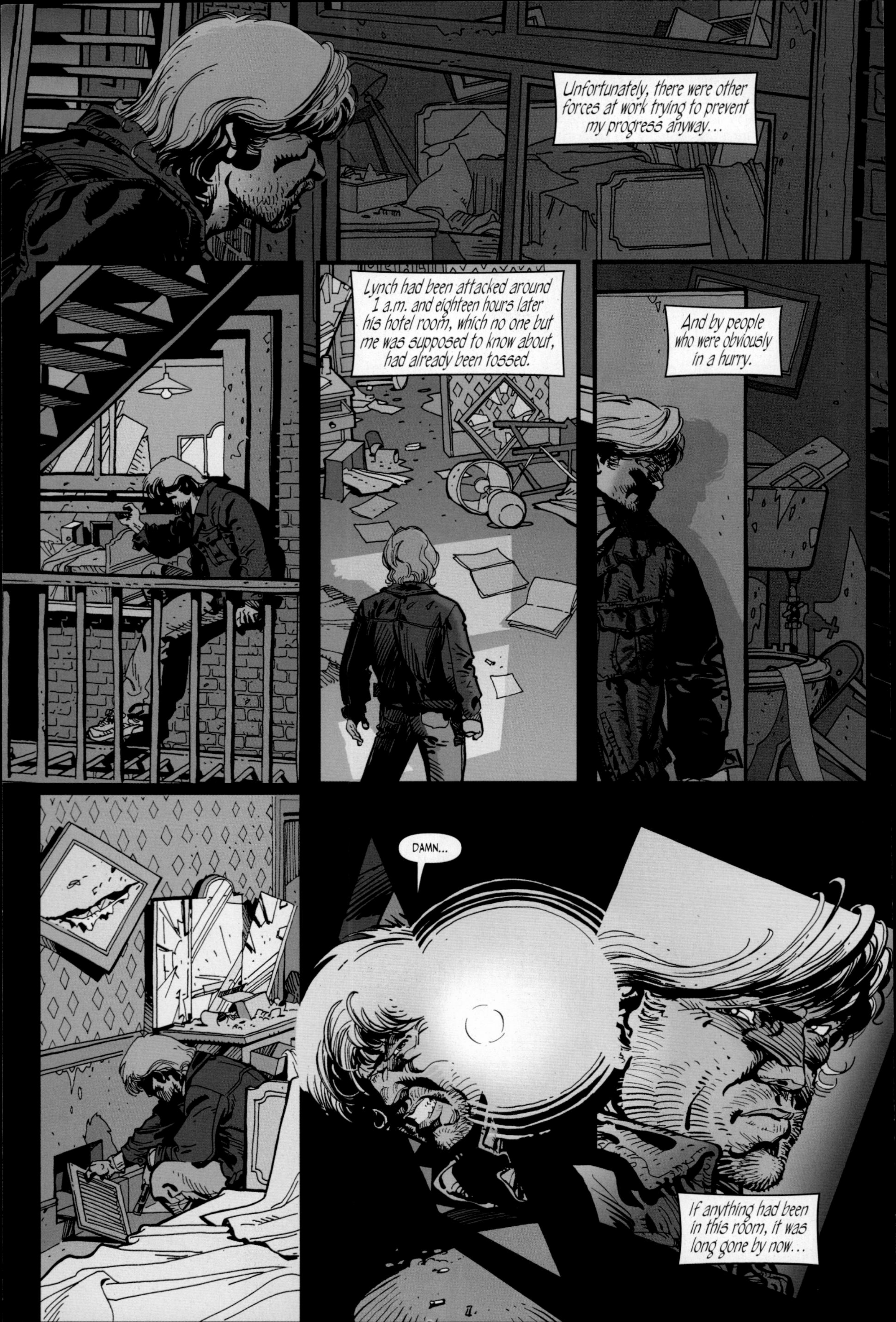
Unfortunately, there were other forces at work trying to prevent my progress anyway...
Lynch had been attacked around 1 a.m. and eighteen hours later his hotel room, which no one but me was supposed to know about, had already been tossed.
And by people who were obviously in a hurry.
DAMN...
If anything had been in this room, it was long gone by now...

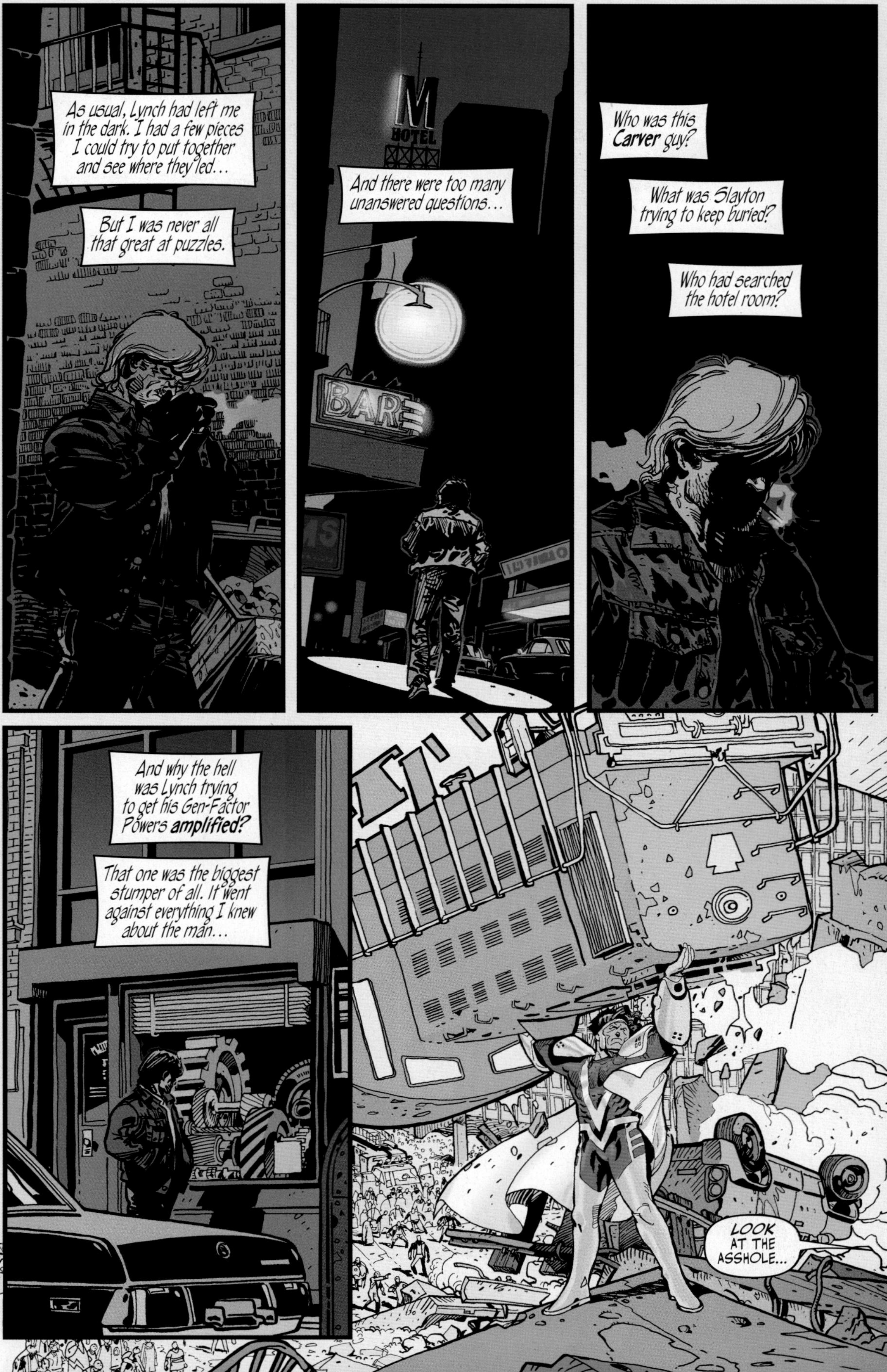
As usual, Lynch had left me in the dark. I had a few pieces I could try to put together and see where they led...
But I was never all that great at puzzles.
M
HOTEL
And there were too many unanswered questions...
BAR
Who was this **Carver** guy?
What was Slayton trying to keep buried?
Who had searched the hotel room?
And why the hell was Lynch trying to get his Gen-Factor Powers **amplified?**
That one was the biggest stumper of all. It went against everything I knew about the man...
LOOK AT THE ASSHOLE...

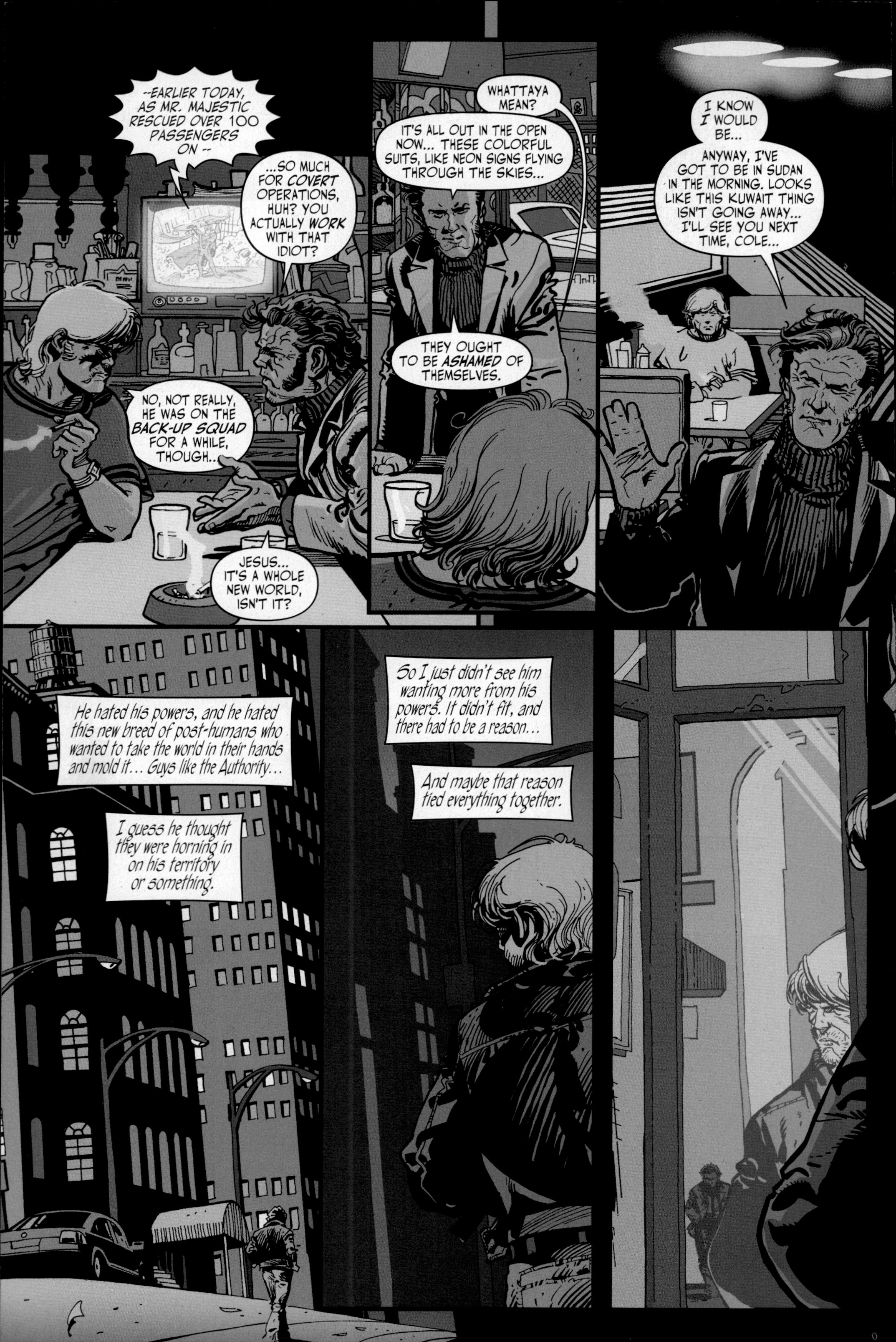
--EARLIER TODAY, AS MR. MAJESTIC RESCUED OVER 100 PASSENGERS ON --
...SO MUCH FOR COVERT OPERATIONS, HUH? YOU ACTUALLY WORK WITH THAT IDIOT?
NO, NOT REALLY, HE WAS ON THE BACK-UP SQUAD FOR A WHILE, THOUGH...
JESUS... IT'S A WHOLE NEW WORLD, ISN'T IT?
WHATTAYA MEAN?
IT'S ALL OUT IN THE OPEN NOW... THESE COLORFUL SUITS, LIKE NEON SIGNS FLYING THROUGH THE SKIES...
THEY OUGHT TO BE ASHAMED OF THEMSELVES.
I KNOW I WOULD BE...
ANYWAY, I'VE GOT TO BE IN SUDAN IN THE MORNING. LOOKS LIKE THIS KUWAIT THING ISN'T GOING AWAY... I'LL SEE YOU NEXT TIME, COLE...
He hated his powers, and he hated this new breed of post-humans who wanted to take the world in their hands and mold it... Guys like the Authority...
I guess he thought they were horning in on his territory or something.
So I just didn't see him wanting more from his powers. It didn't fit, and there had to be a reason...
And maybe that reason tied everything together.

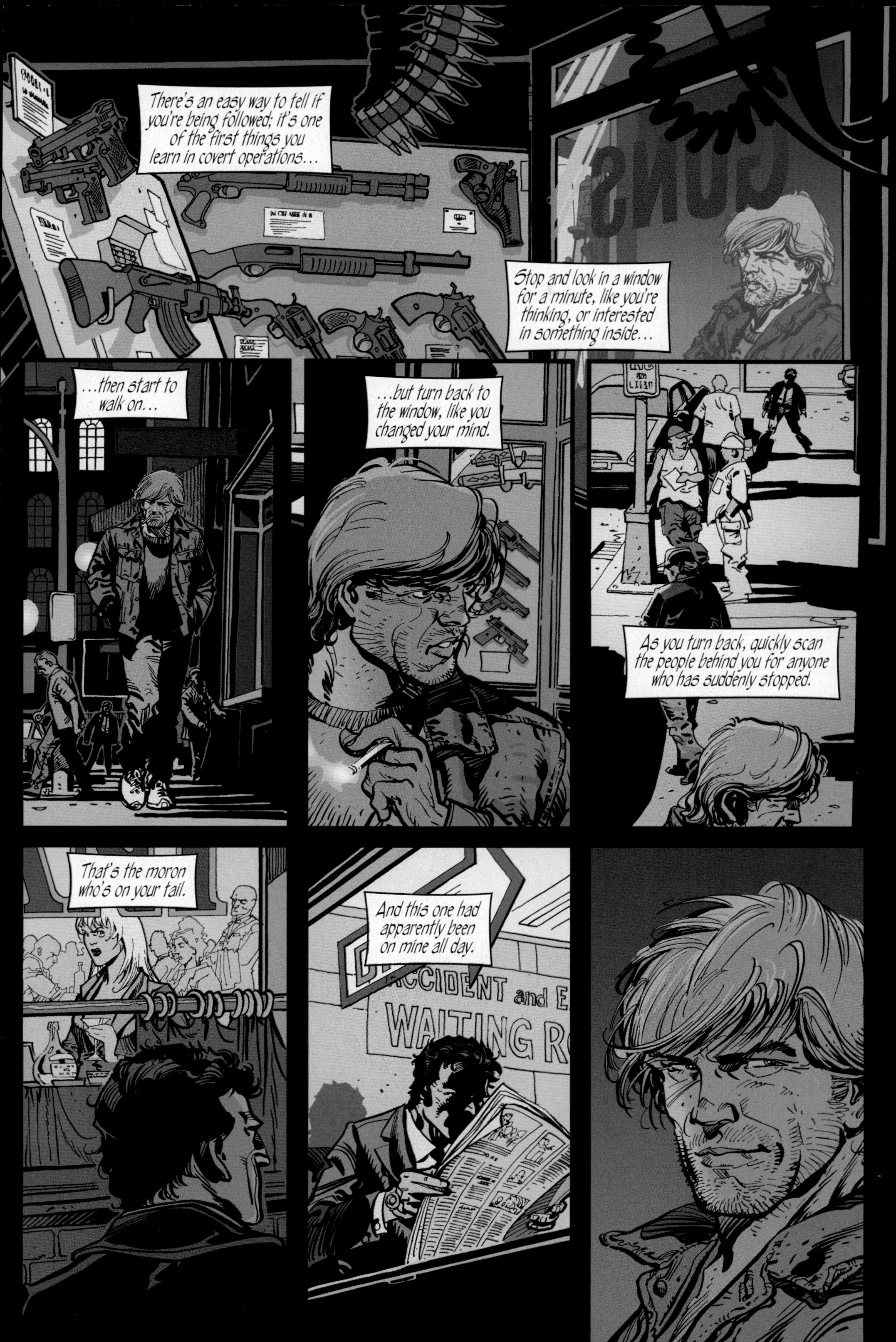
There's an easy way to tell if you're being followed; it's one of the first things you learn in covert operations...
GUNS
Stop and look in a window for a minute, like you're thinking, or interested in something inside...
...then start to walk on...
...but turn back to the window, like you changed your mind.
As you turn back, quickly scan the people behind you for anyone who has suddenly stopped.
That's the moron who's on your tail.
And this one had apparently been on mine all day.
ACCIDENT and E
WAITING R

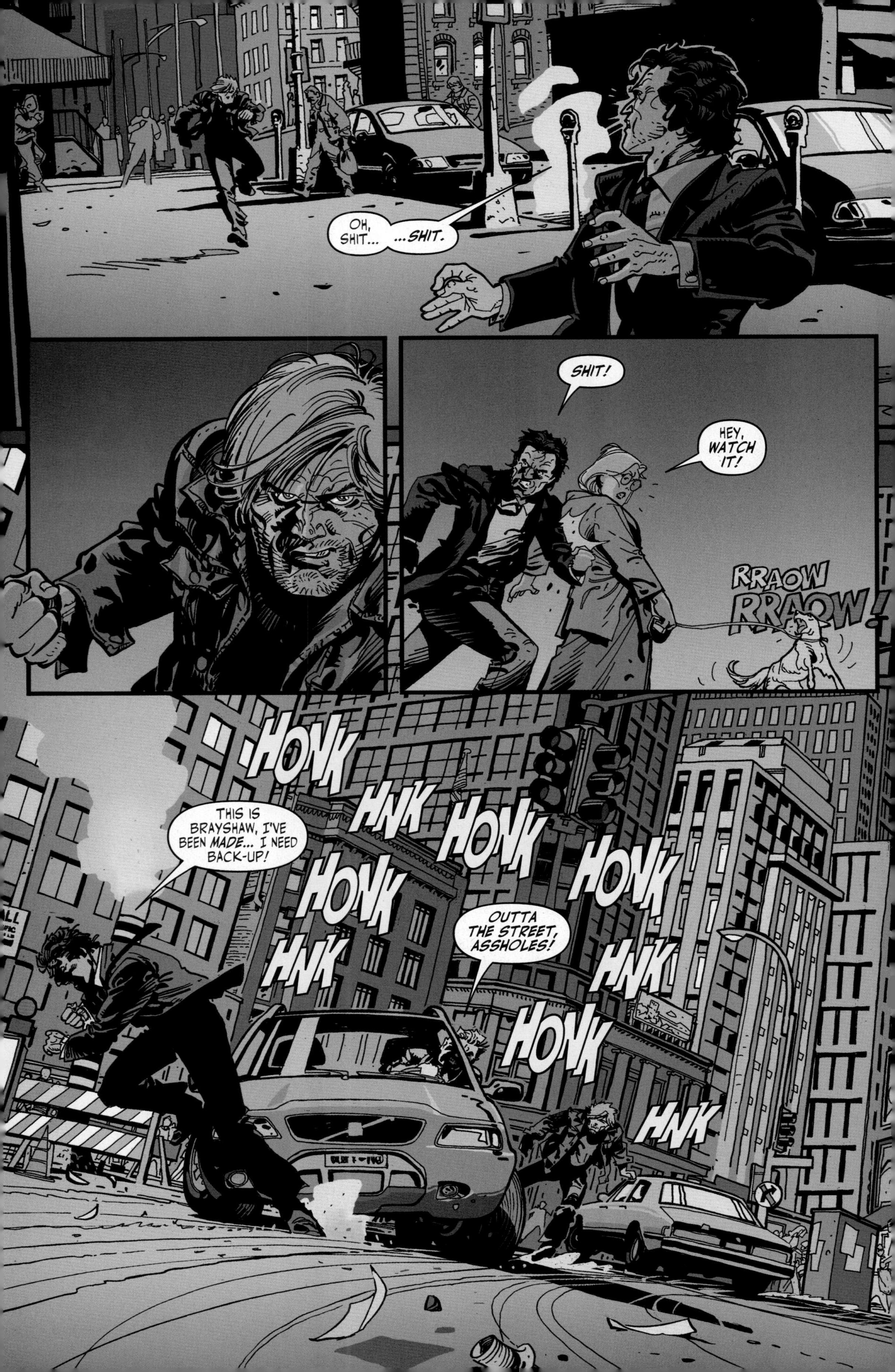
OH, SHIT...
...SHIT.
SHIT!
HEY, WATCH IT!
RRAOW RRAOW!
HONK
HNK
HONK
THIS IS BRAYSHAW, I'VE BEEN MADE... I NEED BACK-UP!
HONK
HNK
HONK
OUTTA THE STREET, ASSHOLES!
HNK
HONK
HNK

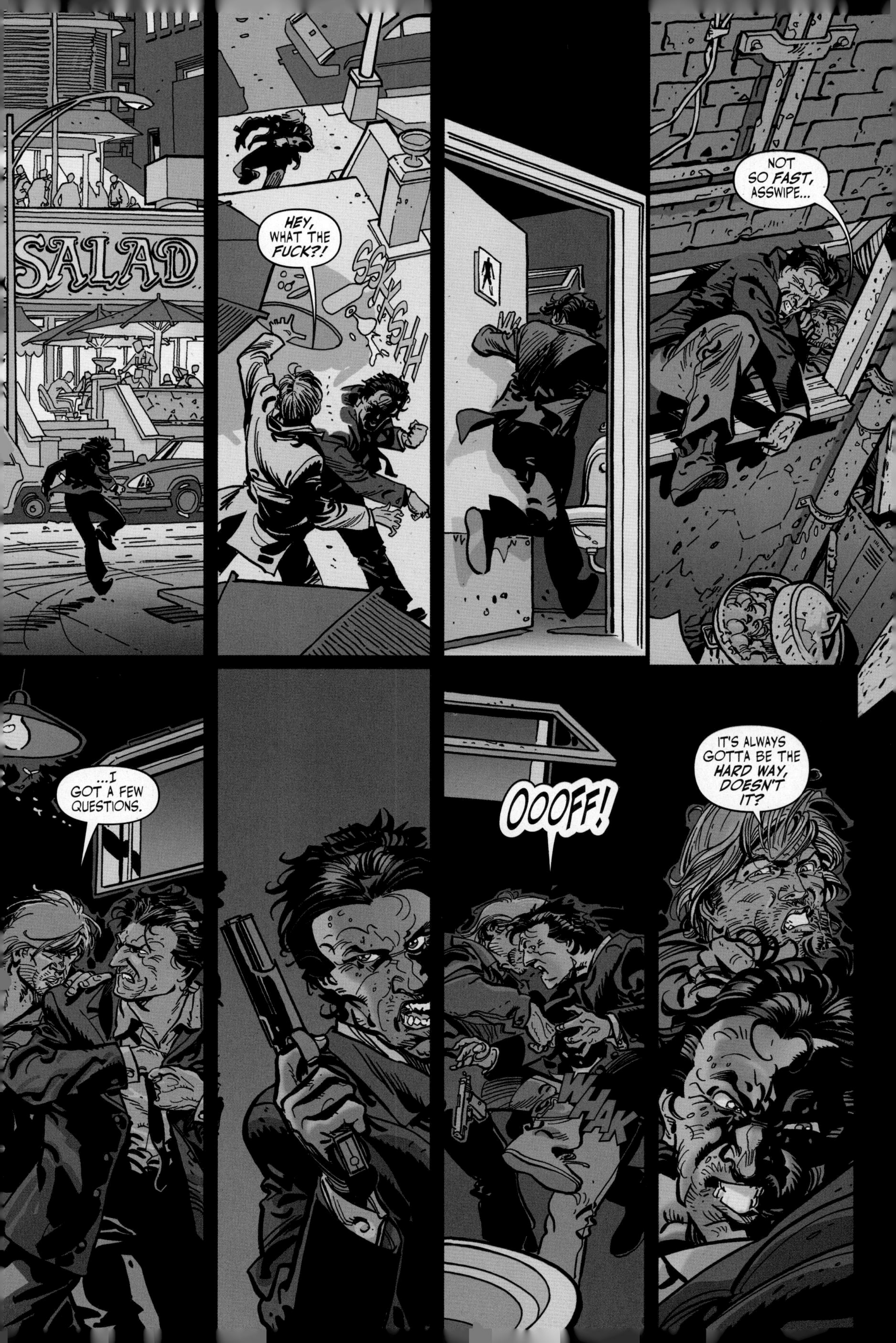
SALAD
HEY, WHAT THE FUCK?!
SSHKSHSH
NOT SO FAST, ASSWIPE...
...I GOT A FEW QUESTIONS.
OOOFF!
WHAK
IT'S ALWAYS GOTTA BE THE HARD WAY, DOESN'T IT?

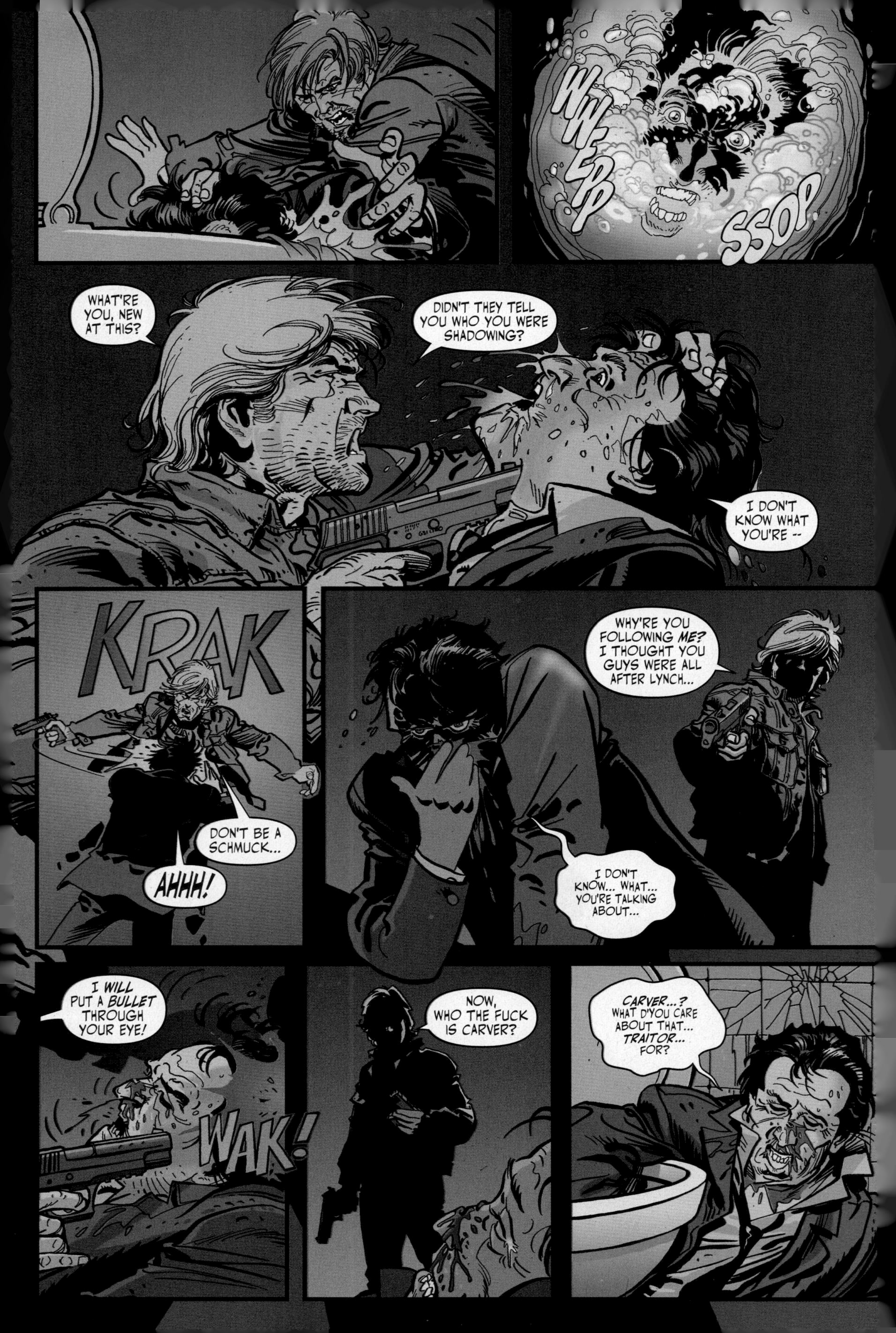
WWEPP
SSOP
WHAT'RE YOU, NEW AT THIS?
DIDN'T THEY TELL YOU WHO YOU WERE SHADOWING?
I DON'T KNOW WHAT YOU'RE --
KRAK
DON'T BE A SCHMUCK...
AHHH!
WHY'RE YOU FOLLOWING ME? I THOUGHT YOU GUYS WERE ALL AFTER LYNCH...
I DON'T KNOW... WHAT... YOU'RE TALKING ABOUT...
I WILL PUT A BULLET THROUGH YOUR EYE!
WAK!
NOW, WHO THE FUCK IS CARVER?
CARVER...? WHAT D'YOU CARE ABOUT THAT... TRAITOR... FOR?

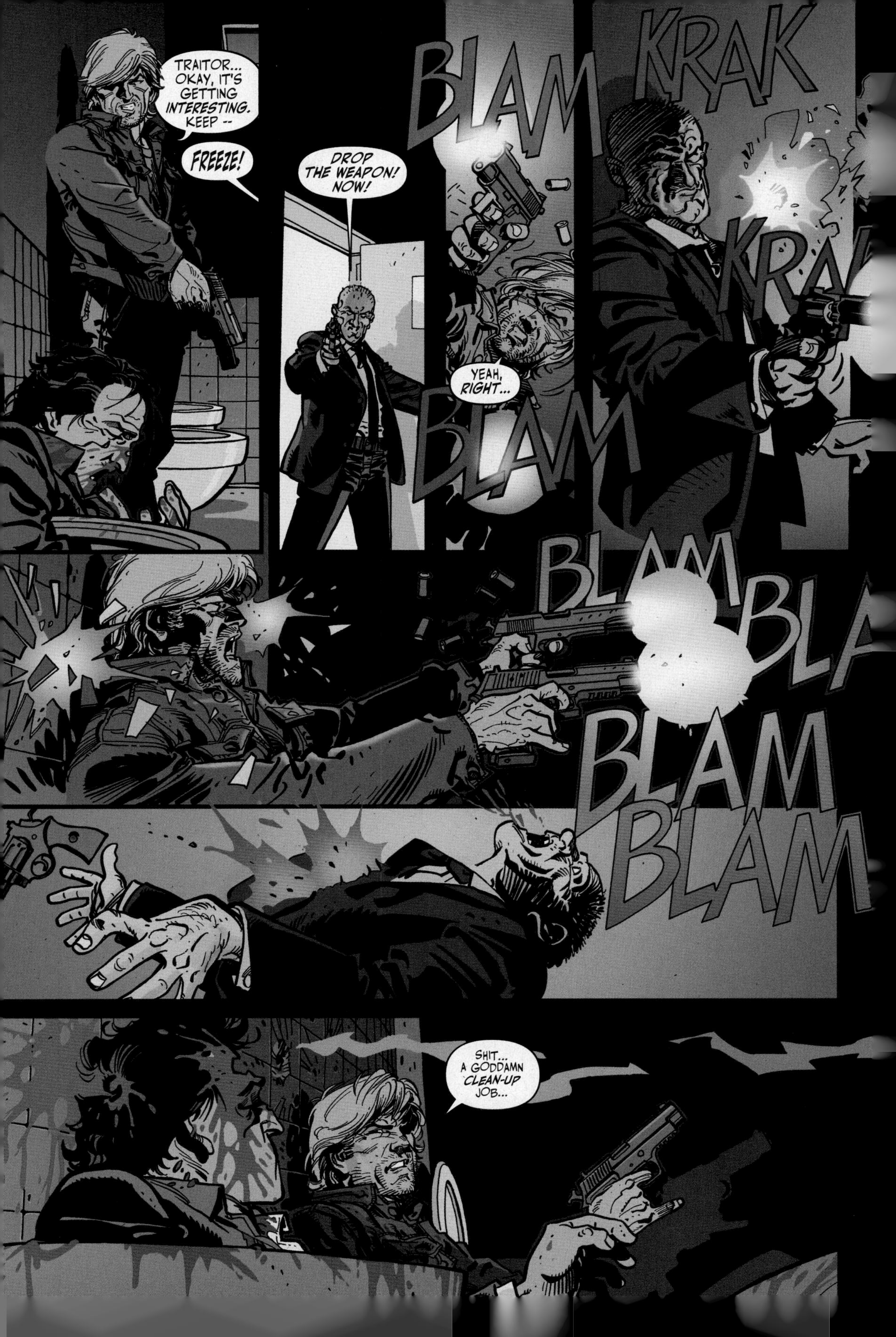
TRAITOR... OKAY, IT'S GETTING INTERESTING. KEEP --
FREEZE!
DROP THE WEAPON! NOW!
BLAM
KRAK
YEAH, RIGHT...
BLAM
KRAK
BLAM
BLAM
BLAM
BLAM
SHIT... A GODDAMN CLEAN-UP JOB...

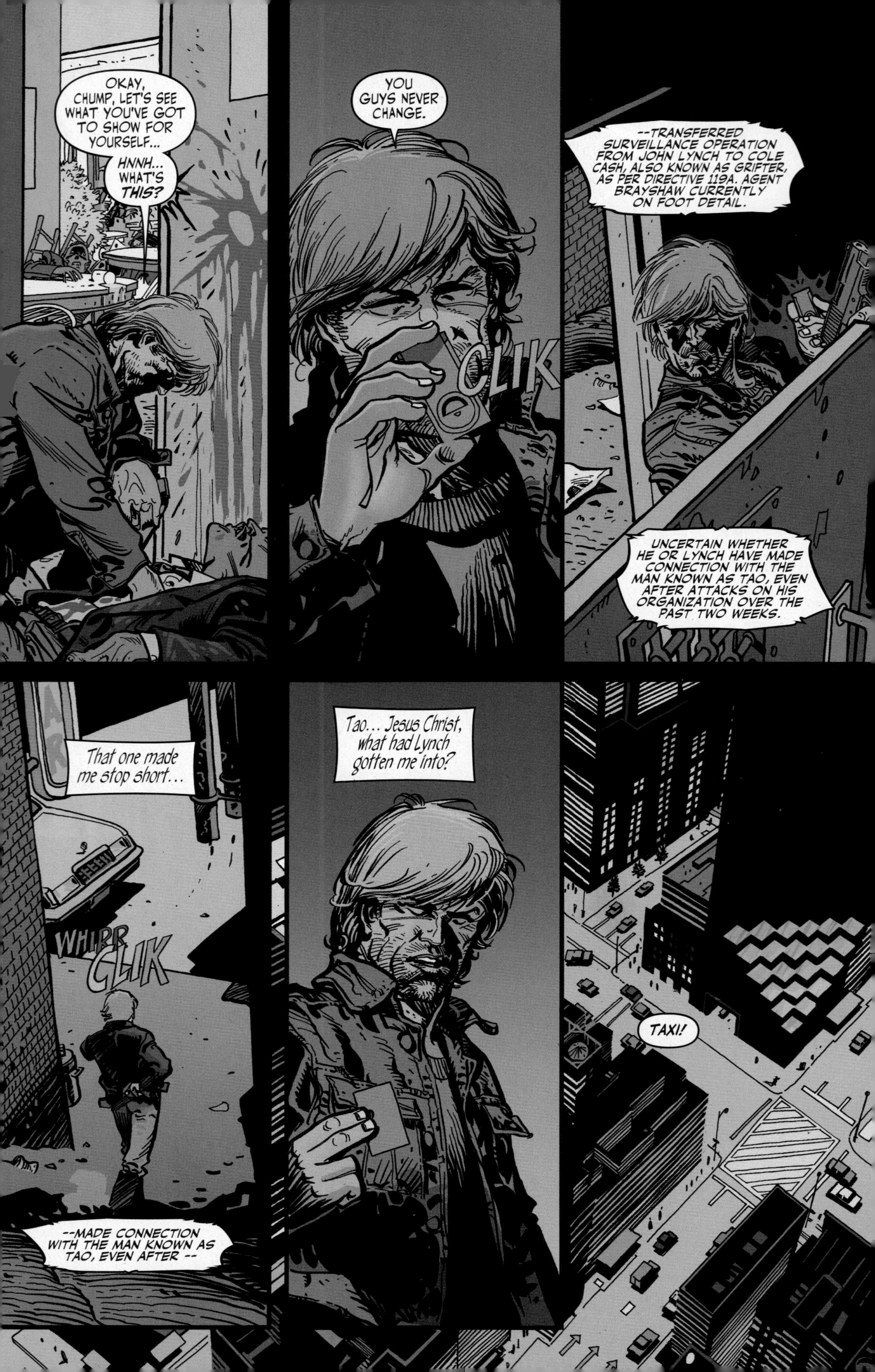
OKAY, CHUMP, LET'S SEE WHAT YOU'VE GOT TO SHOW FOR YOURSELF...
HNNH... WHAT'S *THIS?*
YOU GUYS NEVER CHANGE.
CLIK
--TRANSFERRED SURVEILLANCE OPERATION FROM JOHN LYNCH TO COLE CASH, ALSO KNOWN AS GRIFTER, AS PER DIRECTIVE 119A. AGENT BRAYSHAW CURRENTLY ON FOOT DETAIL.
UNCERTAIN WHETHER HE OR LYNCH HAVE MADE CONNECTION WITH THE MAN KNOWN AS TAO, EVEN AFTER ATTACKS ON HIS ORGANIZATION OVER THE PAST TWO WEEKS.
That one made me stop short...
WHIRR
CLIK
--MADE CONNECTION WITH THE MAN KNOWN AS TAO, EVEN AFTER --
Tao... Jesus Christ, what had Lynch gotten me into?
TAXI!

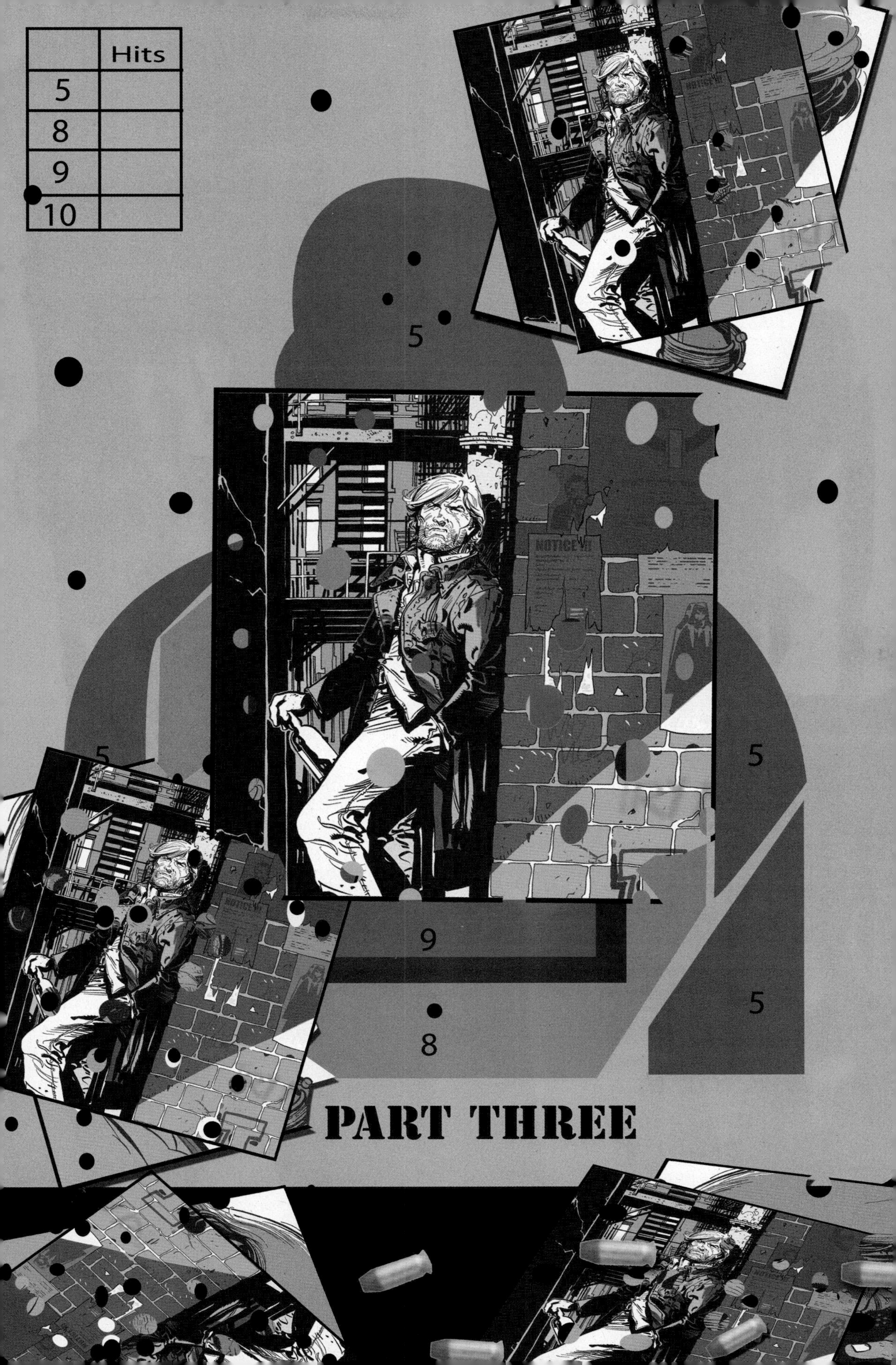
Hits
5
8
9
10
5
5
9
5
8
PART THREE

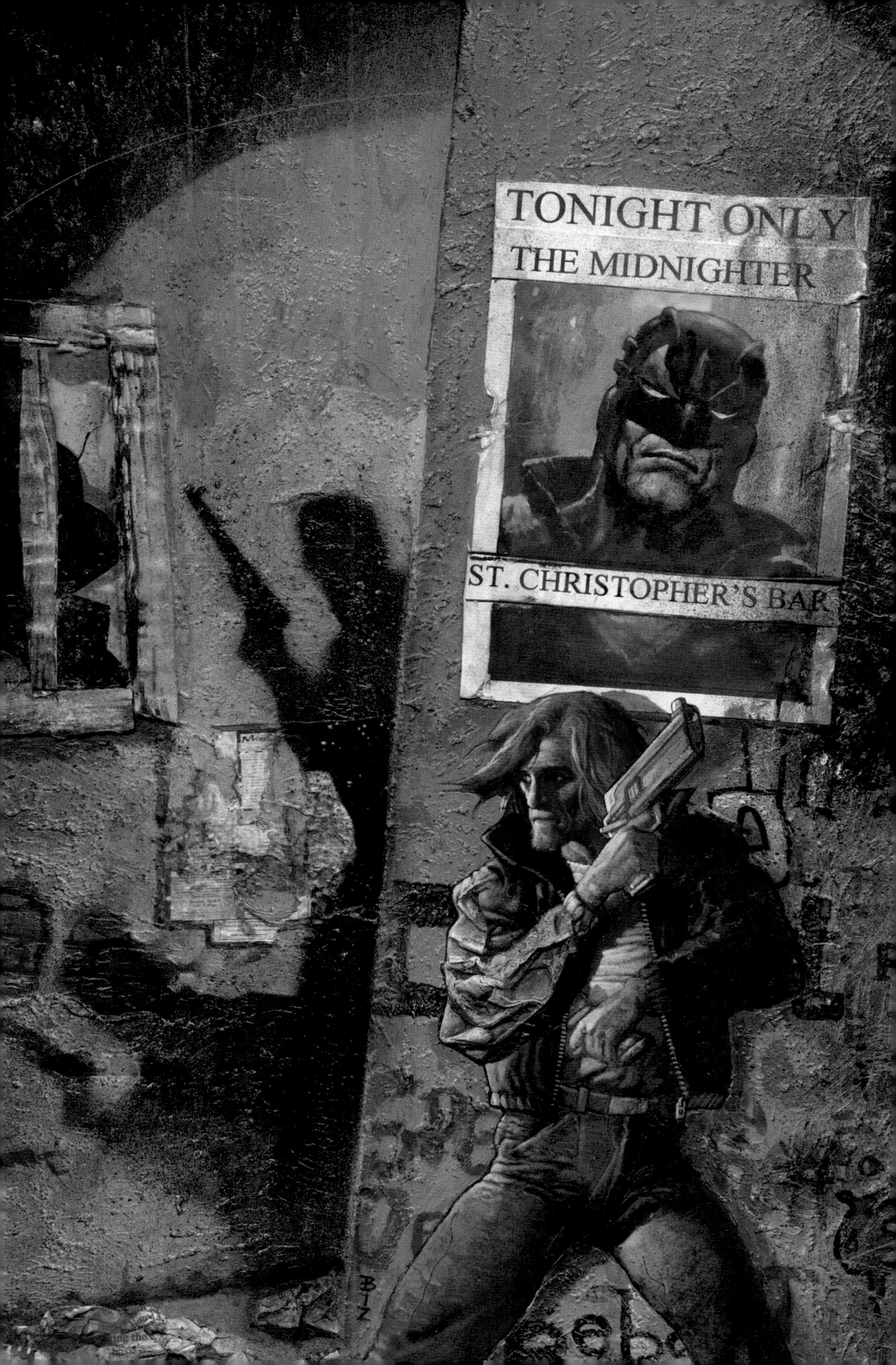
TONIGHT ONLY
THE MIDNIGHTER
ST. CHRISTOPHER'S BAR
BIZ

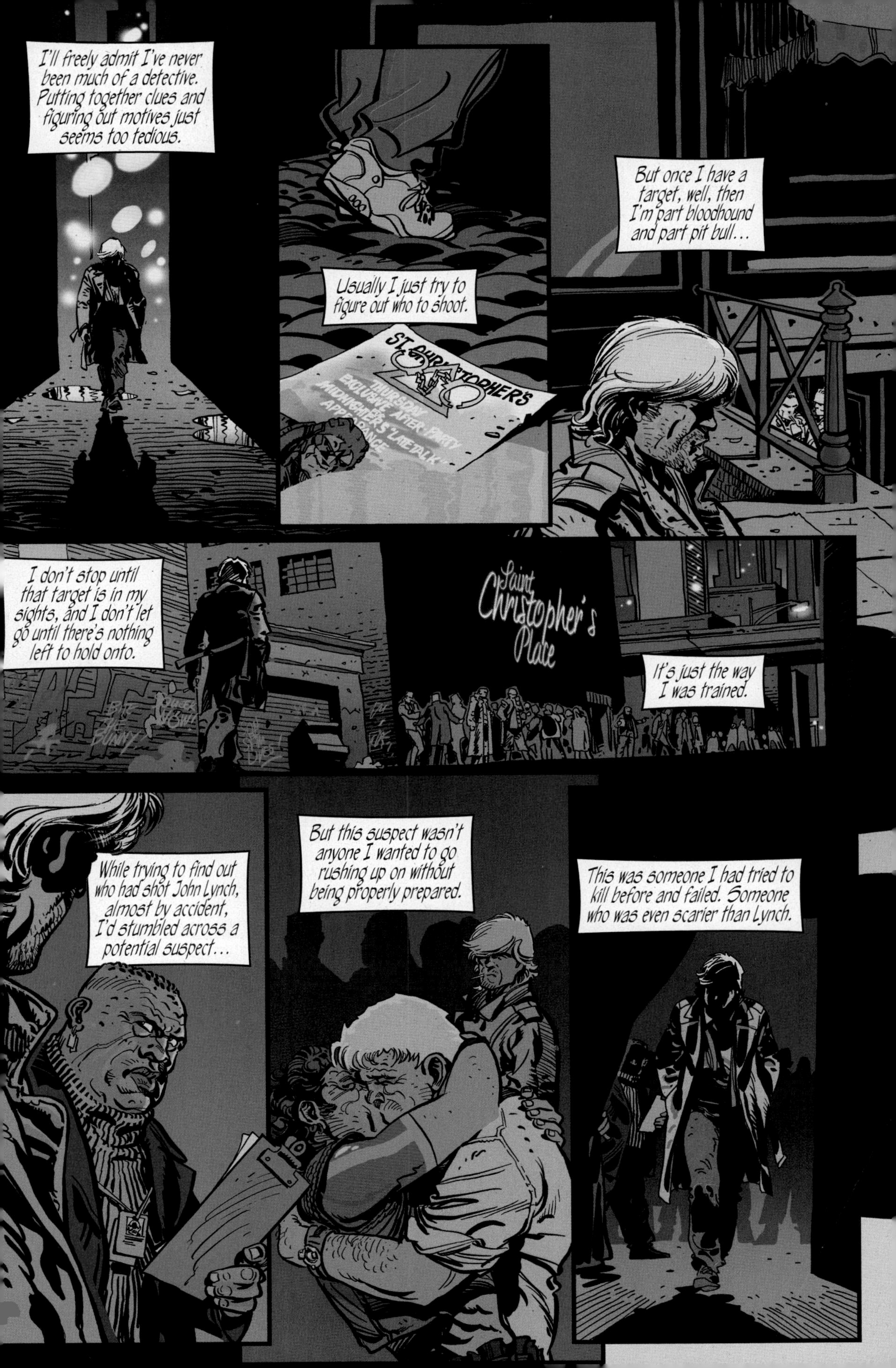
I'll freely admit I've never been much of a detective. Putting together clues and figuring out motives just seems too tedious.
Usually I just try to figure out who to shoot.
THURSDAY
EXCLUSIVE AFTER-PARTY
MIDNIGHTER'S "LATE TALK"
APPEARANCE
But once I have a target, well, then I'm part bloodhound and part pit bull...
I don't stop until that target is in my sights, and I don't let go until there's nothing left to hold onto.
BITE THE BUNNY
Saint Christopher's Place
It's just the way I was trained.
While trying to find out who had shot John Lynch, almost by accident, I'd stumbled across a potential suspect...
But this suspect wasn't anyone I wanted to go rushing up on without being properly prepared.
This was someone I had tried to kill before and failed. Someone who was even scarier than Lynch.

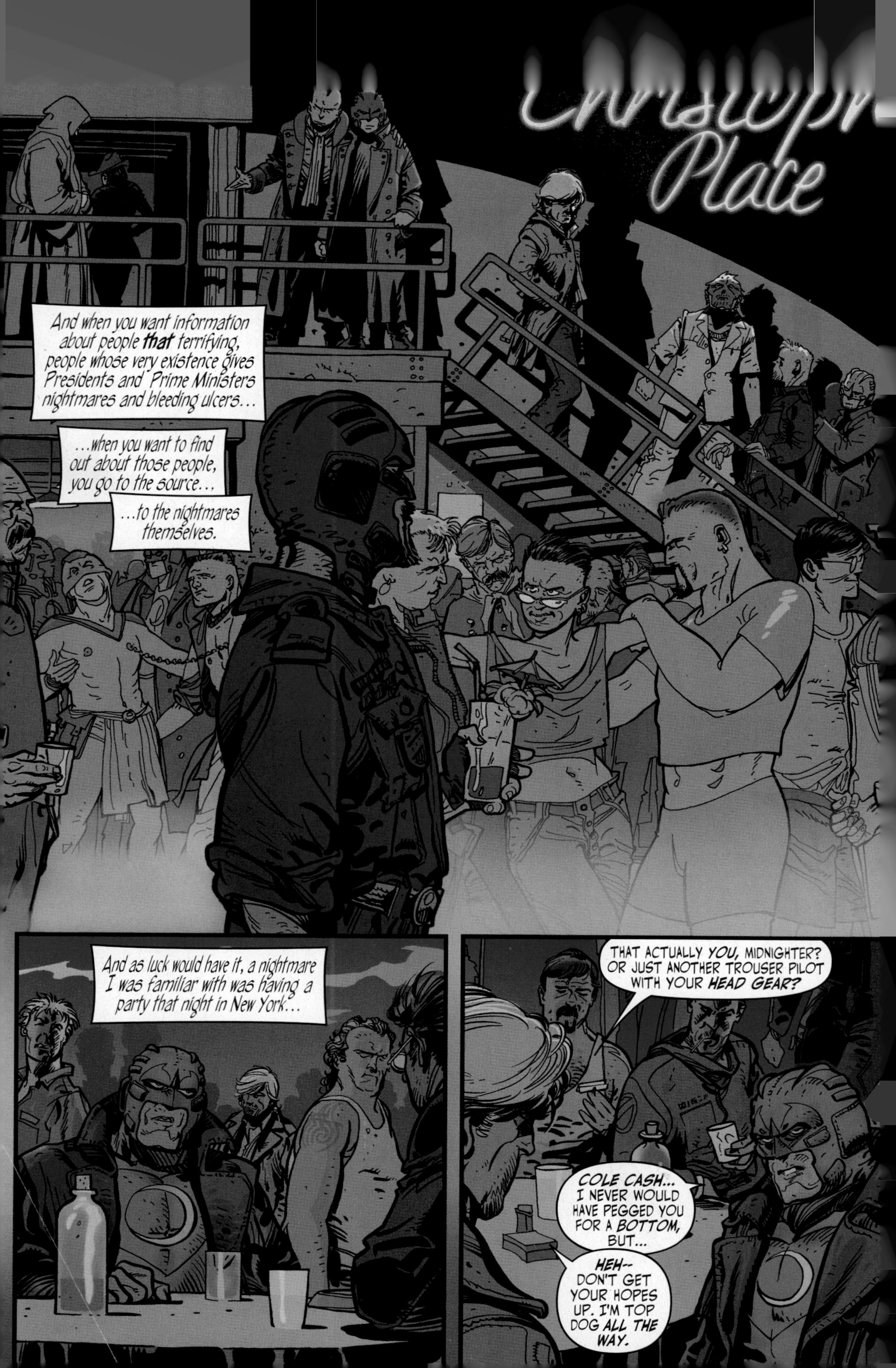
Place
And when you want information about people ***that*** terrifying, people whose very existence gives Presidents and Prime Ministers nightmares and bleeding ulcers...
...when you want to find out about those people, you go to the source...
...to the nightmares themselves.
And as luck would have it, a nightmare I was familiar with was having a party that night in New York...
THAT ACTUALLY *YOU,* MIDNIGHTER? OR JUST ANOTHER TROUSER PILOT WITH YOUR ***HEAD GEAR?***
COLE CASH... I NEVER WOULD HAVE PEGGED YOU FOR A ***BOTTOM,*** BUT...
HEH-- DON'T GET YOUR HOPES UP. I'M TOP DOG ***ALL THE WAY.***

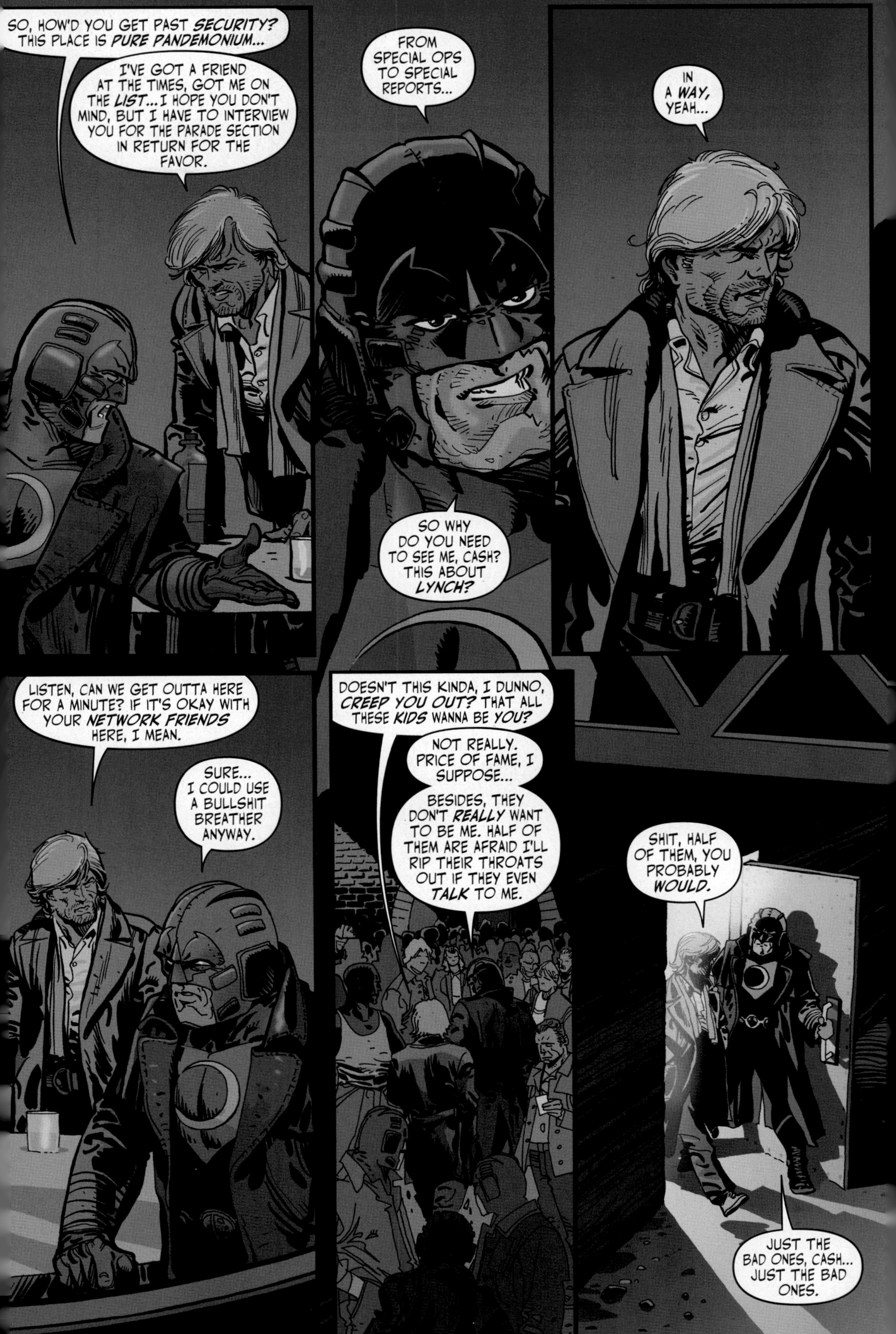
SO, HOW'D YOU GET PAST SECURITY? THIS PLACE IS PURE PANDEMONIUM...
I'VE GOT A FRIEND AT THE TIMES, GOT ME ON THE LIST... I HOPE YOU DON'T MIND, BUT I HAVE TO INTERVIEW YOU FOR THE PARADE SECTION IN RETURN FOR THE FAVOR.
FROM SPECIAL OPS TO SPECIAL REPORTS...
SO WHY DO YOU NEED TO SEE ME, CASH? THIS ABOUT LYNCH?
IN A WAY, YEAH...
LISTEN, CAN WE GET OUTTA HERE FOR A MINUTE? IF IT'S OKAY WITH YOUR NETWORK FRIENDS HERE, I MEAN.
SURE... I COULD USE A BULLSHIT BREATHER ANYWAY.
DOESN'T THIS KINDA, I DUNNO, CREEP YOU OUT? THAT ALL THESE KIDS WANNA BE YOU?
NOT REALLY. PRICE OF FAME, I SUPPOSE...
BESIDES, THEY DON'T REALLY WANT TO BE ME. HALF OF THEM ARE AFRAID I'LL RIP THEIR THROATS OUT IF THEY EVEN TALK TO ME.
SHIT, HALF OF THEM, YOU PROBABLY WOULD.
JUST THE BAD ONES, CASH... JUST THE BAD ONES.

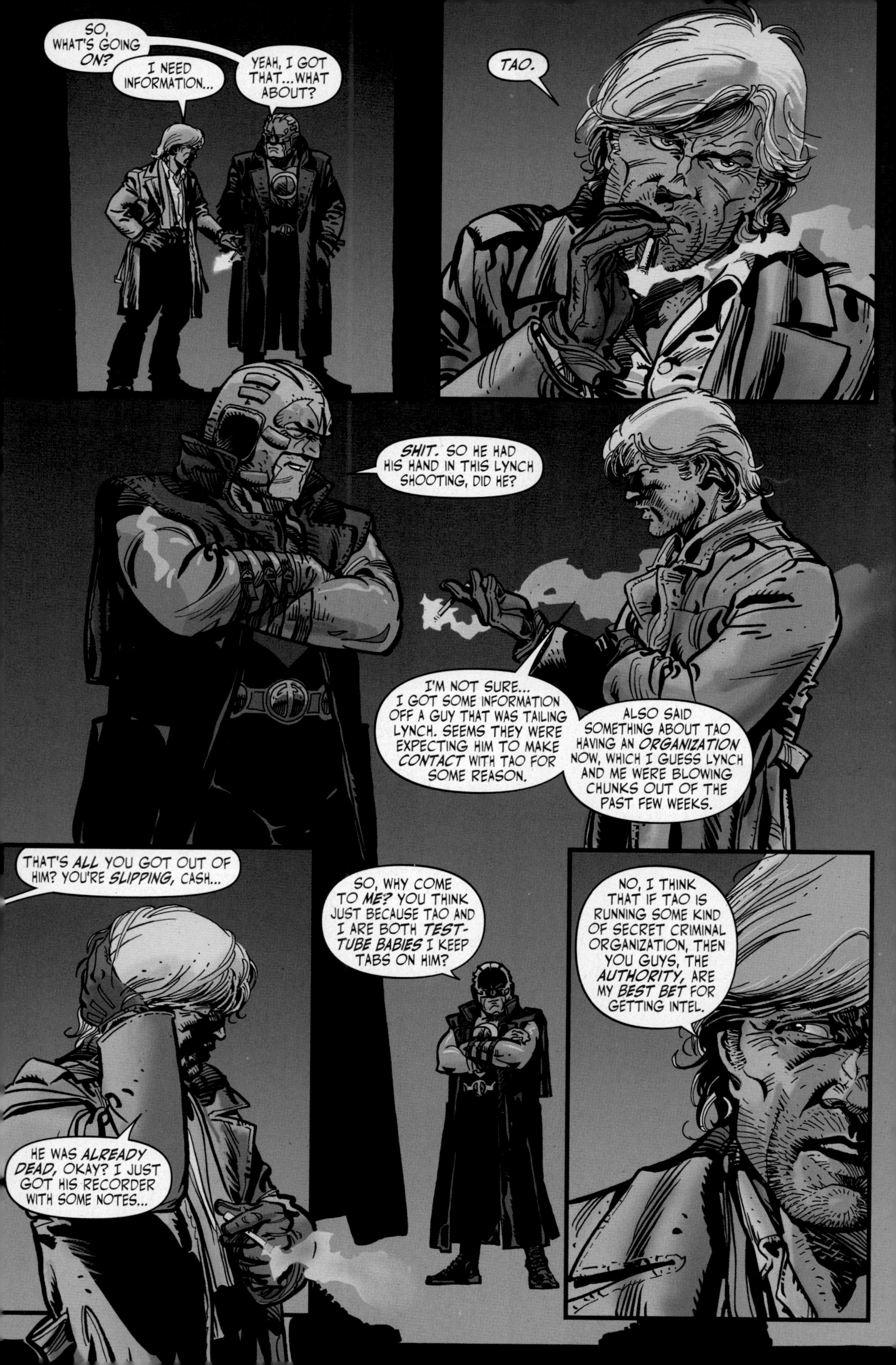
SO, WHAT'S GOING ON?
I NEED INFORMATION...
YEAH, I GOT THAT...WHAT ABOUT?
TAO.
SHIT. SO HE HAD HIS HAND IN THIS LYNCH SHOOTING, DID HE?
I'M NOT SURE... I GOT SOME INFORMATION OFF A GUY THAT WAS TAILING LYNCH. SEEMS THEY WERE EXPECTING HIM TO MAKE CONTACT WITH TAO FOR SOME REASON.
ALSO SAID SOMETHING ABOUT TAO HAVING AN ORGANIZATION NOW, WHICH I GUESS LYNCH AND ME WERE BLOWING CHUNKS OUT OF THE PAST FEW WEEKS.
THAT'S ALL YOU GOT OUT OF HIM? YOU'RE SLIPPING, CASH...
HE WAS ALREADY DEAD, OKAY? I JUST GOT HIS RECORDER WITH SOME NOTES...
SO, WHY COME TO ME? YOU THINK JUST BECAUSE TAO AND I ARE BOTH TEST-TUBE BABIES I KEEP TABS ON HIM?
NO, I THINK THAT IF TAO IS RUNNING SOME KIND OF SECRET CRIMINAL ORGANIZATION, THEN YOU GUYS, THE AUTHORITY, ARE MY BEST BET FOR GETTING INTEL.

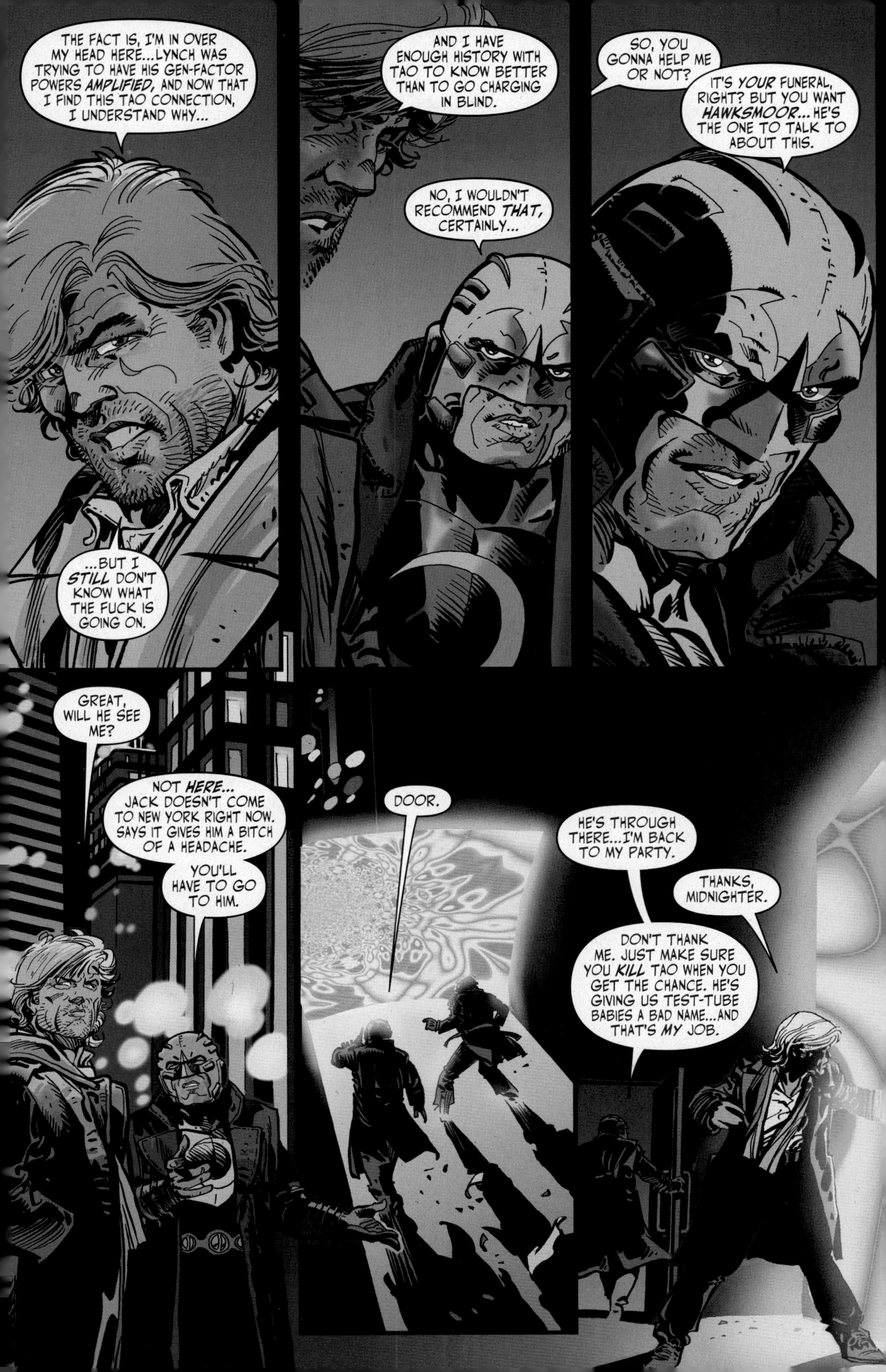
THE FACT IS, I'M IN OVER MY HEAD HERE...LYNCH WAS TRYING TO HAVE HIS GEN-FACTOR POWERS AMPLIFIED, AND NOW THAT I FIND THIS TAO CONNECTION, I UNDERSTAND WHY...
...BUT I STILL DON'T KNOW WHAT THE FUCK IS GOING ON.
AND I HAVE ENOUGH HISTORY WITH TAO TO KNOW BETTER THAN TO GO CHARGING IN BLIND.
NO, I WOULDN'T RECOMMEND THAT, CERTAINLY...
SO, YOU GONNA HELP ME OR NOT?
IT'S YOUR FUNERAL, RIGHT? BUT YOU WANT HAWKSMOOR... HE'S THE ONE TO TALK TO ABOUT THIS.
GREAT, WILL HE SEE ME?
NOT HERE... JACK DOESN'T COME TO NEW YORK RIGHT NOW. SAYS IT GIVES HIM A BITCH OF A HEADACHE.
YOU'LL HAVE TO GO TO HIM.
DOOR.
HE'S THROUGH THERE...I'M BACK TO MY PARTY.
THANKS, MIDNIGHTER.
DON'T THANK ME. JUST MAKE SURE YOU KILL TAO WHEN YOU GET THE CHANCE. HE'S GIVING US TEST-TUBE BABIES A BAD NAME...AND THAT'S MY JOB.

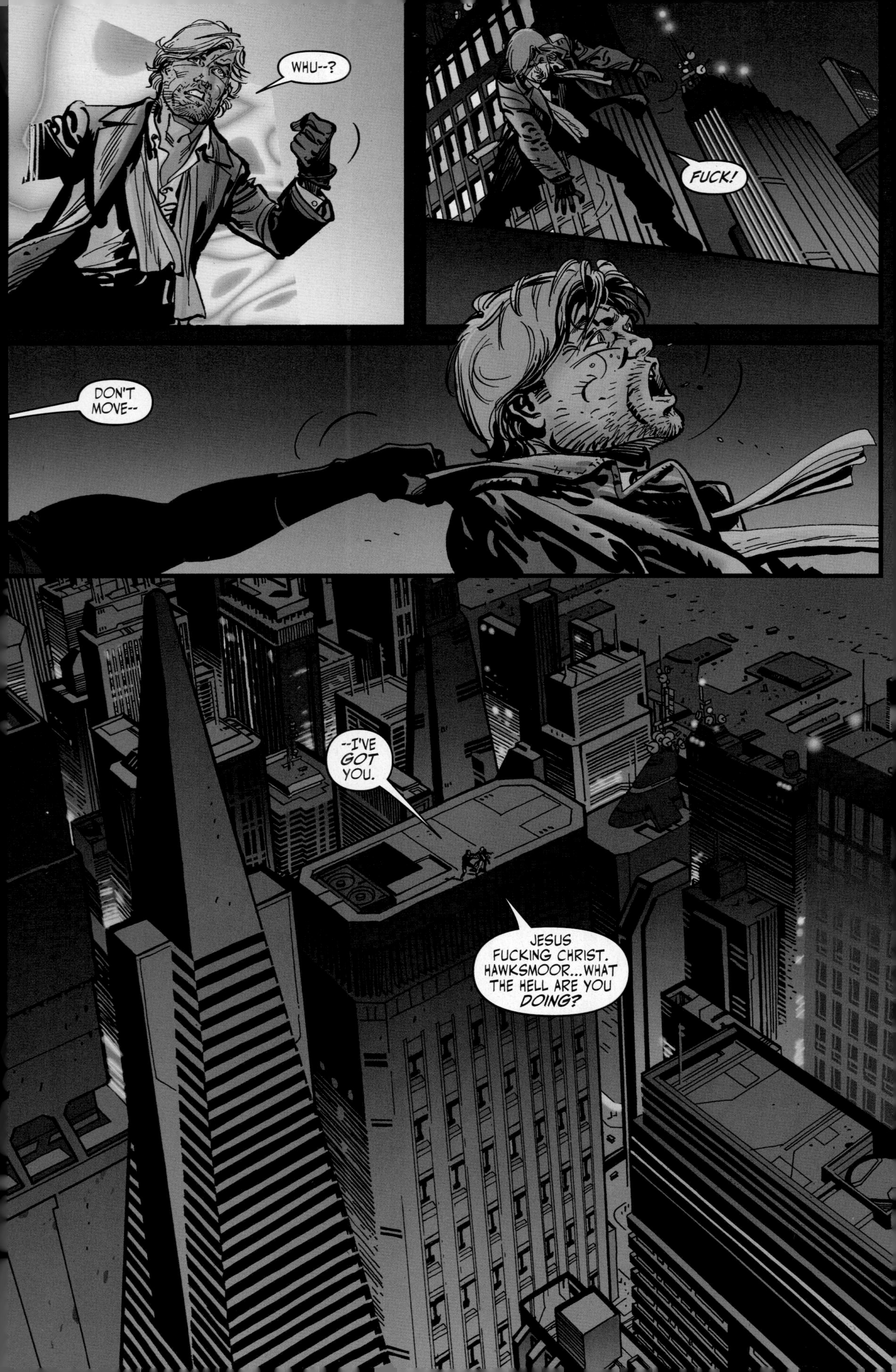
WHU--?
FUCK!
DON'T MOVE--
--I'VE GOT YOU.
JESUS FUCKING CHRIST. HAWKSMOOR...WHAT THE HELL ARE YOU DOING?

JUST HANGING OUT... I WASN'T EXPECTING *YOU*, GRIFTER.

YEAH, MIDNIGHTER SENT ME...DIDN'T BOTHER TELLING ME TO WATCH MY *STEP*, THOUGH.

THAT'S MIDNIGHTER FOR YOU. HE'S NOT *KILLING ANYBODY* TONIGHT, IS HE?

OTHER THAN THIS LAME ATTEMPT ON *ME?* NO.

YOU KNOW WHY I LOVE SAN FRANCISCO, GRIFTER?

BECAUSE BY *RIGHTS*, IT SHOULDN'T BE HERE *AT ALL.* HALF THE CITY IS BUILT ON A LANDFILL, AND THE OTHER HALF ON A BUNCH OF FAULT-LINES. PEOPLE *SHOULDN'T* WANT TO LIVE HERE.

YET, IT'S BEEN THRIVING FOR CENTURIES, ALWAYS JAMMED TO OVERCROWDING. AND FOR EVERY PERSON WHO LEAVES, FIVE MORE ARRIVE WITH STARS IN THEIR EYES.

OF COURSE, THE INTERNET ALMOST RUINED IT...

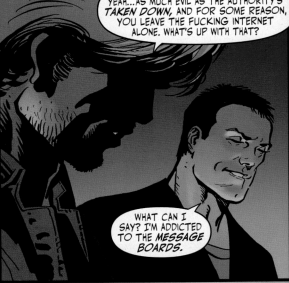

YEAH...AS MUCH EVIL AS THE AUTHORITY'S *TAKEN DOWN,* AND FOR SOME REASON, YOU LEAVE THE FUCKING INTERNET ALONE. WHAT'S UP WITH THAT?

WHAT CAN I SAY? I'M ADDICTED TO THE *MESSAGE BOARDS.*

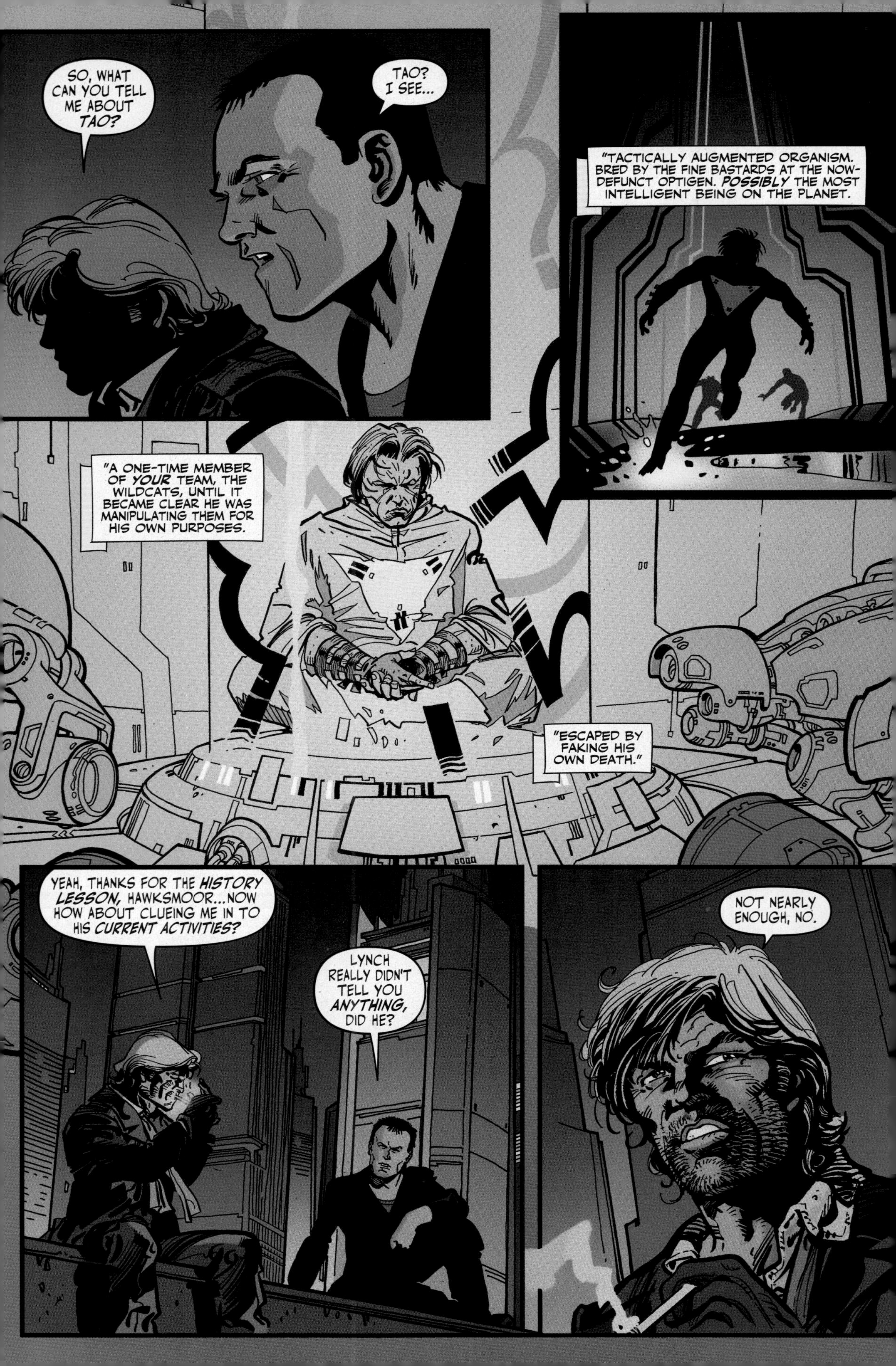
SO, WHAT CAN YOU TELL ME ABOUT *TAO?*
TAO? I SEE...
"TACTICALLY AUGMENTED ORGANISM. BRED BY THE FINE BASTARDS AT THE NOW-DEFUNCT OPTIGEN. *POSSIBLY* THE MOST INTELLIGENT BEING ON THE PLANET.
"A ONE-TIME MEMBER OF *YOUR* TEAM, THE WILDCATS, UNTIL IT BECAME CLEAR HE WAS MANIPULATING THEM FOR HIS OWN PURPOSES.
"ESCAPED BY FAKING HIS OWN DEATH."
YEAH, THANKS FOR THE *HISTORY LESSON,* HAWKSMOOR...NOW HOW ABOUT CLUEING ME IN TO HIS *CURRENT ACTIVITIES?*
LYNCH REALLY DIDN'T TELL YOU *ANYTHING,* DID HE?
NOT NEARLY ENOUGH, NO.

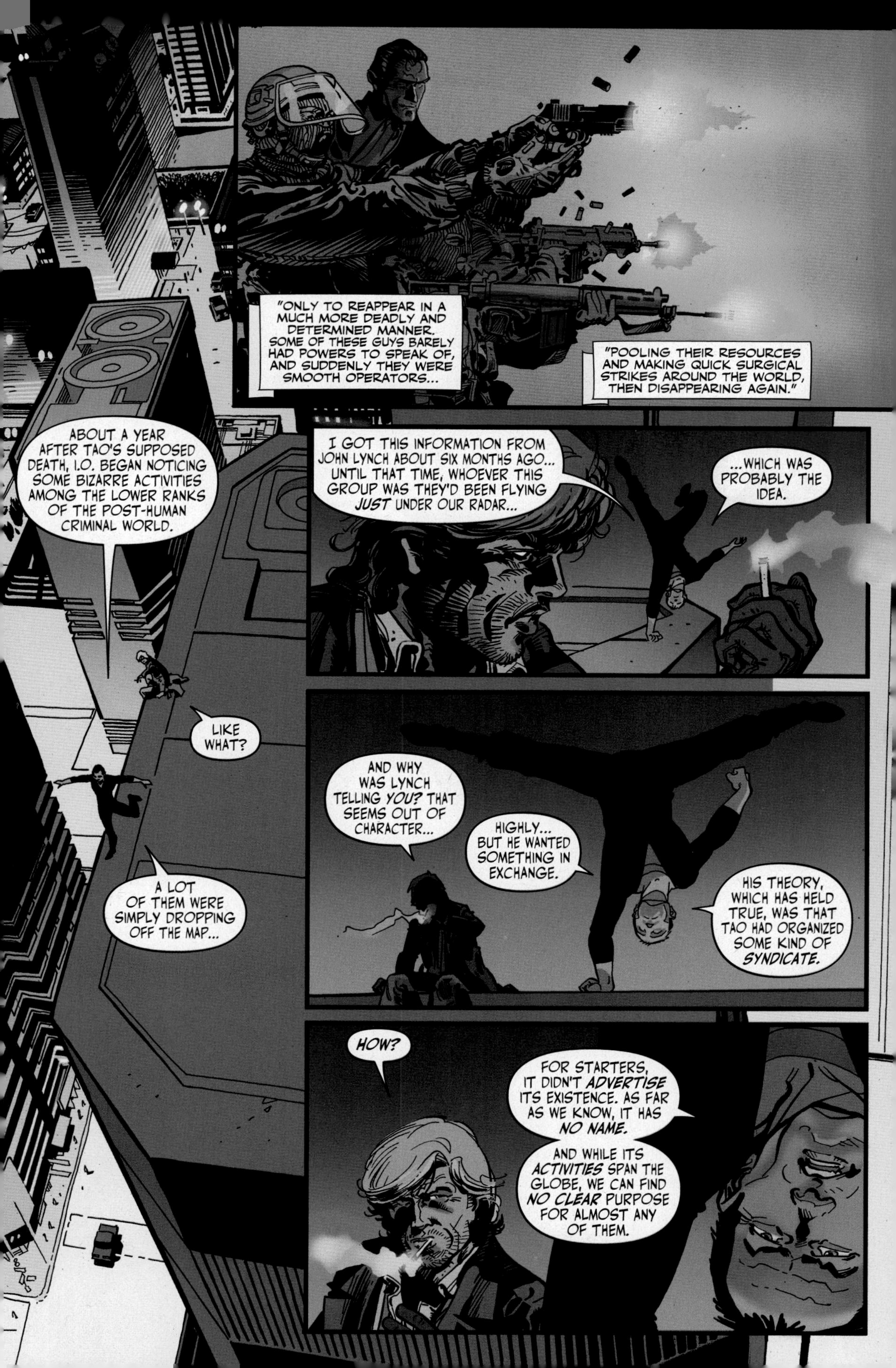
"ONLY TO REAPPEAR IN A MUCH MORE DEADLY AND DETERMINED MANNER. SOME OF THESE GUYS BARELY HAD POWERS TO SPEAK OF, AND SUDDENLY THEY WERE SMOOTH OPERATORS...
"POOLING THEIR RESOURCES AND MAKING QUICK SURGICAL STRIKES AROUND THE WORLD, THEN DISAPPEARING AGAIN."
ABOUT A YEAR AFTER TAO'S SUPPOSED DEATH, I.O. BEGAN NOTICING SOME BIZARRE ACTIVITIES AMONG THE LOWER RANKS OF THE POST-HUMAN CRIMINAL WORLD.
LIKE WHAT?
A LOT OF THEM WERE SIMPLY DROPPING OFF THE MAP...
I GOT THIS INFORMATION FROM JOHN LYNCH ABOUT SIX MONTHS AGO... UNTIL THAT TIME, WHOEVER THIS GROUP WAS THEY'D BEEN FLYING *JUST* UNDER OUR RADAR...
...WHICH WAS PROBABLY THE IDEA.
AND WHY WAS LYNCH TELLING *YOU?* THAT SEEMS OUT OF CHARACTER...
HIGHLY... BUT HE WANTED SOMETHING IN EXCHANGE.
HIS THEORY, WHICH HAS HELD TRUE, WAS THAT TAO HAD ORGANIZED SOME KIND OF *SYNDICATE.*
HOW?
FOR STARTERS, IT DIDN'T *ADVERTISE* ITS EXISTENCE. AS FAR AS WE KNOW, IT HAS *NO NAME.*
AND WHILE ITS *ACTIVITIES* SPAN THE GLOBE, WE CAN FIND *NO CLEAR* PURPOSE FOR ALMOST ANY OF THEM.

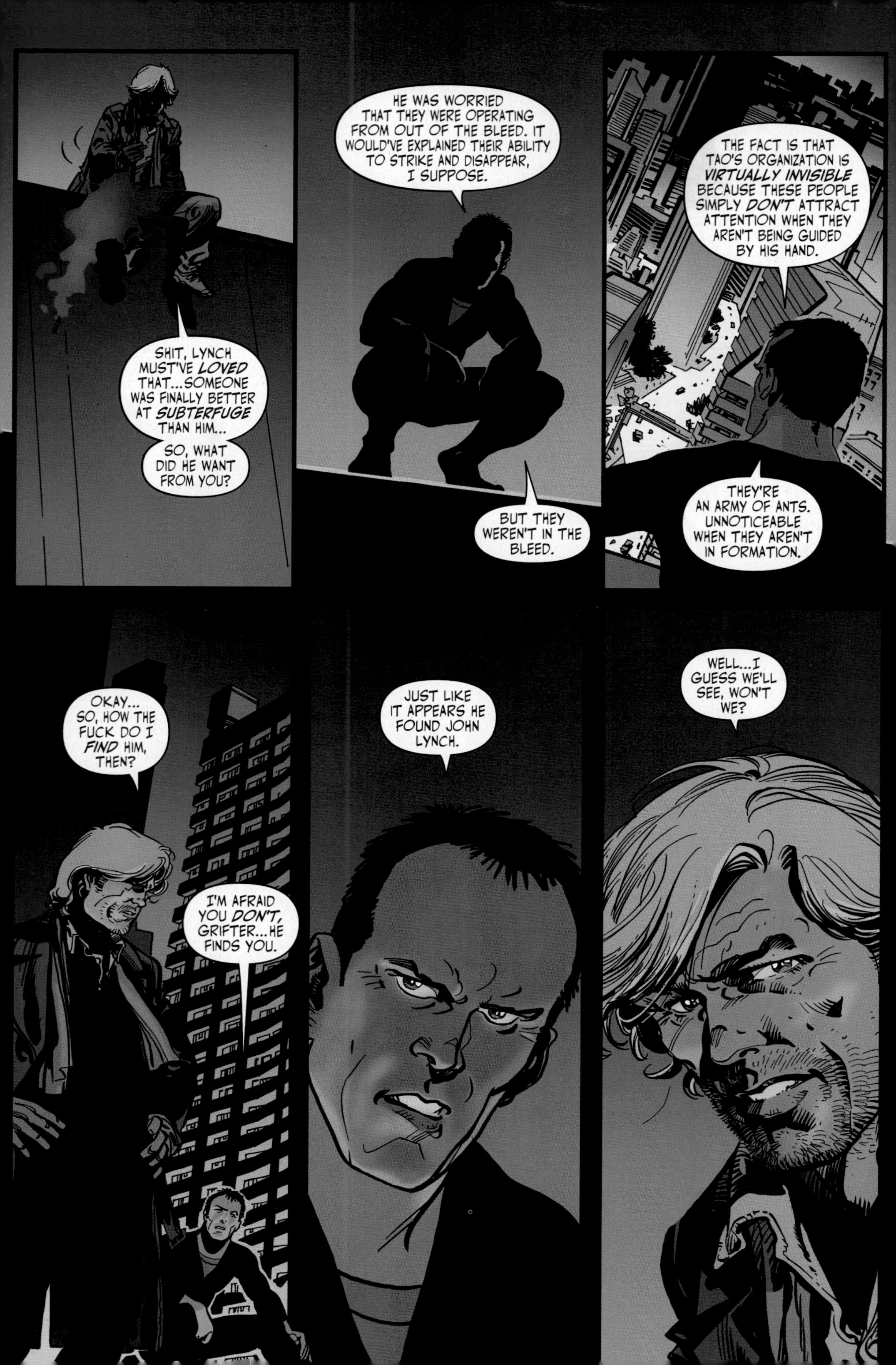
SHIT, LYNCH MUST'VE *LOVED* THAT...SOMEONE WAS FINALLY BETTER AT *SUBTERFUGE* THAN HIM...
SO, WHAT DID HE WANT FROM YOU?
HE WAS WORRIED THAT THEY WERE OPERATING FROM OUT OF THE BLEED. IT WOULD'VE EXPLAINED THEIR ABILITY TO STRIKE AND DISAPPEAR, I SUPPOSE.
BUT THEY WEREN'T IN THE BLEED.
THE FACT IS THAT TAO'S ORGANIZATION IS *VIRTUALLY INVISIBLE* BECAUSE THESE PEOPLE SIMPLY *DON'T* ATTRACT ATTENTION WHEN THEY AREN'T BEING GUIDED BY HIS HAND.
THEY'RE AN ARMY OF ANTS. UNNOTICEABLE WHEN THEY AREN'T IN FORMATION.
OKAY... SO, HOW THE FUCK DO I *FIND* HIM, THEN?
I'M AFRAID YOU *DON'T*, GRIFTER...HE FINDS YOU.
JUST LIKE IT APPEARS HE FOUND JOHN LYNCH.
WELL...I GUESS WE'LL SEE, WON'T WE?

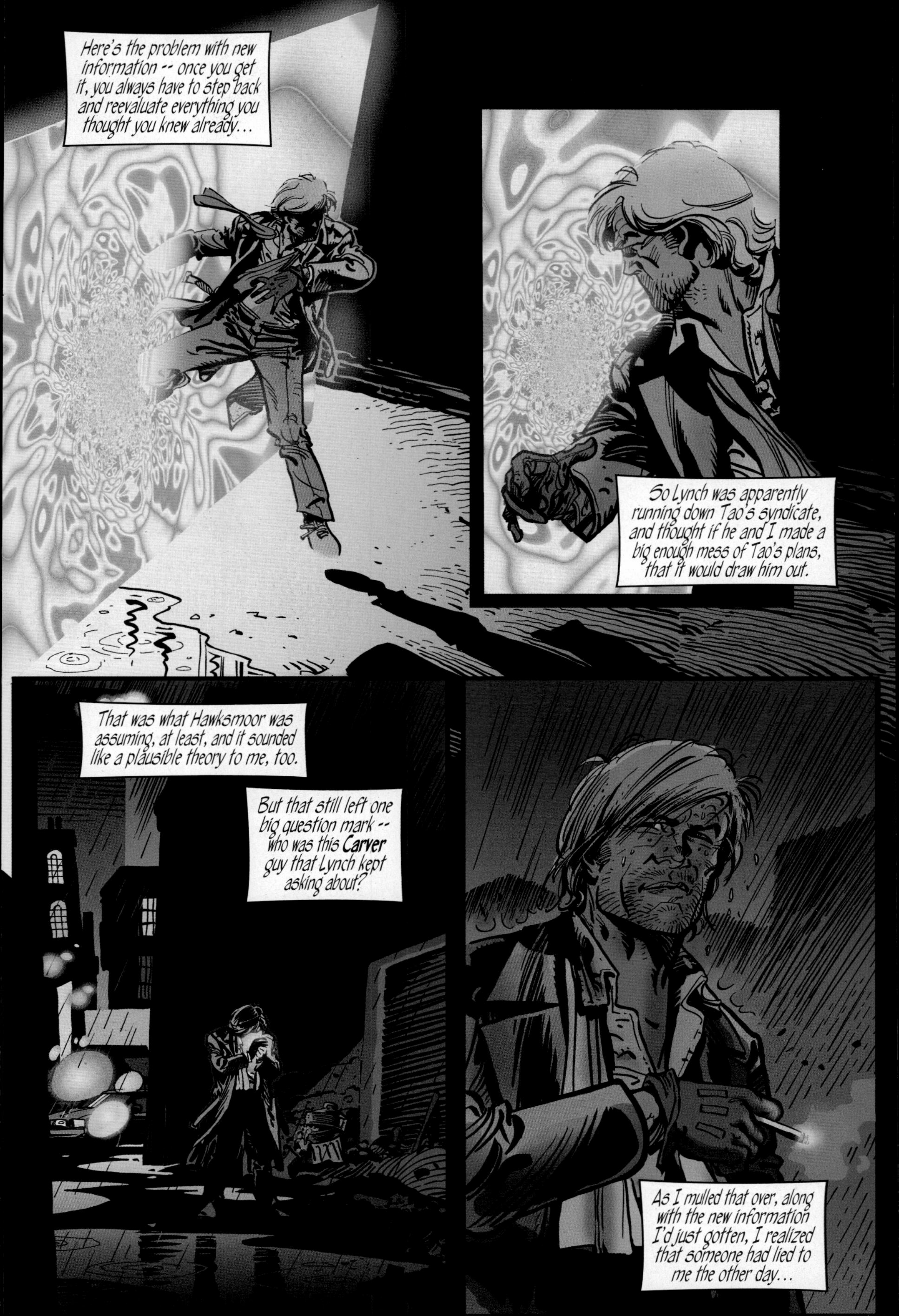
Here's the problem with new information -- once you get it, you always have to step back and reevaluate everything you thought you knew already...
So Lynch was apparently running down Tao's syndicate, and thought if he and I made a big enough mess of Tao's plans, that it would draw him out.
That was what Hawksmoor was assuming, at least, and it sounded like a plausible theory to me, too.
But that still left one big question mark -- who was this **Carver** guy that Lynch kept asking about?
As I mulled that over, along with the new information I'd just gotten, I realized that someone had lied to me the other day...

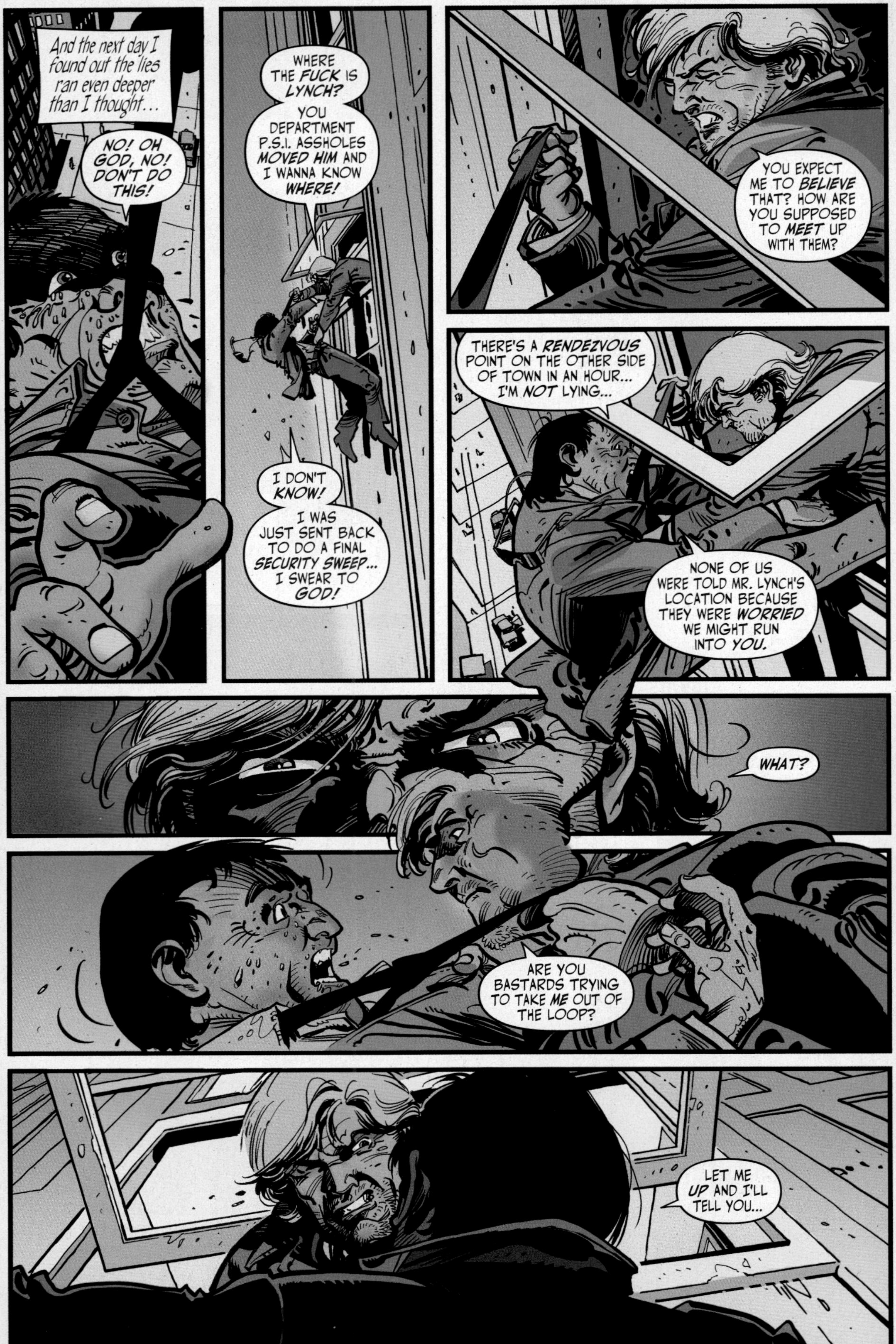
And the next day I found out the lies ran even deeper than I thought...
NO! OH GOD, NO! DON'T DO THIS!
WHERE THE FUCK IS LYNCH?
YOU DEPARTMENT P.S.I. ASSHOLES MOVED HIM AND I WANNA KNOW WHERE!
I DON'T KNOW!
I WAS JUST SENT BACK TO DO A FINAL SECURITY SWEEP... I SWEAR TO GOD!
YOU EXPECT ME TO BELIEVE THAT? HOW ARE YOU SUPPOSED TO MEET UP WITH THEM?
THERE'S A RENDEZVOUS POINT ON THE OTHER SIDE OF TOWN IN AN HOUR... I'M NOT LYING...
NONE OF US WERE TOLD MR. LYNCH'S LOCATION BECAUSE THEY WERE WORRIED WE MIGHT RUN INTO YOU.
WHAT?
ARE YOU BASTARDS TRYING TO TAKE ME OUT OF THE LOOP?
LET ME UP AND I'LL TELL YOU...

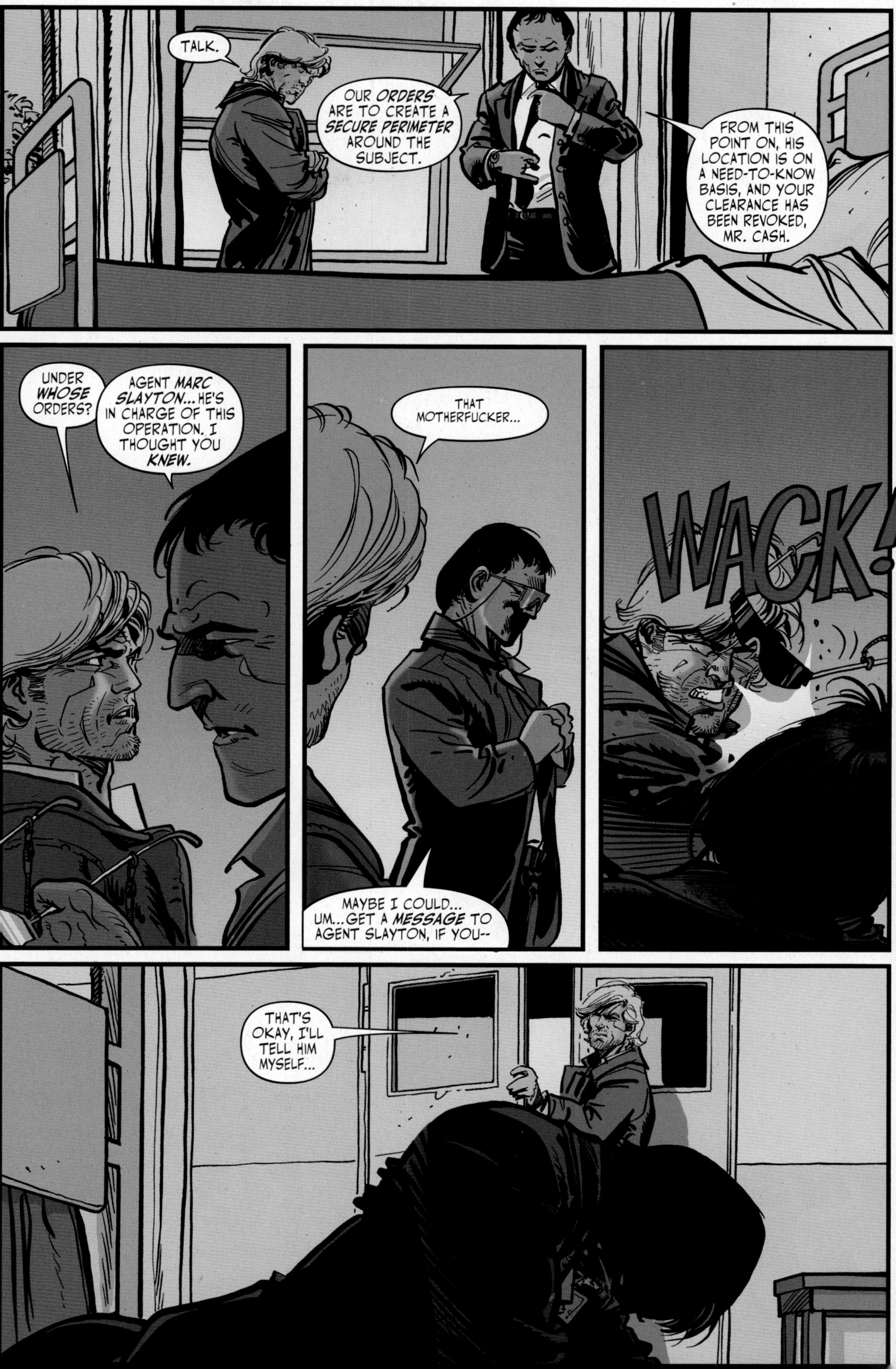
TALK.
OUR ORDERS ARE TO CREATE A SECURE PERIMETER AROUND THE SUBJECT.
FROM THIS POINT ON, HIS LOCATION IS ON A NEED-TO-KNOW BASIS, AND YOUR CLEARANCE HAS BEEN REVOKED, MR. CASH.
UNDER WHOSE ORDERS?
AGENT MARC SLAYTON... HE'S IN CHARGE OF THIS OPERATION. I THOUGHT YOU KNEW.
THAT MOTHERFUCKER...
MAYBE I COULD... UM...GET A MESSAGE TO AGENT SLAYTON, IF YOU--
WACK!
THAT'S OKAY, I'LL TELL HIM MYSELF...

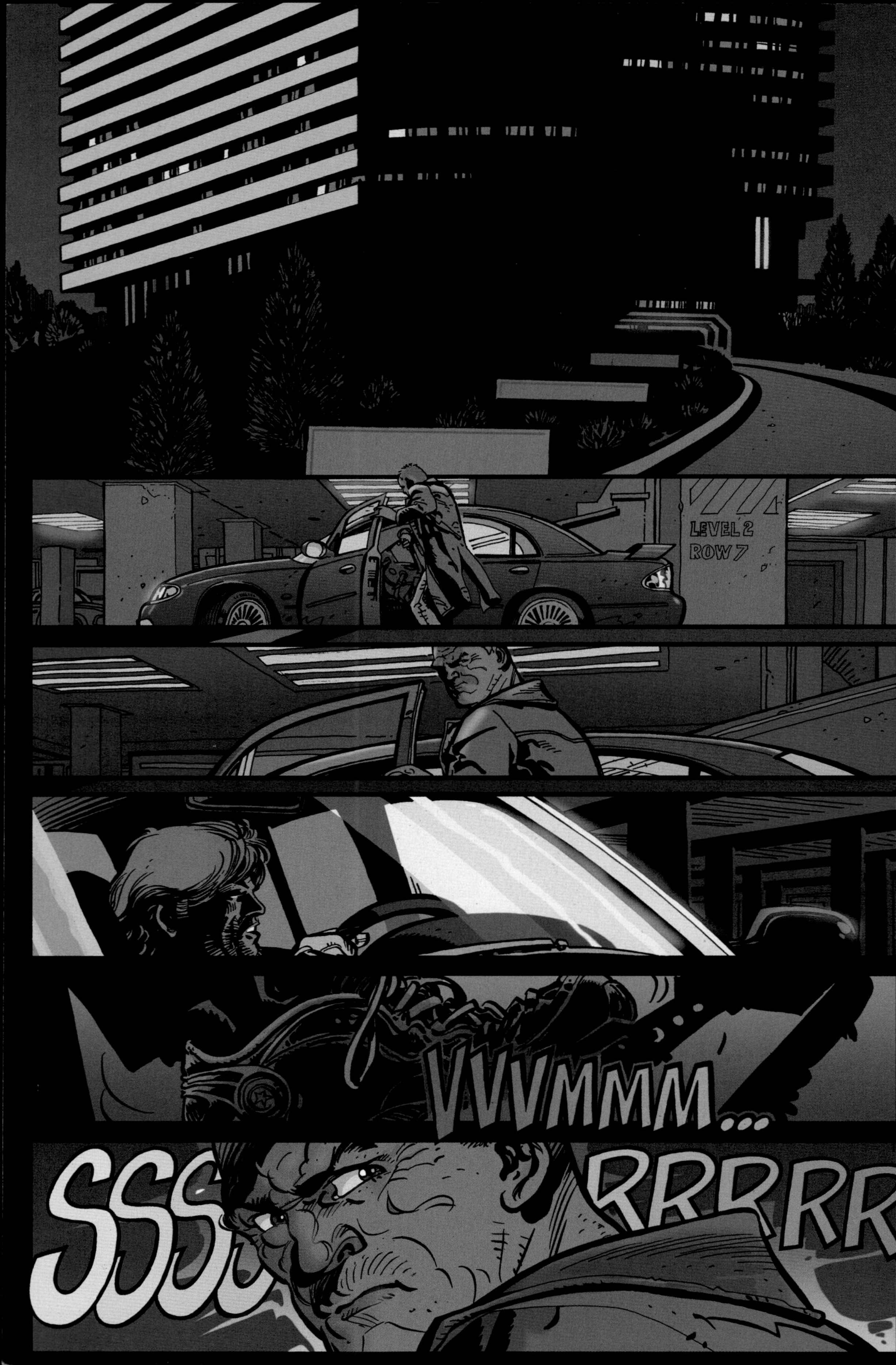
LEVEL 2
ROW 7
VVVMMM...
SSS
RRRRR

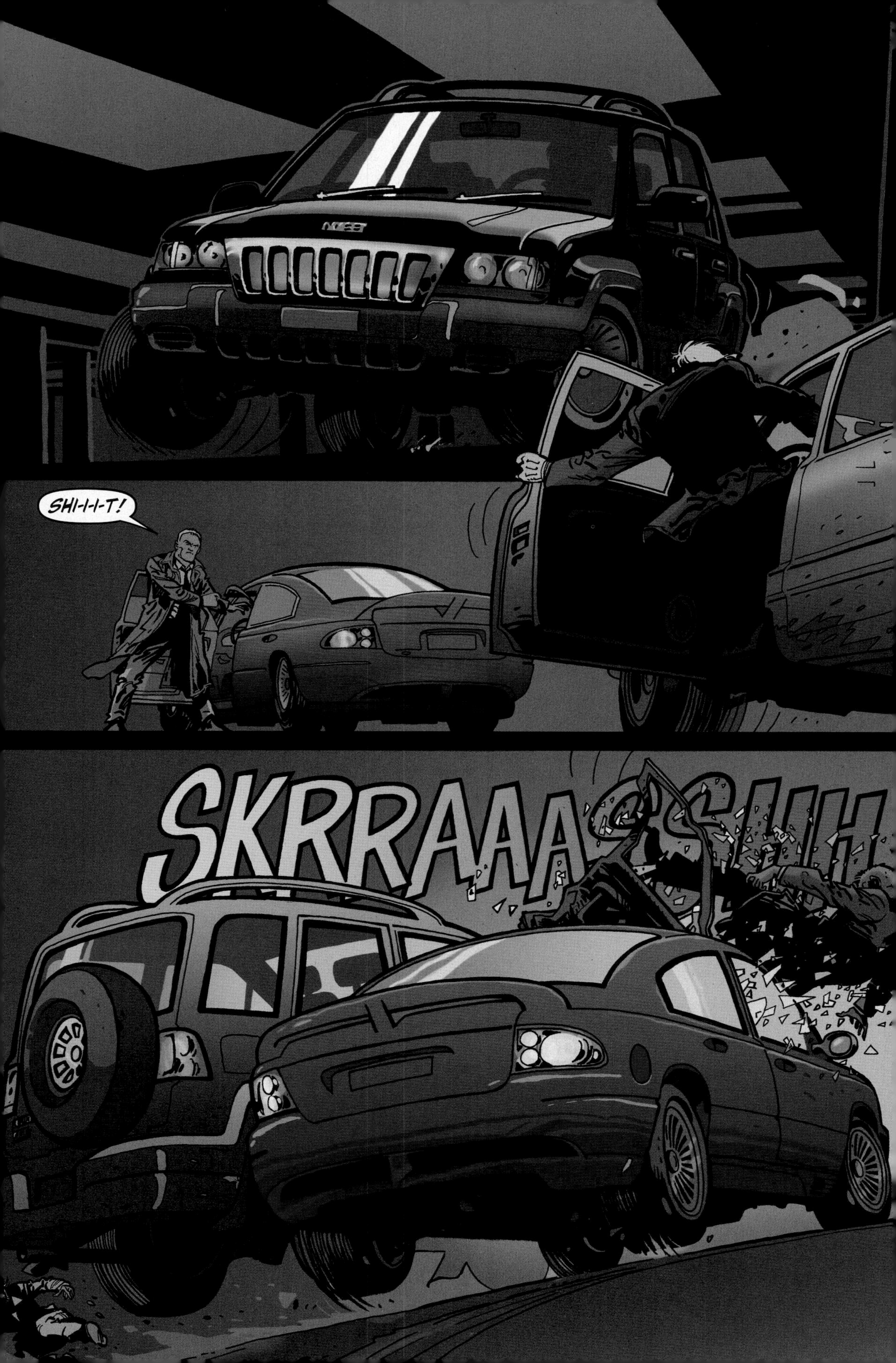
SHI-I-I-T!
SKRRAAASSHH

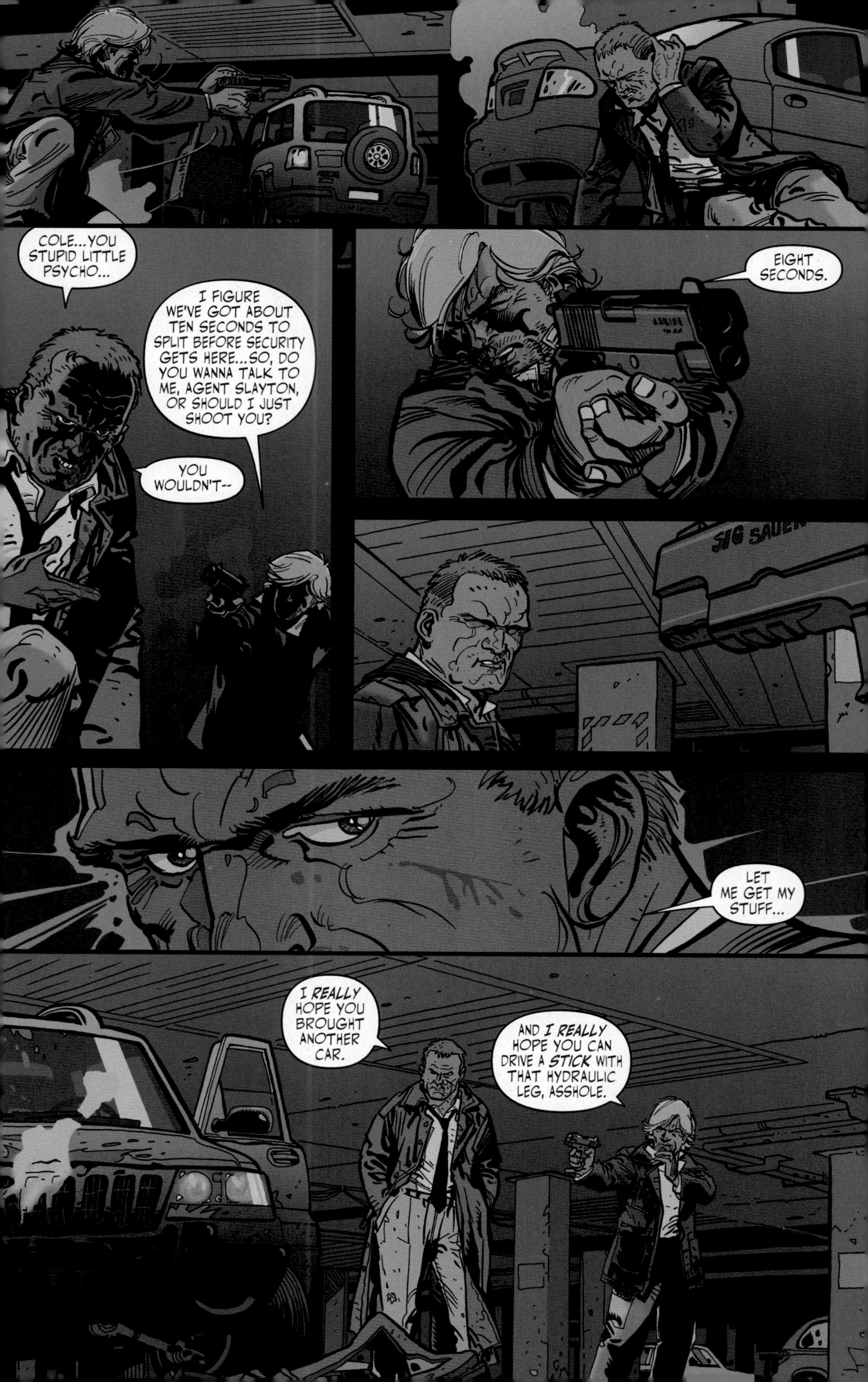

COLE...YOU STUPID LITTLE PSYCHO...
I FIGURE WE'VE GOT ABOUT TEN SECONDS TO SPLIT BEFORE SECURITY GETS HERE...SO, DO YOU WANNA TALK TO ME, AGENT SLAYTON, OR SHOULD I JUST SHOOT YOU?
YOU WOULDN'T--
EIGHT SECONDS.
SIG SAUER
LET ME GET MY STUFF...
I REALLY HOPE YOU BROUGHT ANOTHER CAR.
AND I REALLY HOPE YOU CAN DRIVE A STICK WITH THAT HYDRAULIC LEG, ASSHOLE.

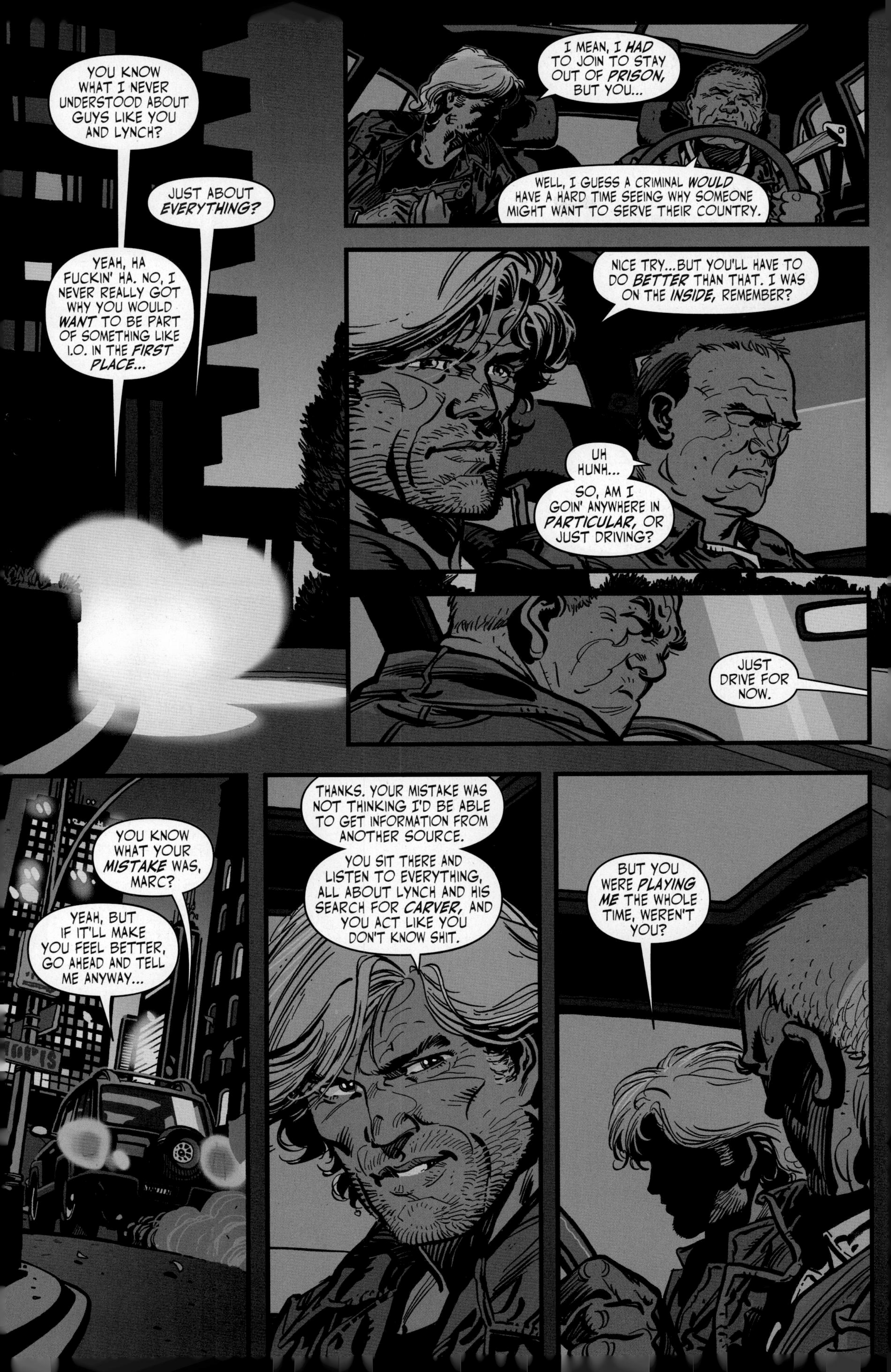
YOU KNOW WHAT I NEVER UNDERSTOOD ABOUT GUYS LIKE YOU AND LYNCH?
JUST ABOUT *EVERYTHING?*
YEAH, HA FUCKIN' HA. NO, I NEVER REALLY GOT WHY YOU WOULD *WANT* TO BE PART OF SOMETHING LIKE I.O. IN THE *FIRST PLACE...*
I MEAN, I *HAD* TO JOIN TO STAY OUT OF *PRISON,* BUT YOU...
WELL, I GUESS A CRIMINAL *WOULD* HAVE A HARD TIME SEEING WHY SOMEONE MIGHT WANT TO SERVE THEIR COUNTRY.
NICE TRY...BUT YOU'LL HAVE TO DO *BETTER* THAN THAT. I WAS ON THE *INSIDE,* REMEMBER?
UH HUNH...
SO, AM I GOIN' ANYWHERE IN *PARTICULAR,* OR JUST DRIVING?
JUST DRIVE FOR NOW.
YOU KNOW WHAT YOUR *MISTAKE* WAS, MARC?
YEAH, BUT IF IT'LL MAKE YOU FEEL BETTER, GO AHEAD AND TELL ME ANYWAY...
THANKS. YOUR MISTAKE WAS NOT THINKING I'D BE ABLE TO GET INFORMATION FROM ANOTHER SOURCE.
YOU SIT THERE AND LISTEN TO EVERYTHING, ALL ABOUT LYNCH AND HIS SEARCH FOR *CARVER,* AND YOU ACT LIKE YOU DON'T KNOW SHIT.
BUT YOU WERE *PLAYING ME* THE WHOLE TIME, WEREN'T YOU?

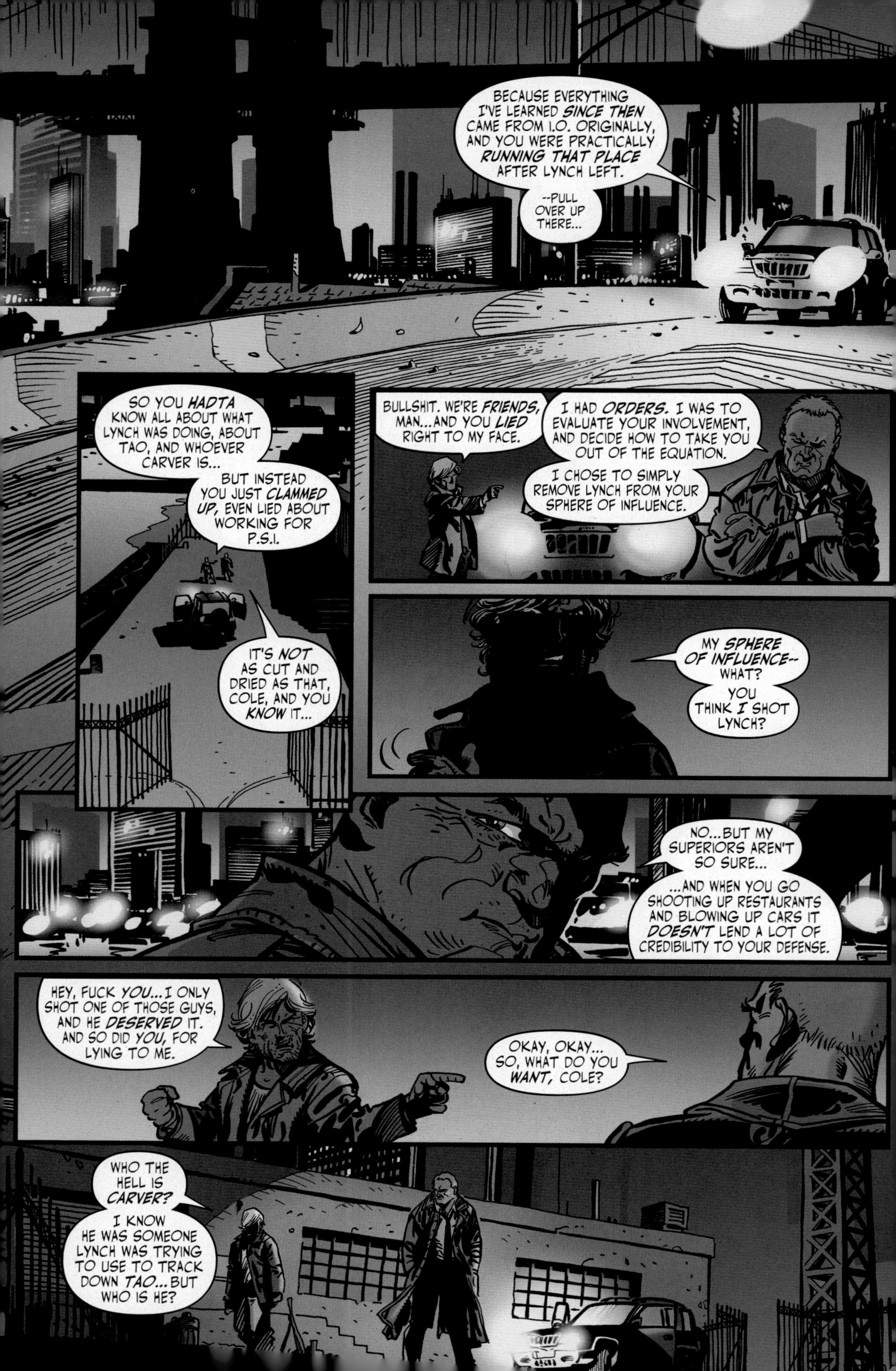
BECAUSE EVERYTHING I'VE LEARNED SINCE THEN CAME FROM I.O. ORIGINALLY, AND YOU WERE PRACTICALLY RUNNING THAT PLACE AFTER LYNCH LEFT.
--PULL OVER UP THERE...
SO YOU HADTA KNOW ALL ABOUT WHAT LYNCH WAS DOING, ABOUT TAO, AND WHOEVER CARVER IS...
BUT INSTEAD YOU JUST CLAMMED UP, EVEN LIED ABOUT WORKING FOR P.S.I.
IT'S NOT AS CUT AND DRIED AS THAT, COLE, AND YOU KNOW IT...
BULLSHIT. WE'RE FRIENDS, MAN...AND YOU LIED RIGHT TO MY FACE.
I HAD ORDERS. I WAS TO EVALUATE YOUR INVOLVEMENT, AND DECIDE HOW TO TAKE YOU OUT OF THE EQUATION.
I CHOSE TO SIMPLY REMOVE LYNCH FROM YOUR SPHERE OF INFLUENCE.
MY SPHERE OF INFLUENCE-- WHAT?
YOU THINK I SHOT LYNCH?
NO...BUT MY SUPERIORS AREN'T SO SURE...
...AND WHEN YOU GO SHOOTING UP RESTAURANTS AND BLOWING UP CARS IT DOESN'T LEND A LOT OF CREDIBILITY TO YOUR DEFENSE.
HEY, FUCK YOU...I ONLY SHOT ONE OF THOSE GUYS, AND HE DESERVED IT. AND SO DID YOU, FOR LYING TO ME.
OKAY, OKAY... SO, WHAT DO YOU WANT, COLE?
WHO THE HELL IS CARVER?
I KNOW HE WAS SOMEONE LYNCH WAS TRYING TO USE TO TRACK DOWN TAO...BUT WHO IS HE?

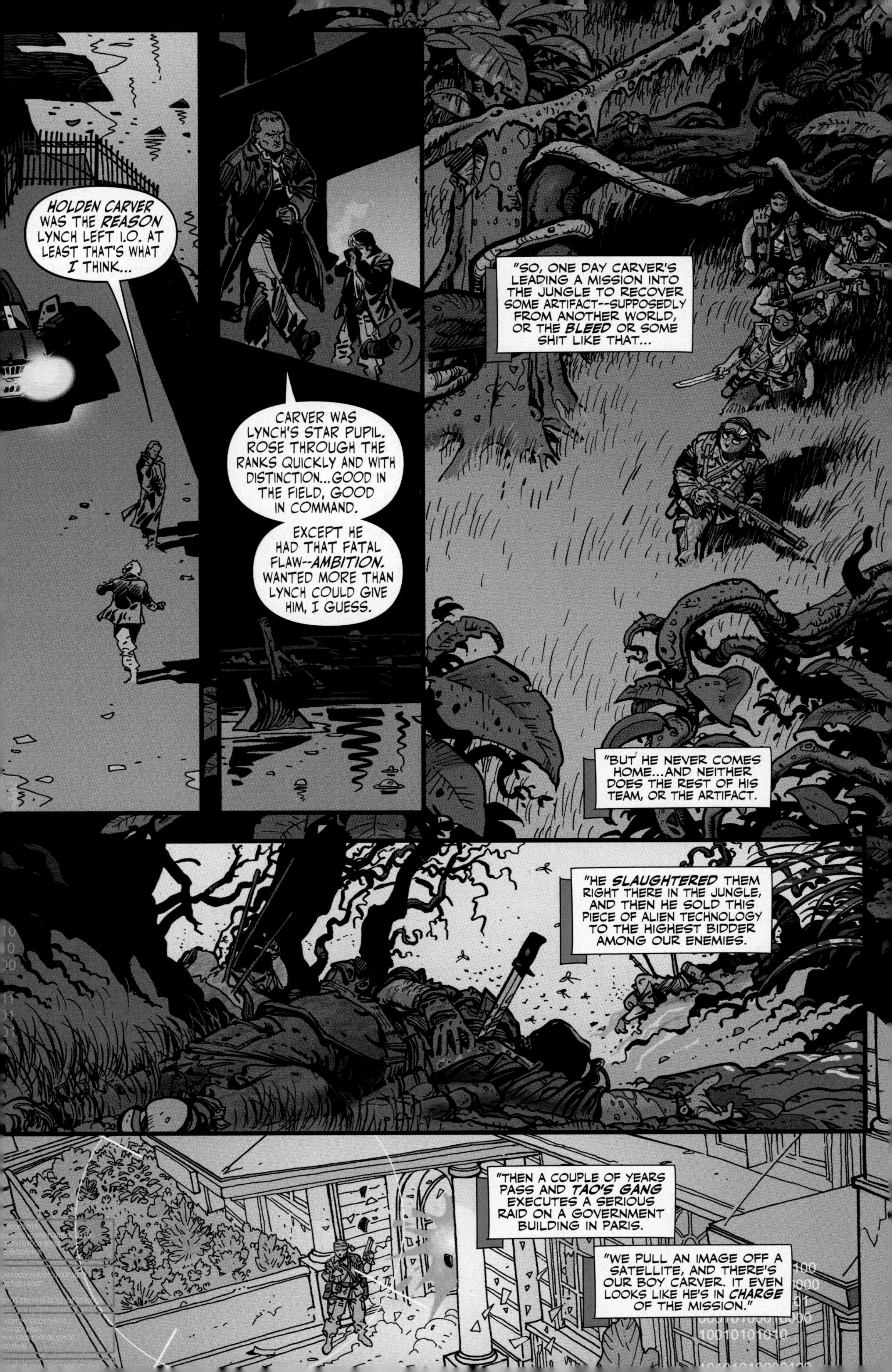
HOLDEN CARVER WAS THE REASON LYNCH LEFT I.O. AT LEAST THAT'S WHAT I THINK...
CARVER WAS LYNCH'S STAR PUPIL. ROSE THROUGH THE RANKS QUICKLY AND WITH DISTINCTION...GOOD IN THE FIELD, GOOD IN COMMAND.
EXCEPT HE HAD THAT FATAL FLAW--AMBITION. WANTED MORE THAN LYNCH COULD GIVE HIM, I GUESS.
"SO, ONE DAY CARVER'S LEADING A MISSION INTO THE JUNGLE TO RECOVER SOME ARTIFACT--SUPPOSEDLY FROM ANOTHER WORLD, OR THE BLEED OR SOME SHIT LIKE THAT...
"BUT HE NEVER COMES HOME...AND NEITHER DOES THE REST OF HIS TEAM, OR THE ARTIFACT.
"HE SLAUGHTERED THEM RIGHT THERE IN THE JUNGLE, AND THEN HE SOLD THIS PIECE OF ALIEN TECHNOLOGY TO THE HIGHEST BIDDER AMONG OUR ENEMIES.
"THEN A COUPLE OF YEARS PASS AND TAO'S GANG EXECUTES A SERIOUS RAID ON A GOVERNMENT BUILDING IN PARIS.
"WE PULL AN IMAGE OFF A SATELLITE, AND THERE'S OUR BOY CARVER. IT EVEN LOOKS LIKE HE'S IN CHARGE OF THE MISSION."

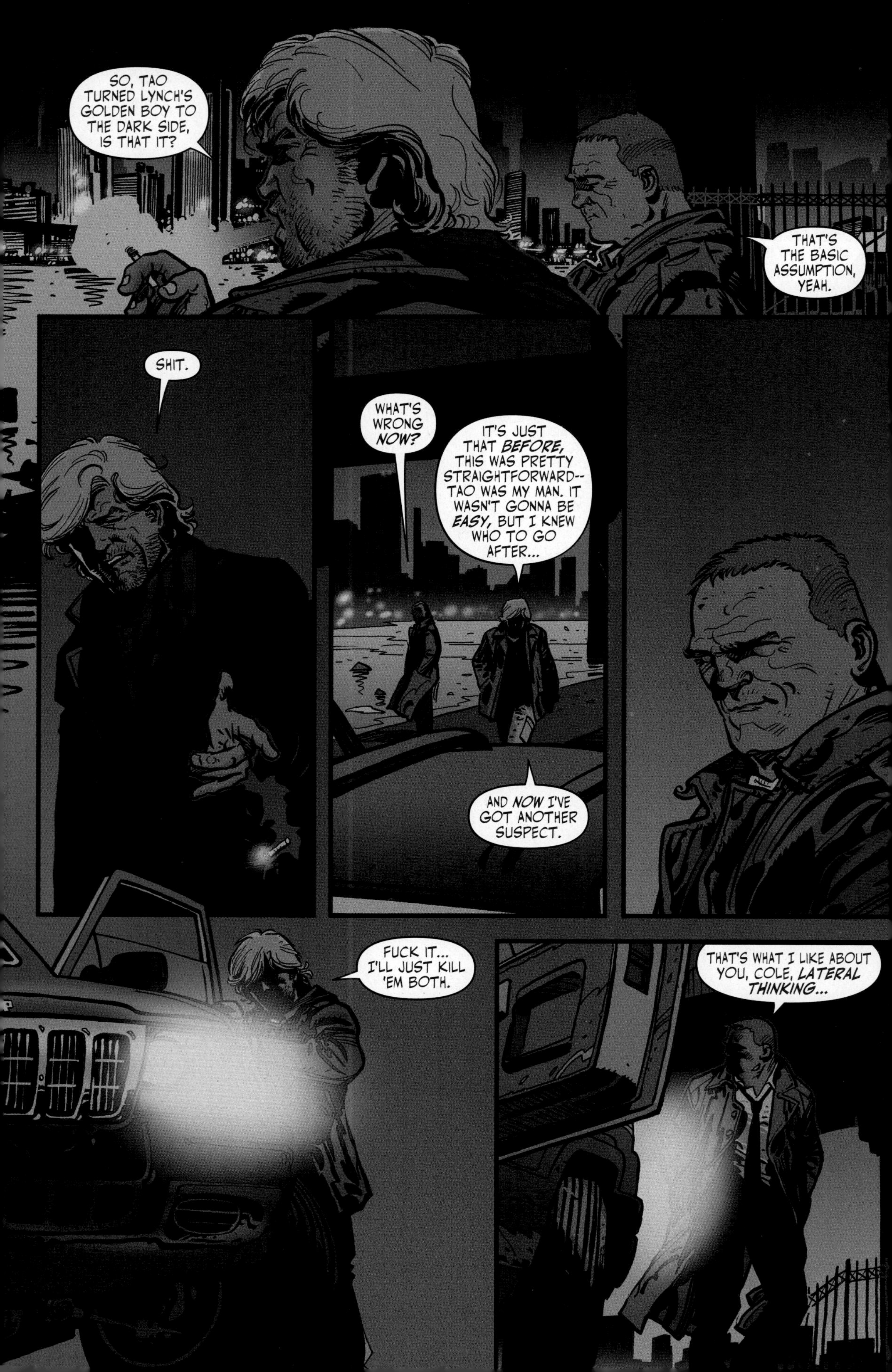
SO, TAO TURNED LYNCH'S GOLDEN BOY TO THE DARK SIDE, IS THAT IT?
THAT'S THE BASIC ASSUMPTION, YEAH.
SHIT.
WHAT'S WRONG *NOW?*
IT'S JUST THAT *BEFORE,* THIS WAS PRETTY STRAIGHTFORWARD-- TAO WAS MY MAN. IT WASN'T GONNA BE *EASY,* BUT I KNEW WHO TO GO AFTER...
AND *NOW* I'VE GOT ANOTHER SUSPECT.
FUCK IT... I'LL JUST KILL 'EM BOTH.
THAT'S WHAT I LIKE ABOUT YOU, COLE, *LATERAL THINKING...*

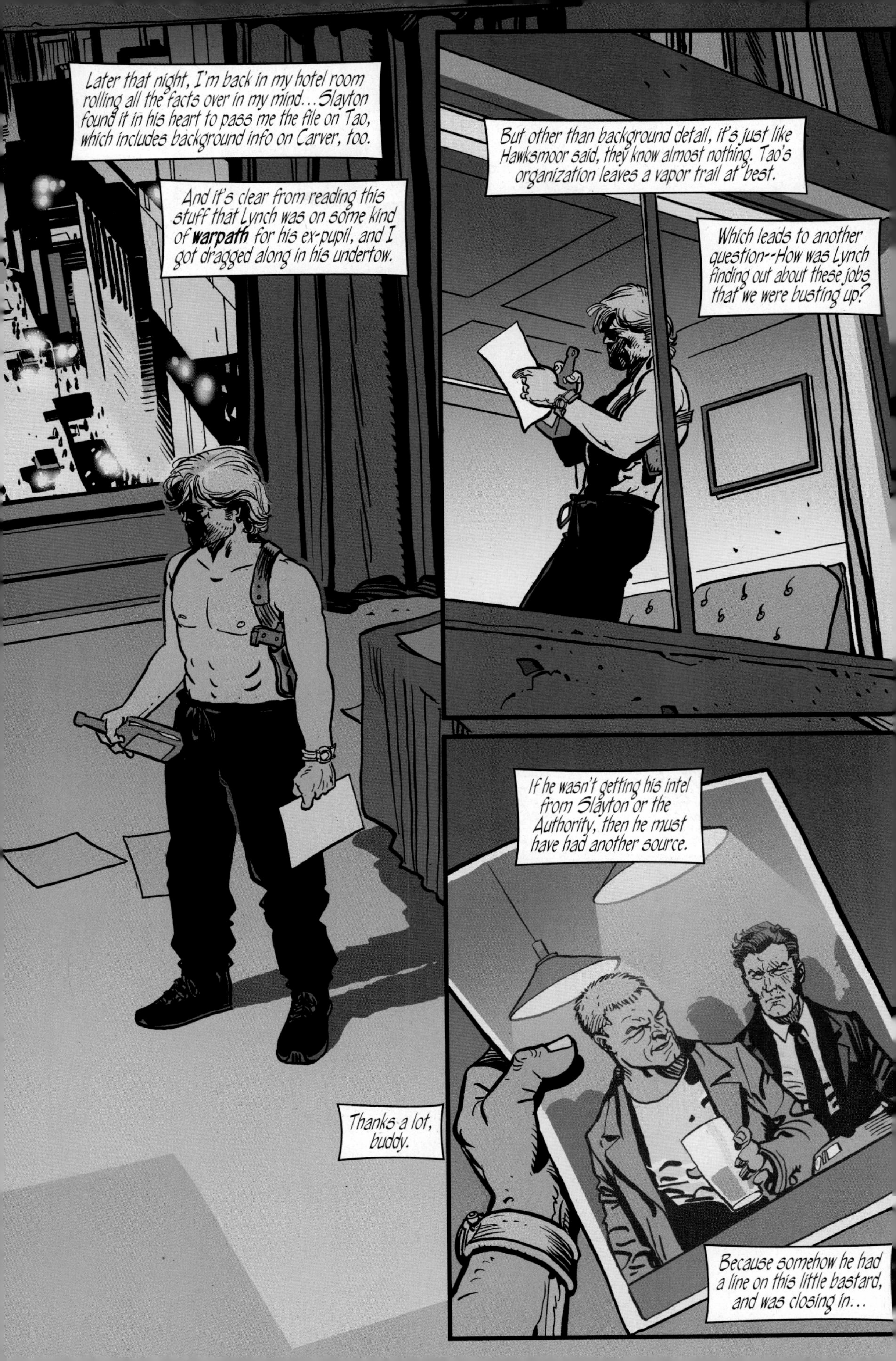
Later that night, I'm back in my hotel room rolling all the facts over in my mind... Slayton found it in his heart to pass me the file on Tao, which includes background info on Carver, too.
And it's clear from reading this stuff that Lynch was on some kind of **warpath** for his ex-pupil, and I got dragged along in his undertow.
Thanks a lot, buddy.
But other than background detail, it's just like Hawksmoor said, they know almost nothing. Tao's organization leaves a vapor trail at best.
Which leads to another question--How was Lynch finding out about these jobs that we were busting up?
If he wasn't getting his intel from Slayton or the Authority, then he must have had another source.
Because somehow he had a line on this little bastard, and was closing in...

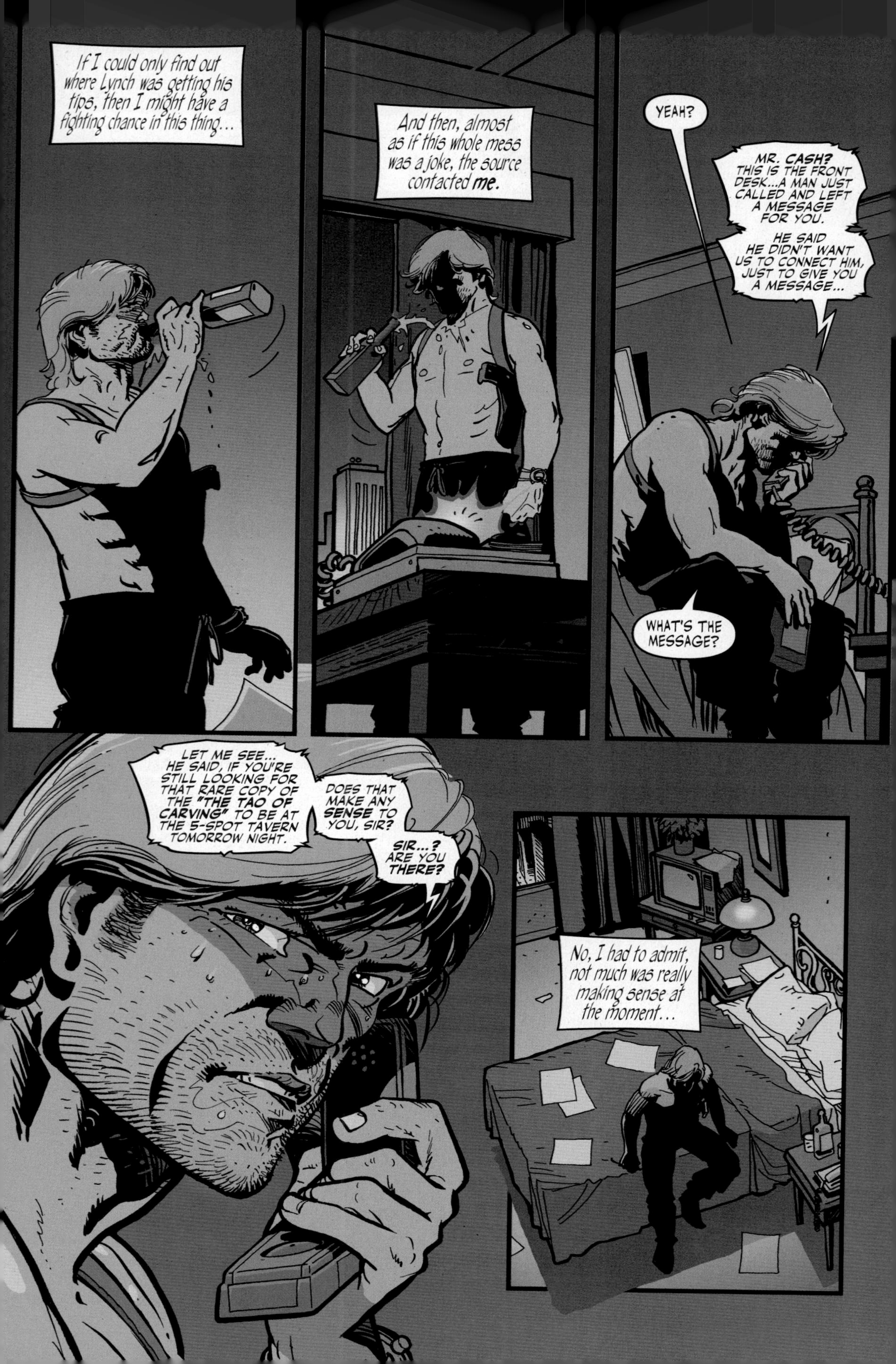
If I could only find out where Lynch was getting his tips, then I might have a fighting chance in this thing...
And then, almost as if this whole mess was a joke, the source contacted **me.**
YEAH?
MR. **CASH?** THIS IS THE FRONT DESK...A MAN JUST CALLED AND LEFT A MESSAGE FOR YOU.
HE SAID HE DIDN'T WANT US TO CONNECT HIM, JUST TO GIVE YOU A MESSAGE...
WHAT'S THE MESSAGE?
LET ME SEE... HE SAID, IF YOU'RE STILL LOOKING FOR THAT RARE COPY OF THE **"THE TAO OF CARVING"** TO BE AT THE 5-SPOT TAVERN TOMORROW NIGHT.
DOES THAT MAKE ANY **SENSE** TO YOU, SIR?
SIR...? ARE YOU **THERE?**
No, I had to admit, not much was really making sense at the moment...

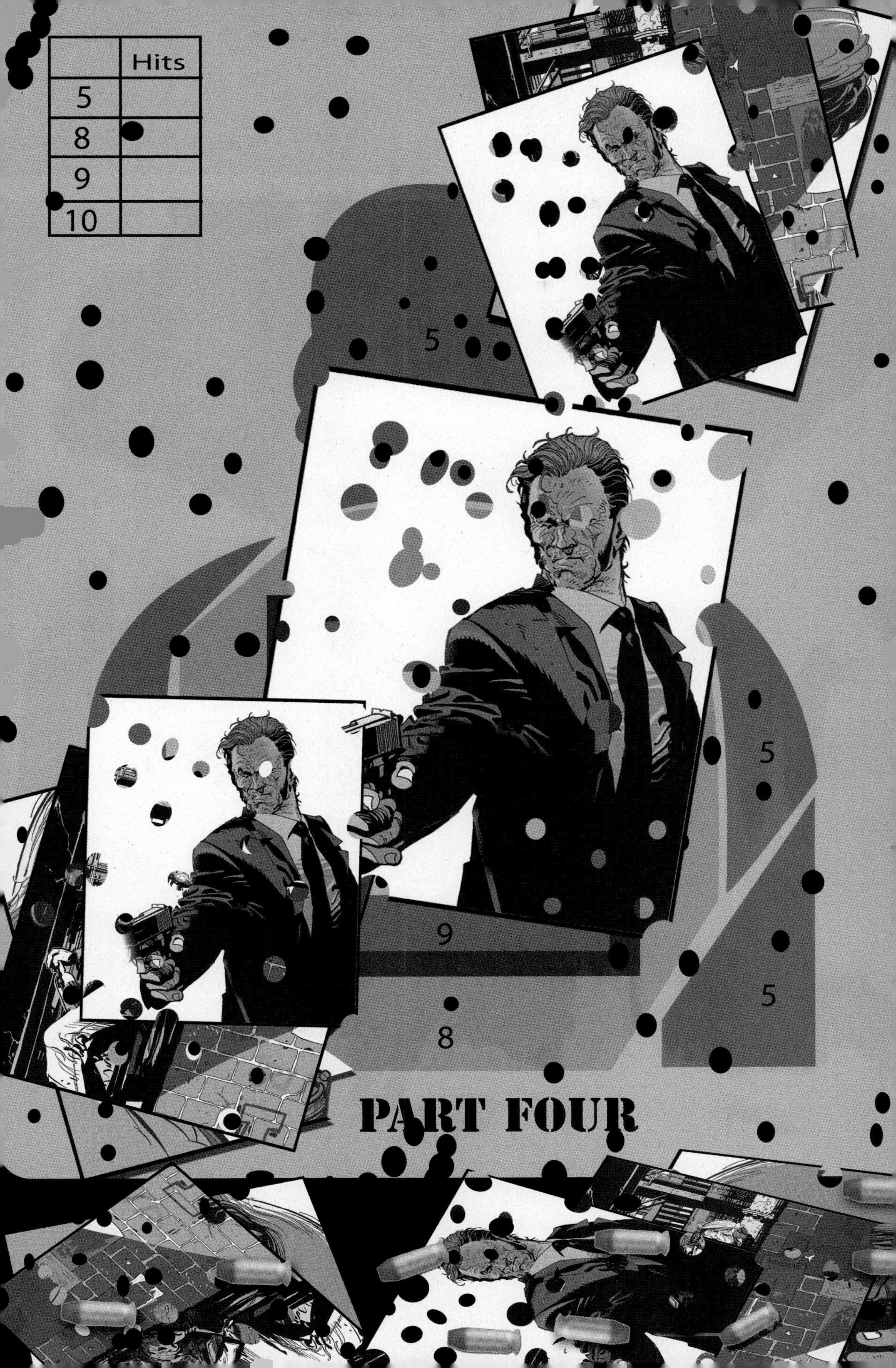
Hits
5
8
9
10
5
5
9
5
8

PART FOUR

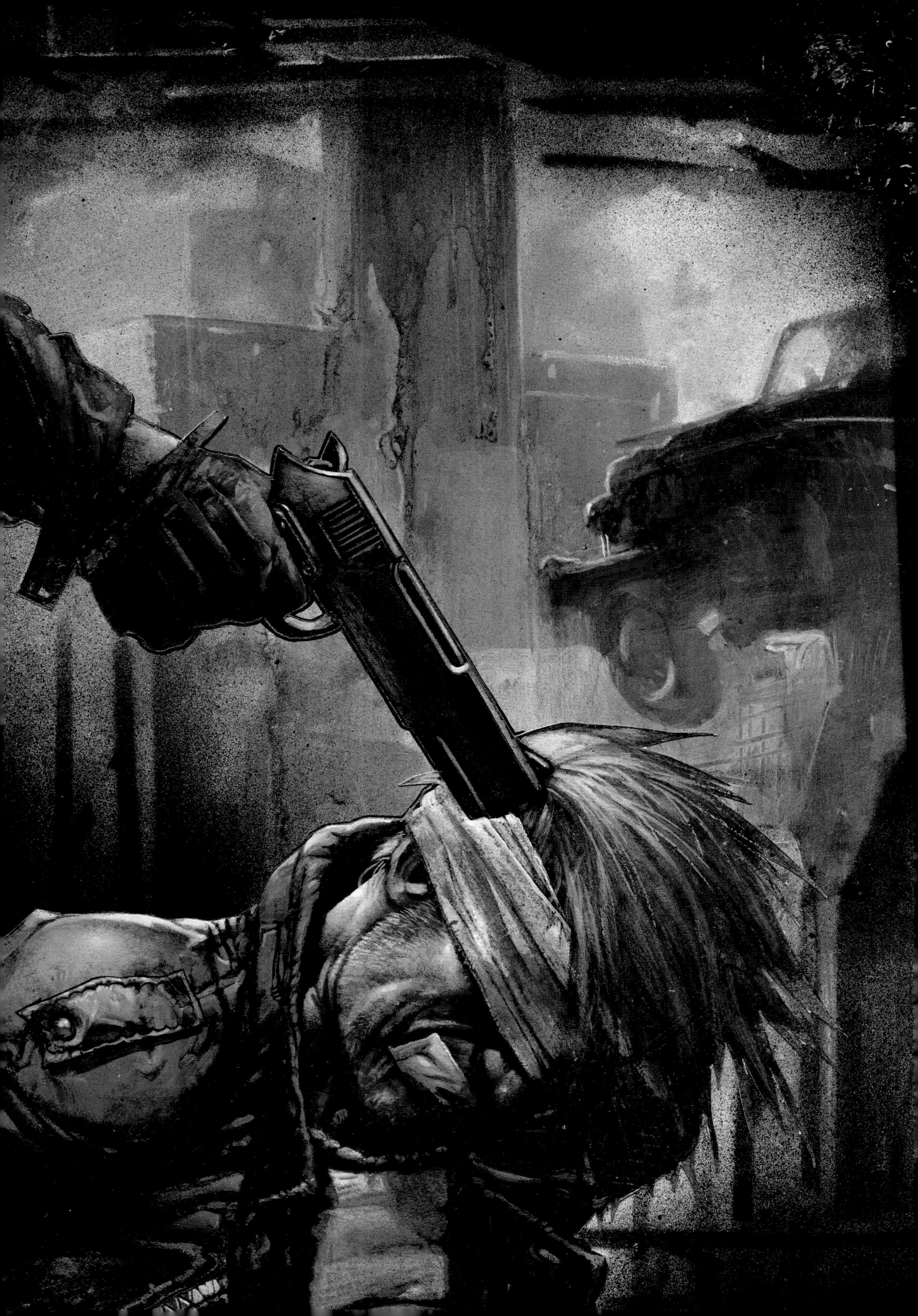

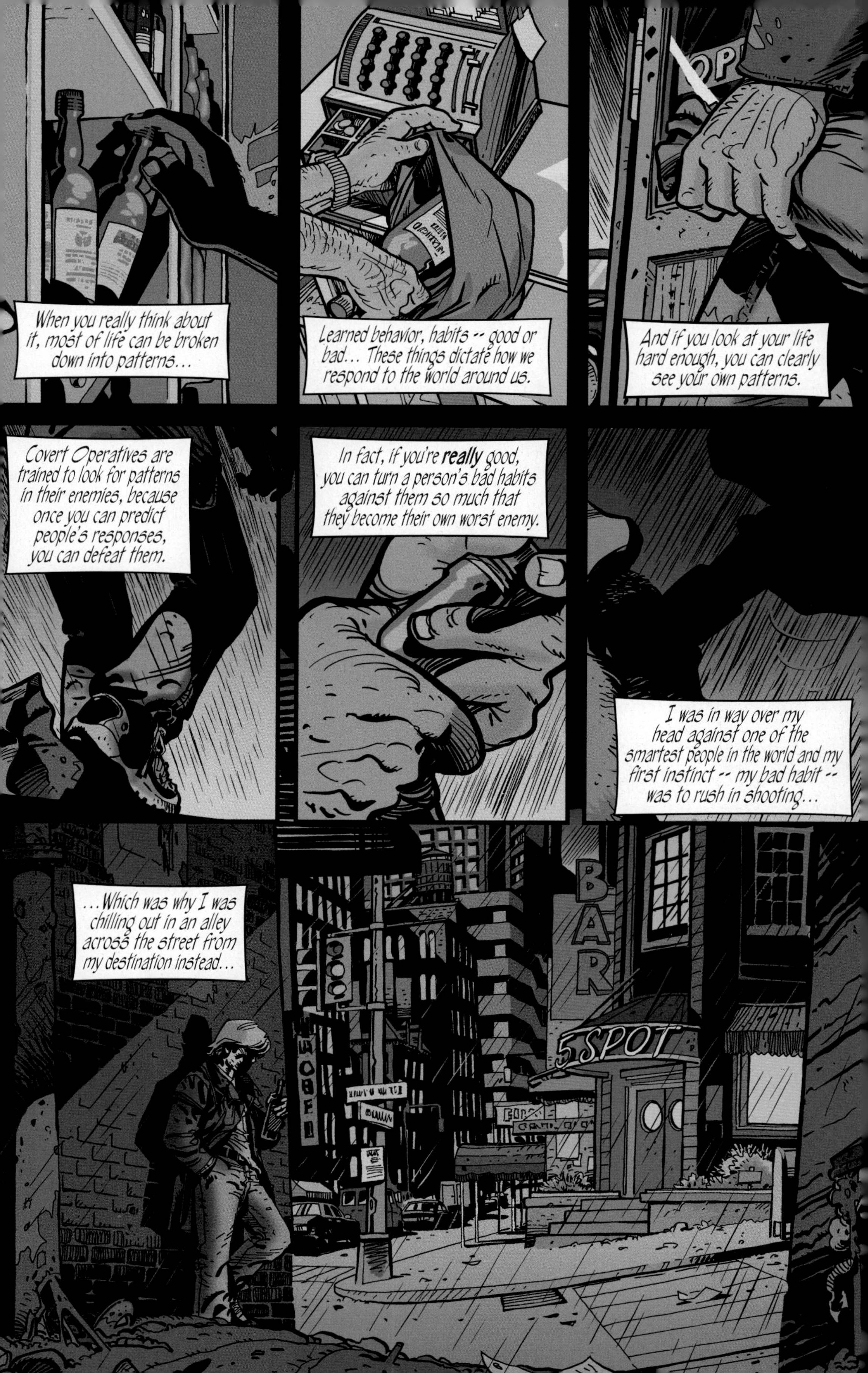
When you really think about it, most of life can be broken down into patterns...
Learned behavior, habits -- good or bad... These things dictate how we respond to the world around us.
And if you look at your life hard enough, you can clearly see your own patterns.
Covert Operatives are trained to look for patterns in their enemies, because once you can predict people's responses, you can defeat them.
In fact, if you're **really** good, you can turn a person's bad habits against them so much that they become their own worst enemy.
I was in way over my head against one of the smartest people in the world and my first instinct -- my bad habit -- was to rush in shooting...
...Which was why I was chilling out in an alley across the street from my destination instead...
BAR
5 SPOT

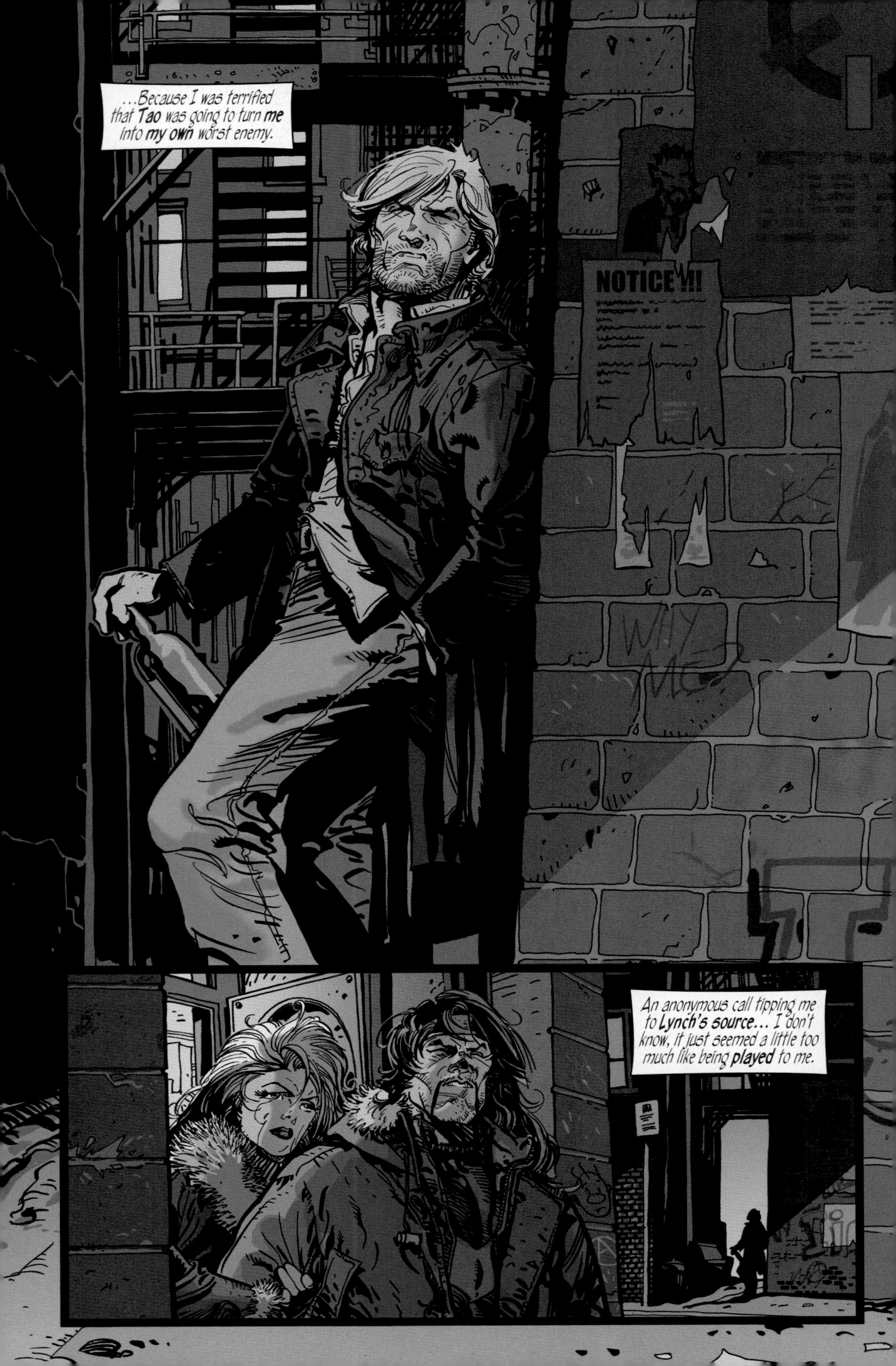
...Because I was terrified that Tao was going to turn me into my own worst enemy.
NOTICE !!!
WHY ME?
An anonymous call tipping me to Lynch's source... I don't know, it just seemed a little too much like being played to me.

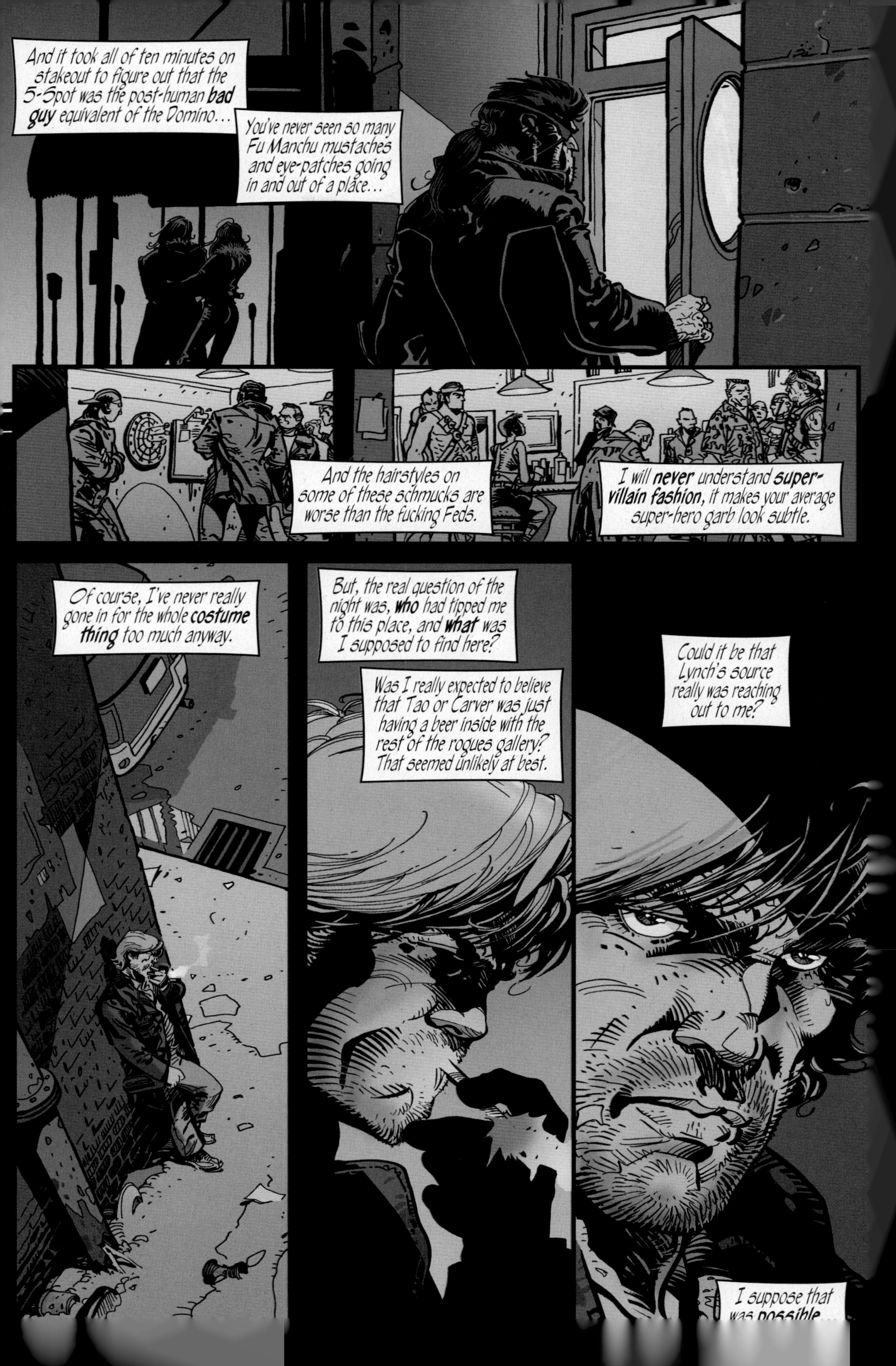
And it took all of ten minutes on stakeout to figure out that the 5-Spot was the post-human **bad guy** equivalent of the Domino...
You've never seen so many Fu Manchu mustaches and eye-patches going in and out of a place...
And the hairstyles on some of these schmucks are worse than the fucking Feds.
I will **never** understand **super-villain fashion**, it makes your average super-hero garb look subtle.
Of course, I've never really gone in for the whole **costume thing** too much anyway.
But, the real question of the night was, **who** had tipped me to this place, and **what** was I supposed to find here?
Was I really expected to believe that Tao or Carver was just having a beer inside with the rest of the rogues gallery? That seemed unlikely at best.
Could it be that Lynch's source really was reaching out to me?
I suppose that was **possible**...

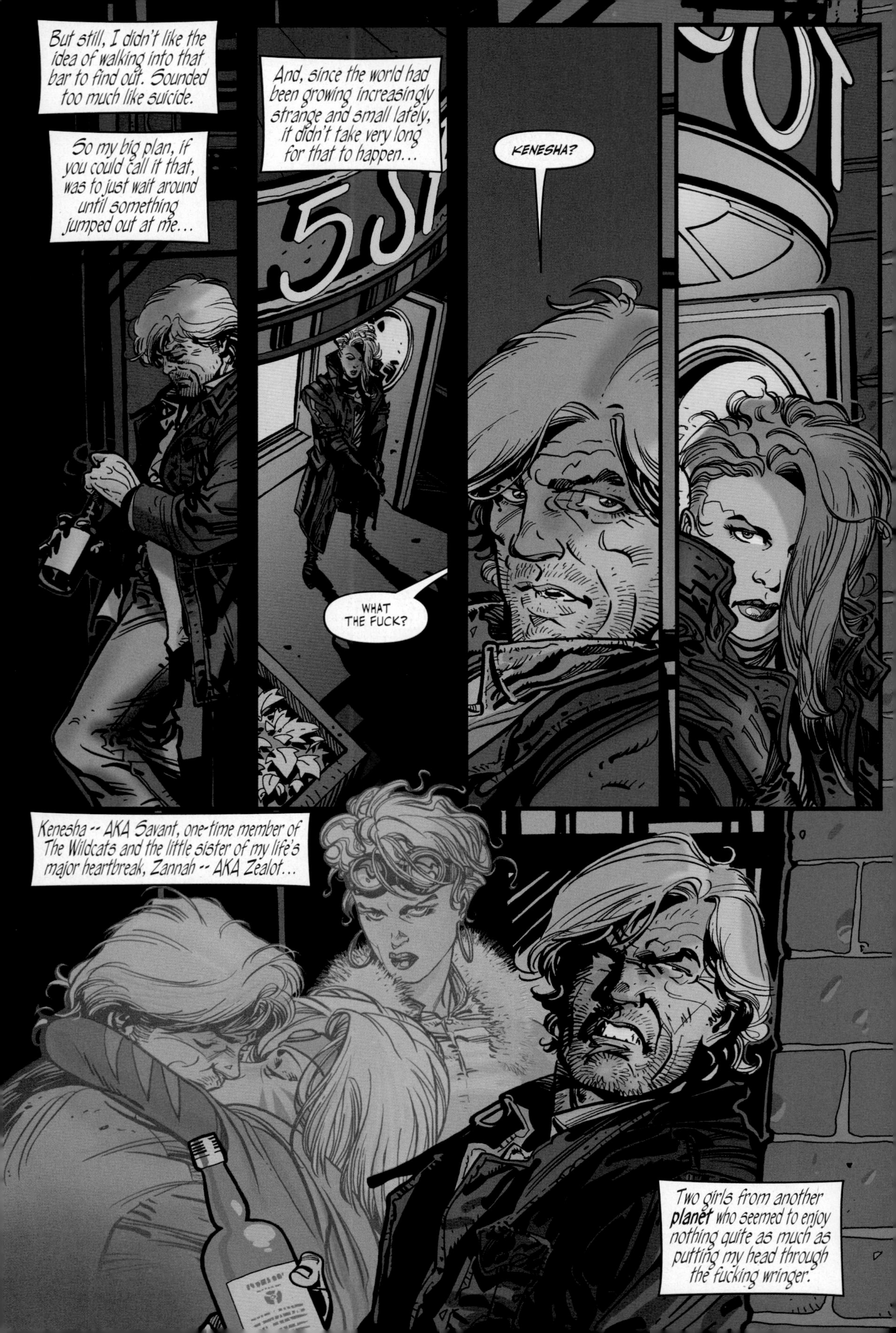
But still, I didn't like the idea of walking into that bar to find out. Sounded too much like suicide.
So my big plan, if you could call it that, was to just wait around until something jumped out at me...
And, since the world had been growing increasingly strange and small lately, it didn't take very long for that to happen...
WHAT THE FUCK?
KENESHA?
Kenesha -- AKA Savant, one-time member of The Wildcats and the little sister of my life's major heartbreak, Zannah -- AKA Zealot...
Two girls from another planet who seemed to enjoy nothing quite as much as putting my head through the fucking wringer.

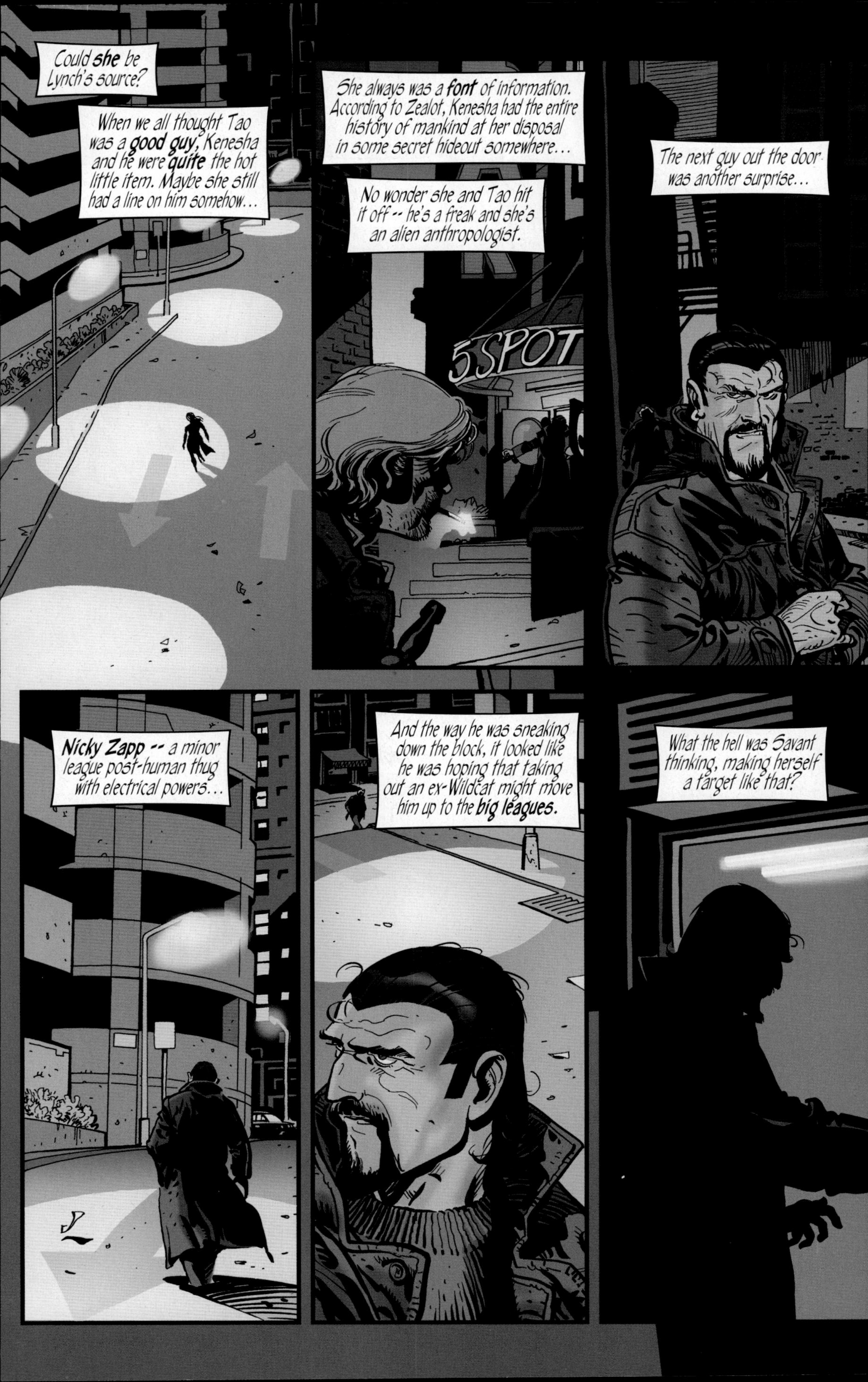
Could she be Lynch's source?
When we all thought Tao was a good guy, Kenesha and he were quite the hot little item. Maybe she still had a line on him somehow...
She always was a font of information. According to Zealot, Kenesha had the entire history of mankind at her disposal in some secret hideout somewhere...
No wonder she and Tao hit it off -- he's a freak and she's an alien anthropologist.
5 SPOT
The next guy out the door was another surprise...
Nicky Zapp -- a minor league post-human thug with electrical powers...
And the way he was sneaking down the block, it looked like he was hoping that taking out an ex-Wildcat might move him up to the big leagues.
What the hell was Savant thinking, making herself a target like that?

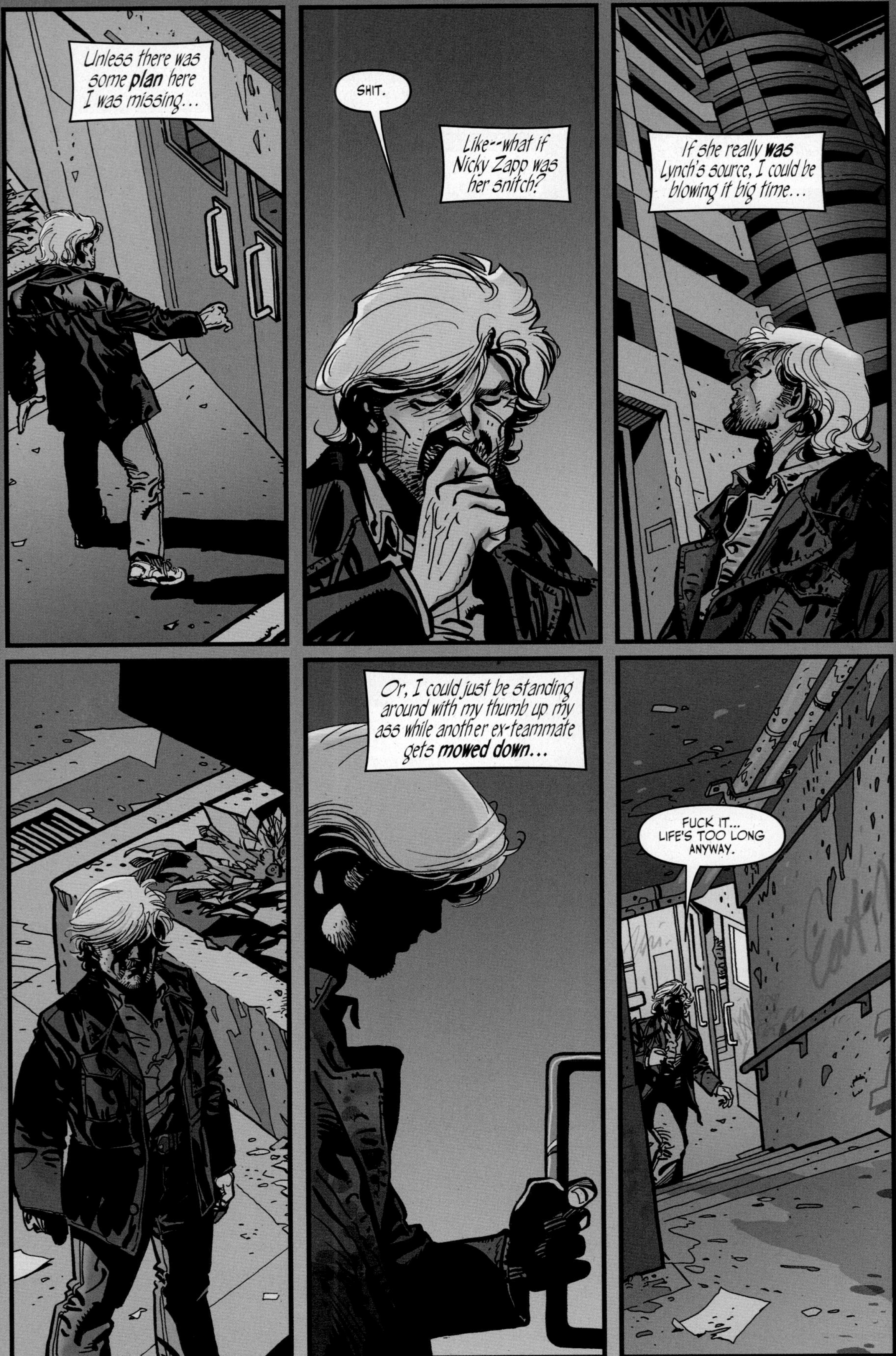
Unless there was some **plan** here I was missing...
SHIT.
Like--what if Nicky Zapp was her snitch?
If she really **was** Lynch's source, I could be blowing it big time...
Or, I could just be standing around with my thumb up my ass while another ex-teammate gets **mowed down**...
FUCK IT... LIFE'S TOO LONG ANYWAY.

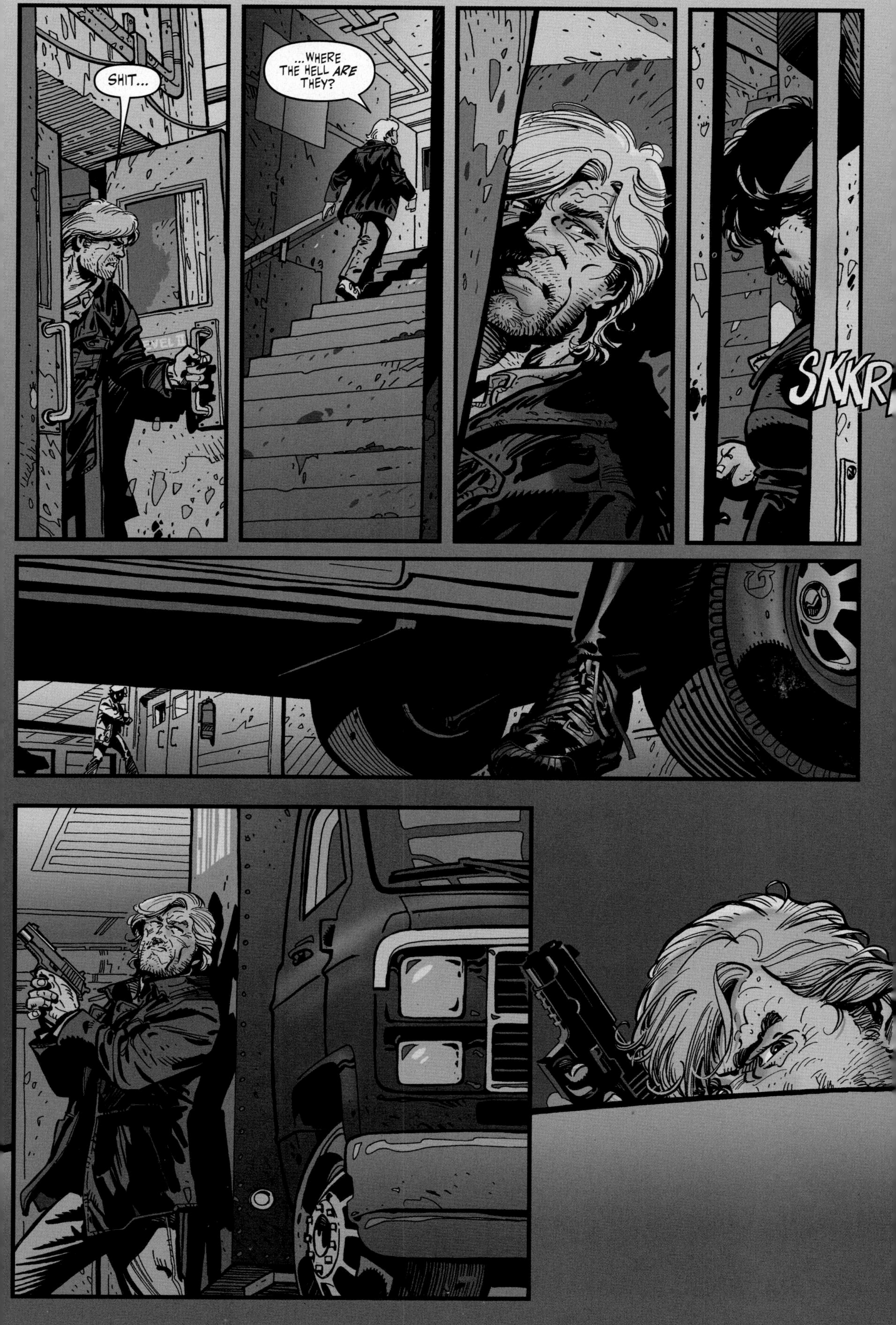

SHIT...
...WHERE THE HELL ARE THEY?
SKKR

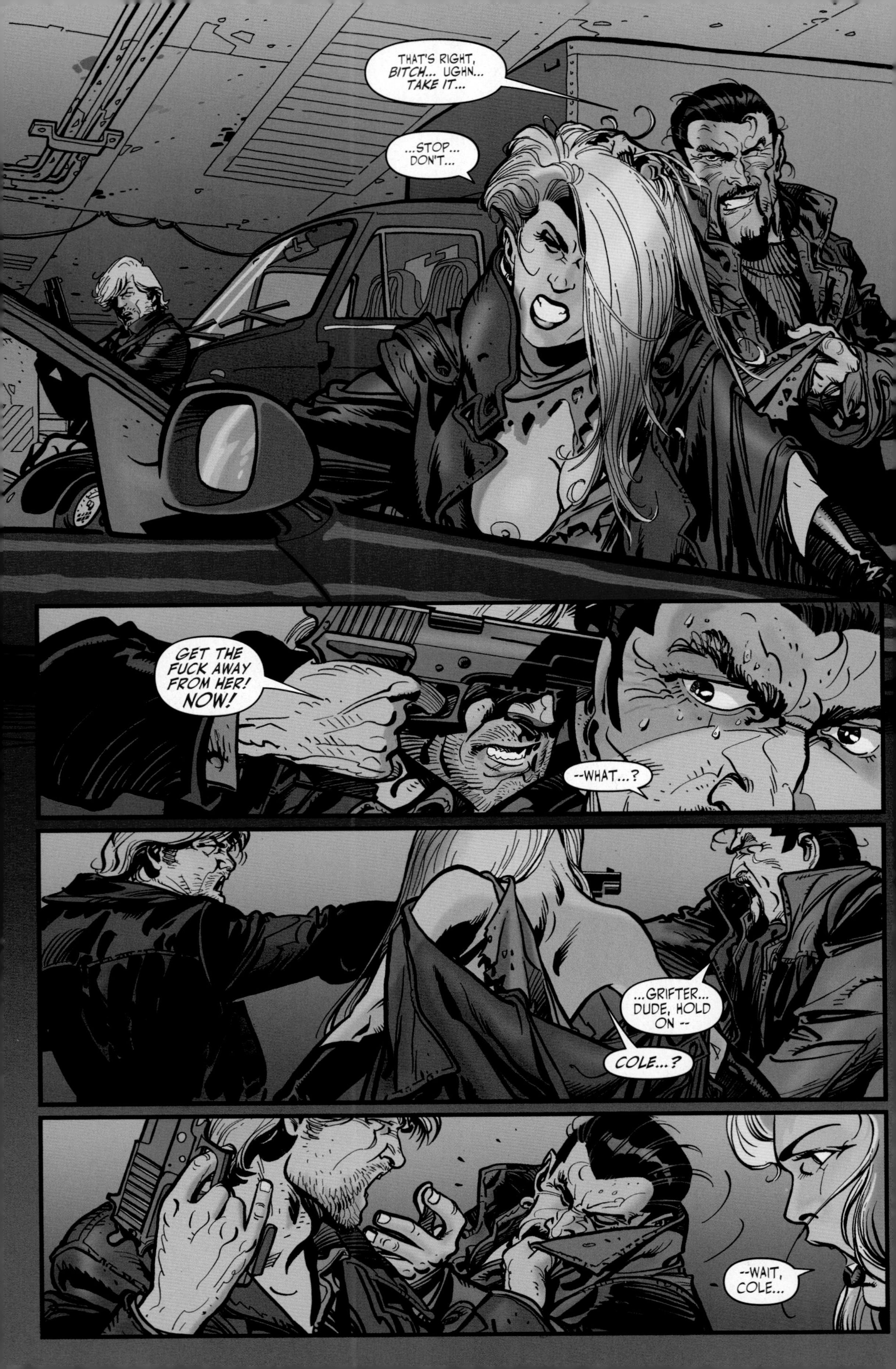
THAT'S RIGHT, BITCH... UGHN... TAKE IT...
...STOP... DON'T...
GET THE FUCK AWAY FROM HER! NOW!
--WHAT...?
...GRIFTER... DUDE, HOLD ON --
COLE...?
--WAIT, COLE...

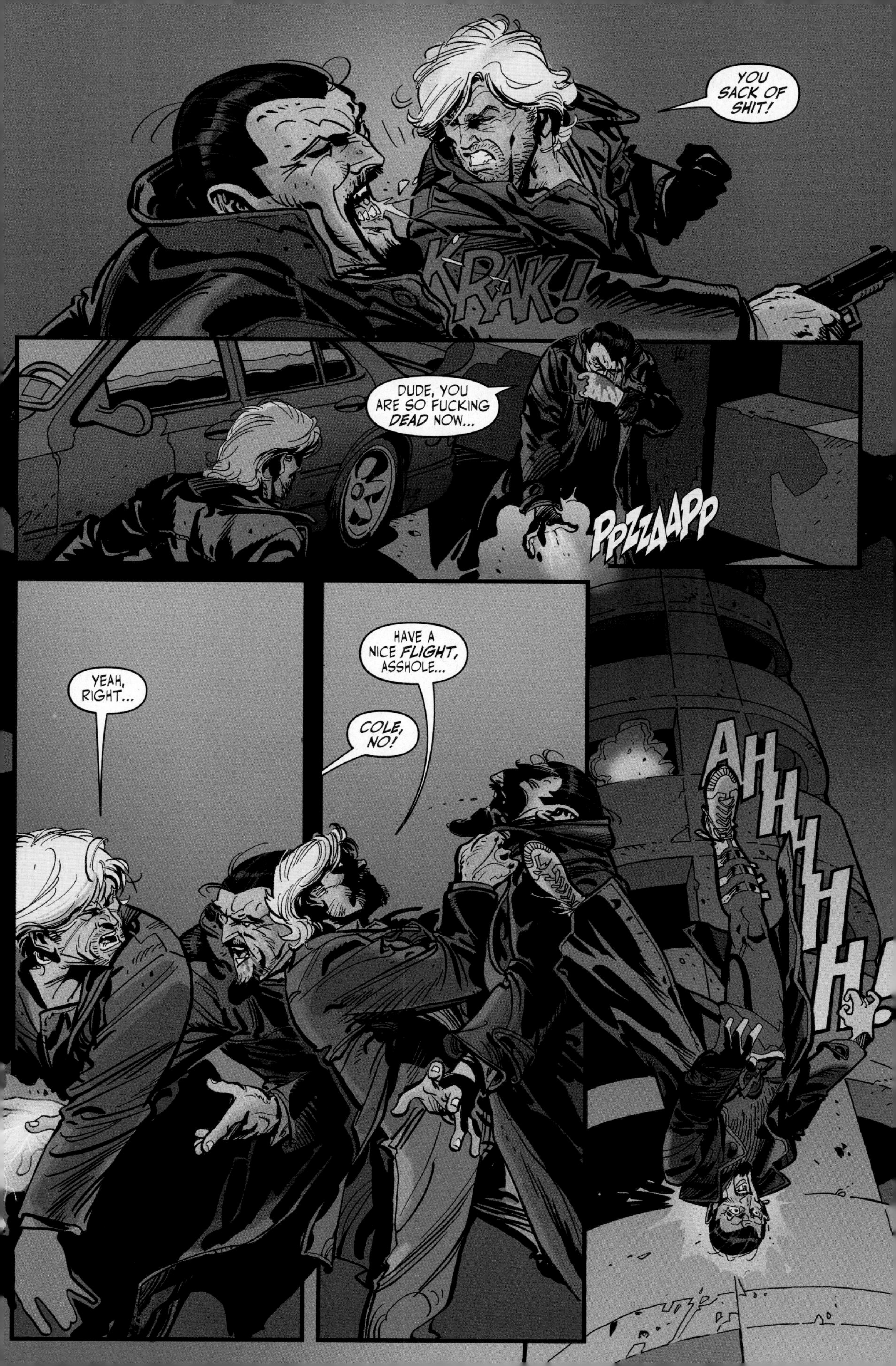
YOU SACK OF SHIT!
KRAK!
DUDE, YOU ARE SO FUCKING DEAD NOW...
PPZZZAAPP
YEAH, RIGHT...
HAVE A NICE FLIGHT, ASSHOLE...
COLE, NO!
AHHHHHH!

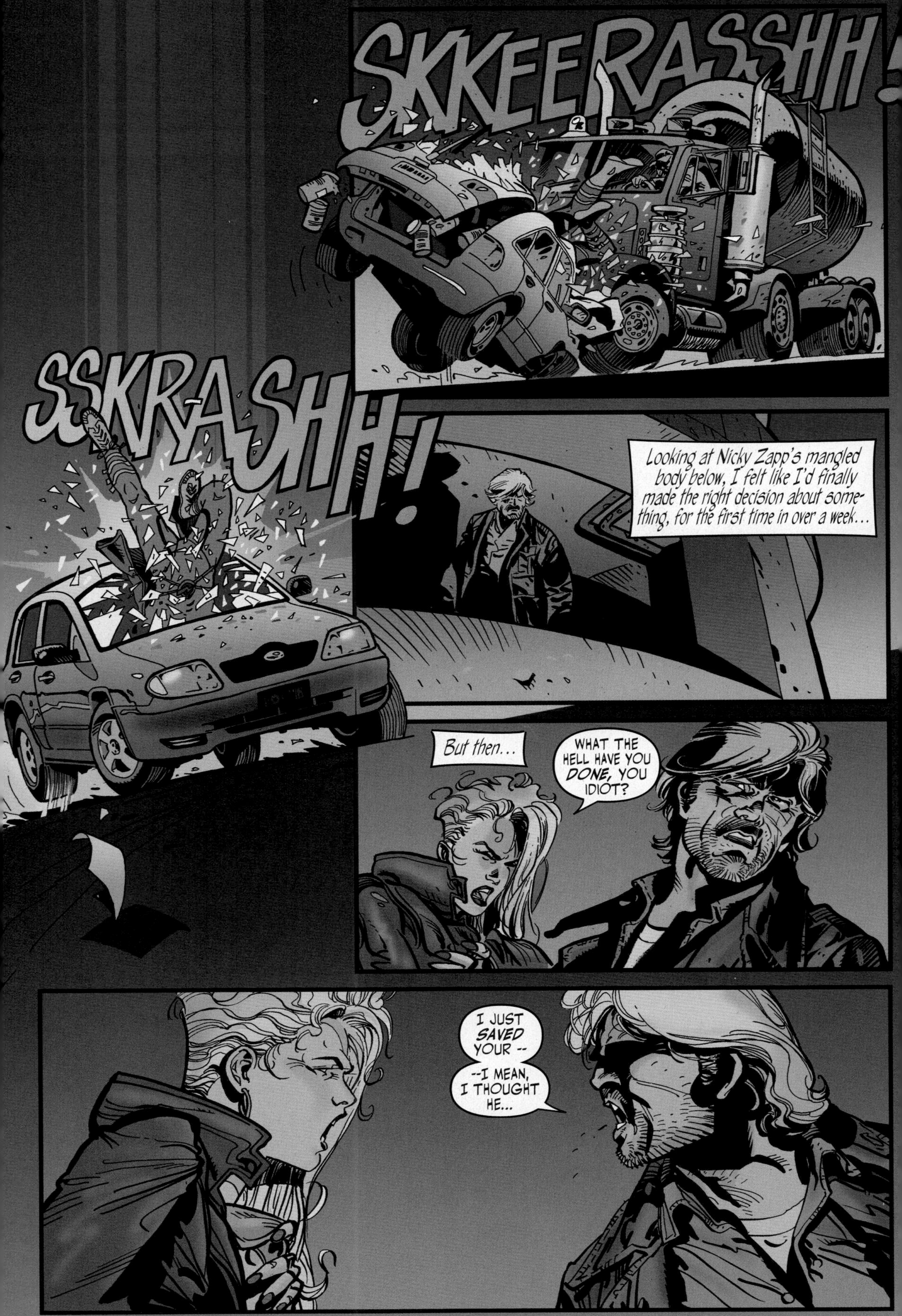
SKKEERASSHH!
SSKRASHH!
Looking at Nicky Zapp's mangled body below, I felt like I'd finally made the right decision about something, for the first time in over a week...
But then...
WHAT THE HELL HAVE YOU DONE, YOU IDIOT?
I JUST SAVED YOUR --
--I MEAN, I THOUGHT HE...

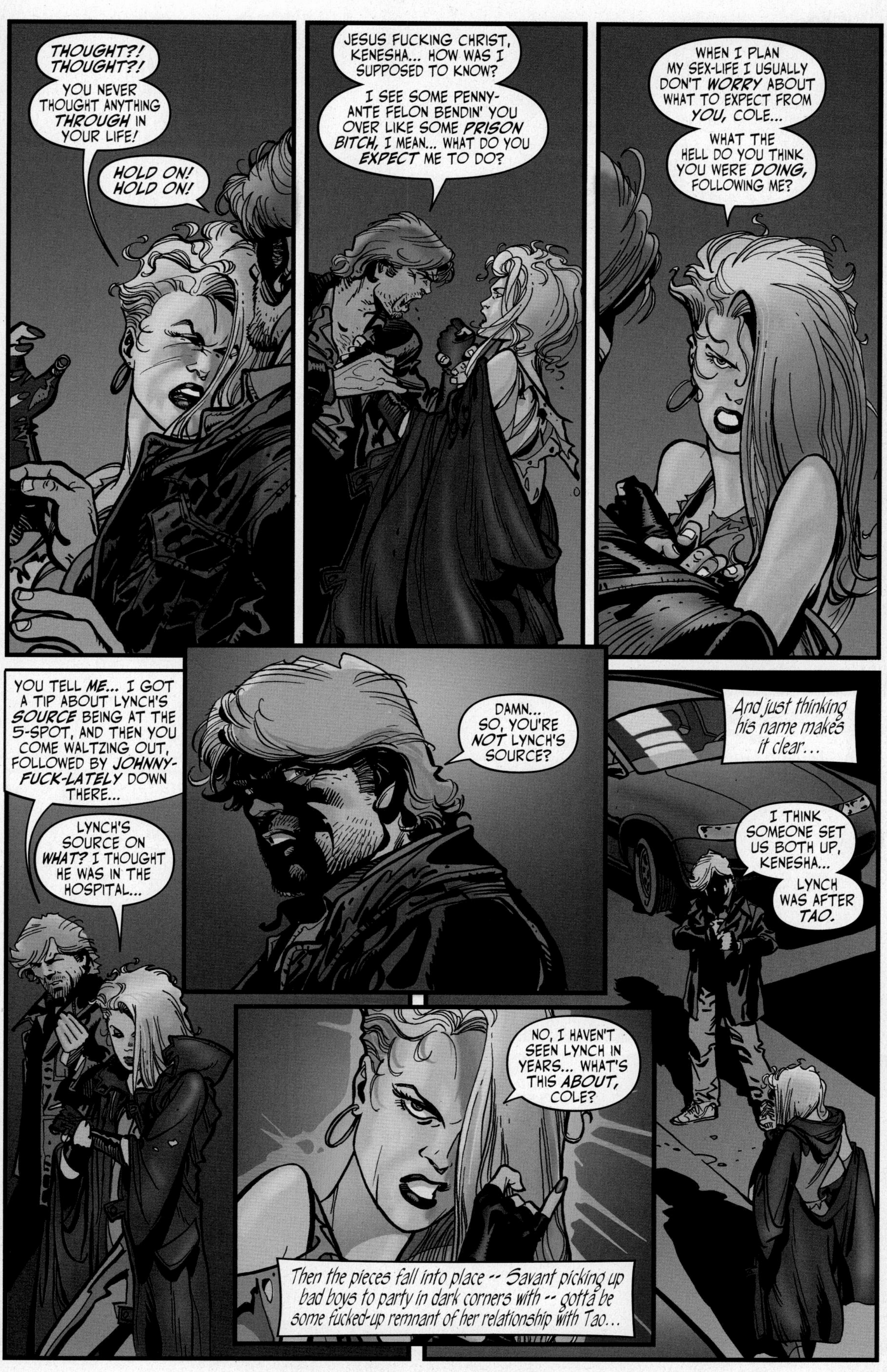

THOUGHT?! THOUGHT?!
YOU NEVER THOUGHT ANYTHING THROUGH IN YOUR LIFE!
HOLD ON! HOLD ON!
JESUS FUCKING CHRIST, KENESHA... HOW WAS I SUPPOSED TO KNOW?
I SEE SOME PENNY-ANTE FELON BENDIN' YOU OVER LIKE SOME PRISON BITCH, I MEAN... WHAT DO YOU EXPECT ME TO DO?
WHEN I PLAN MY SEX-LIFE I USUALLY DON'T WORRY ABOUT WHAT TO EXPECT FROM YOU, COLE...
WHAT THE HELL DO YOU THINK YOU WERE DOING, FOLLOWING ME?
YOU TELL ME... I GOT A TIP ABOUT LYNCH'S SOURCE BEING AT THE 5-SPOT, AND THEN YOU COME WALTZING OUT, FOLLOWED BY JOHNNY-FUCK-LATELY DOWN THERE...
LYNCH'S SOURCE ON WHAT? I THOUGHT HE WAS IN THE HOSPITAL...
DAMN... SO, YOU'RE NOT LYNCH'S SOURCE?
NO, I HAVEN'T SEEN LYNCH IN YEARS... WHAT'S THIS ABOUT, COLE?
Then the pieces fall into place -- Savant picking up bad boys to party in dark corners with -- gotta be some fucked-up remnant of her relationship with Tao...
And just thinking his name makes it clear...
I THINK SOMEONE SET US BOTH UP, KENESHA...
LYNCH WAS AFTER TAO.

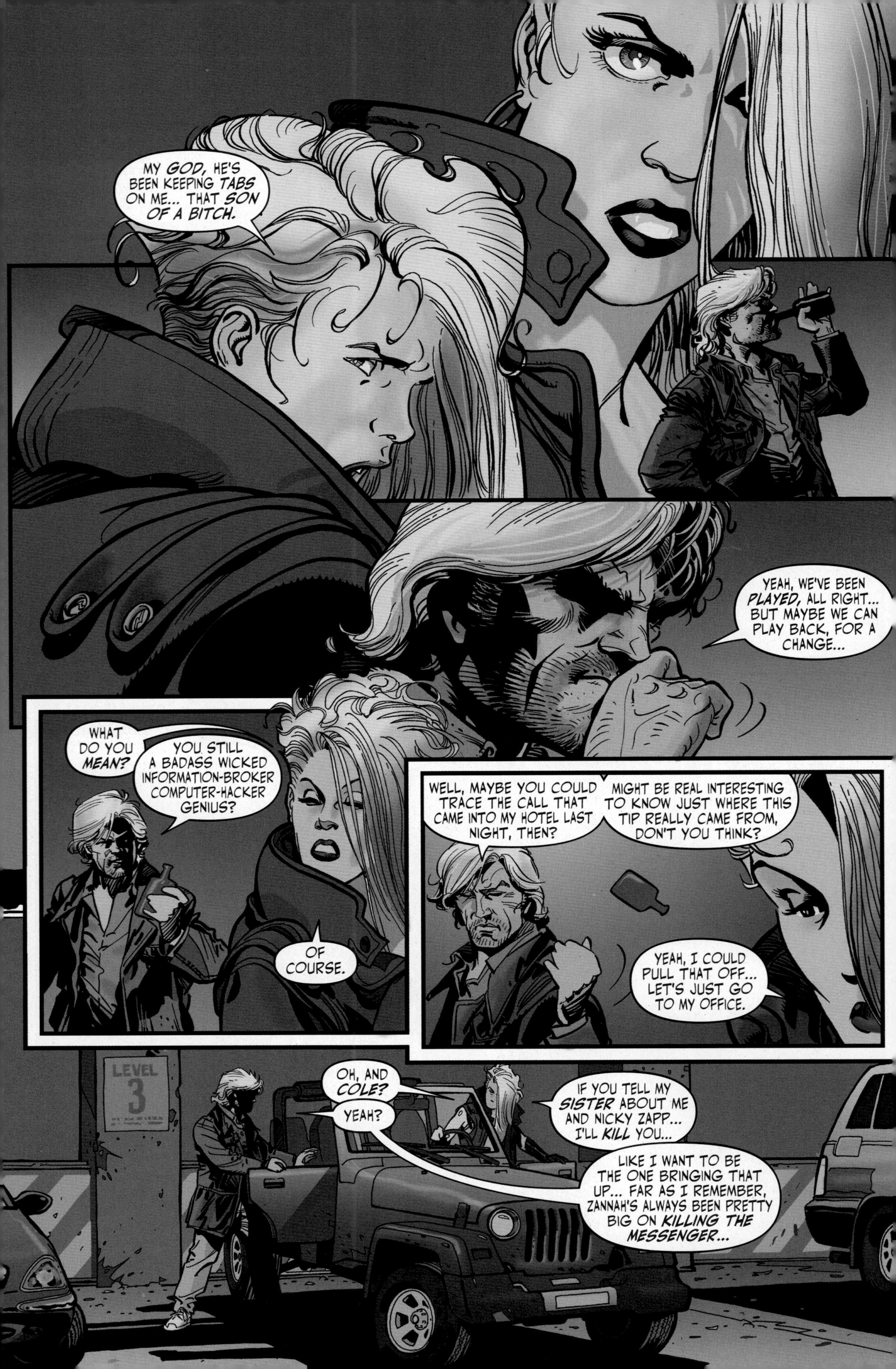
MY GOD, HE'S BEEN KEEPING TABS ON ME... THAT SON OF A BITCH.
YEAH, WE'VE BEEN PLAYED, ALL RIGHT... BUT MAYBE WE CAN PLAY BACK, FOR A CHANGE...
WHAT DO YOU MEAN?
YOU STILL A BADASS WICKED INFORMATION-BROKER COMPUTER-HACKER GENIUS?
OF COURSE.
WELL, MAYBE YOU COULD TRACE THE CALL THAT CAME INTO MY HOTEL LAST NIGHT, THEN?
MIGHT BE REAL INTERESTING TO KNOW JUST WHERE THIS TIP REALLY CAME FROM, DON'T YOU THINK?
YEAH, I COULD PULL THAT OFF... LET'S JUST GO TO MY OFFICE.
LEVEL 3
OH, AND COLE?
YEAH?
IF YOU TELL MY SISTER ABOUT ME AND NICKY ZAPP... I'LL KILL YOU...
LIKE I WANT TO BE THE ONE BRINGING THAT UP... FAR AS I REMEMBER, ZANNAH'S ALWAYS BEEN PRETTY BIG ON KILLING THE MESSENGER...

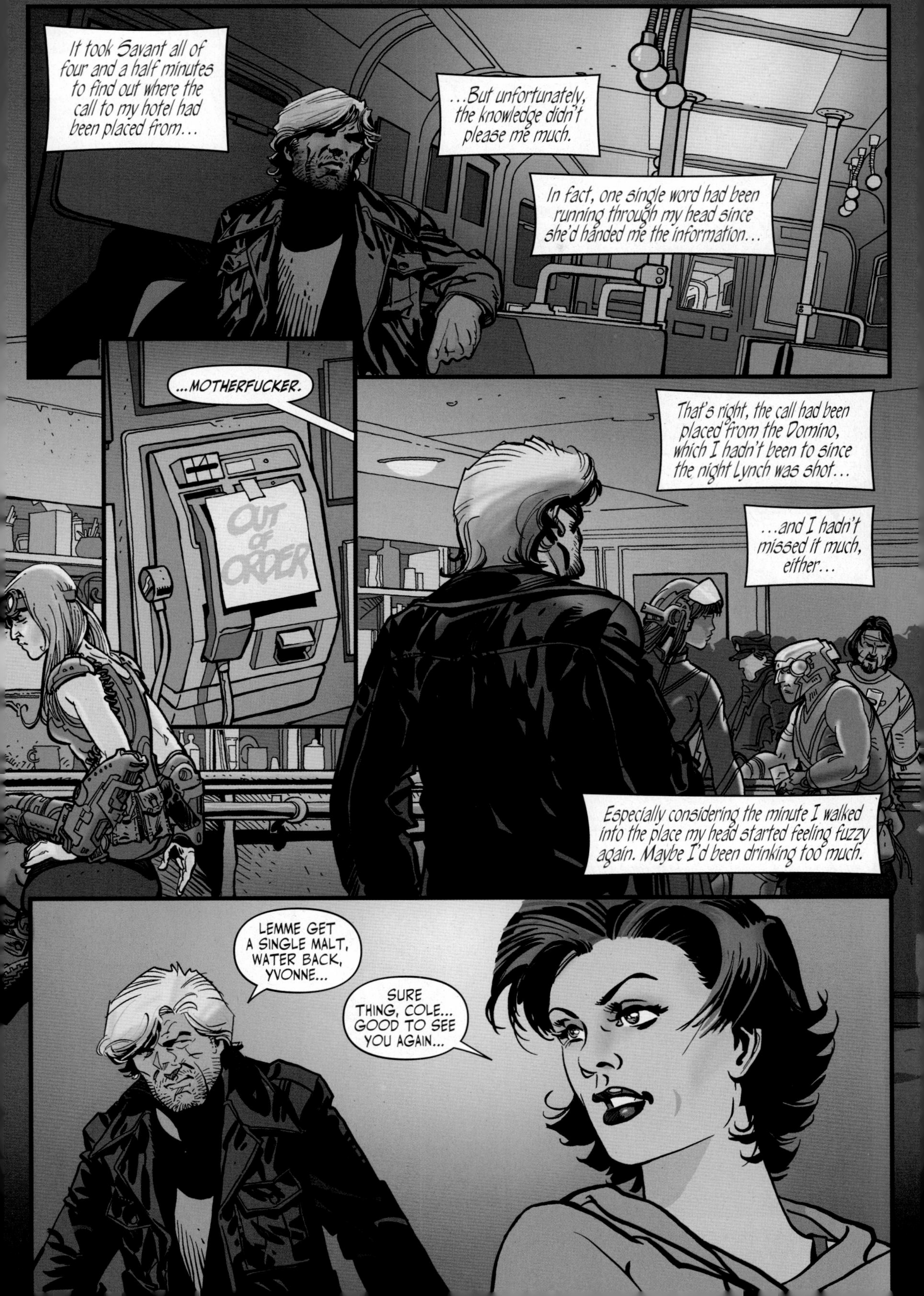
It took Savant all of four and a half minutes to find out where the call to my hotel had been placed from...
...But unfortunately, the knowledge didn't please me much.
In fact, one single word had been running through my head since she'd handed me the information...
...MOTHERFUCKER.
OUT OF ORDER
That's right, the call had been placed from the Domino, which I hadn't been to since the night Lynch was shot...
...and I hadn't missed it much, either...
Especially considering the minute I walked into the place my head started feeling fuzzy again. Maybe I'd been drinking too much.
LEMME GET A SINGLE MALT, WATER BACK, YVONNE...
SURE THING, COLE... GOOD TO SEE YOU AGAIN...

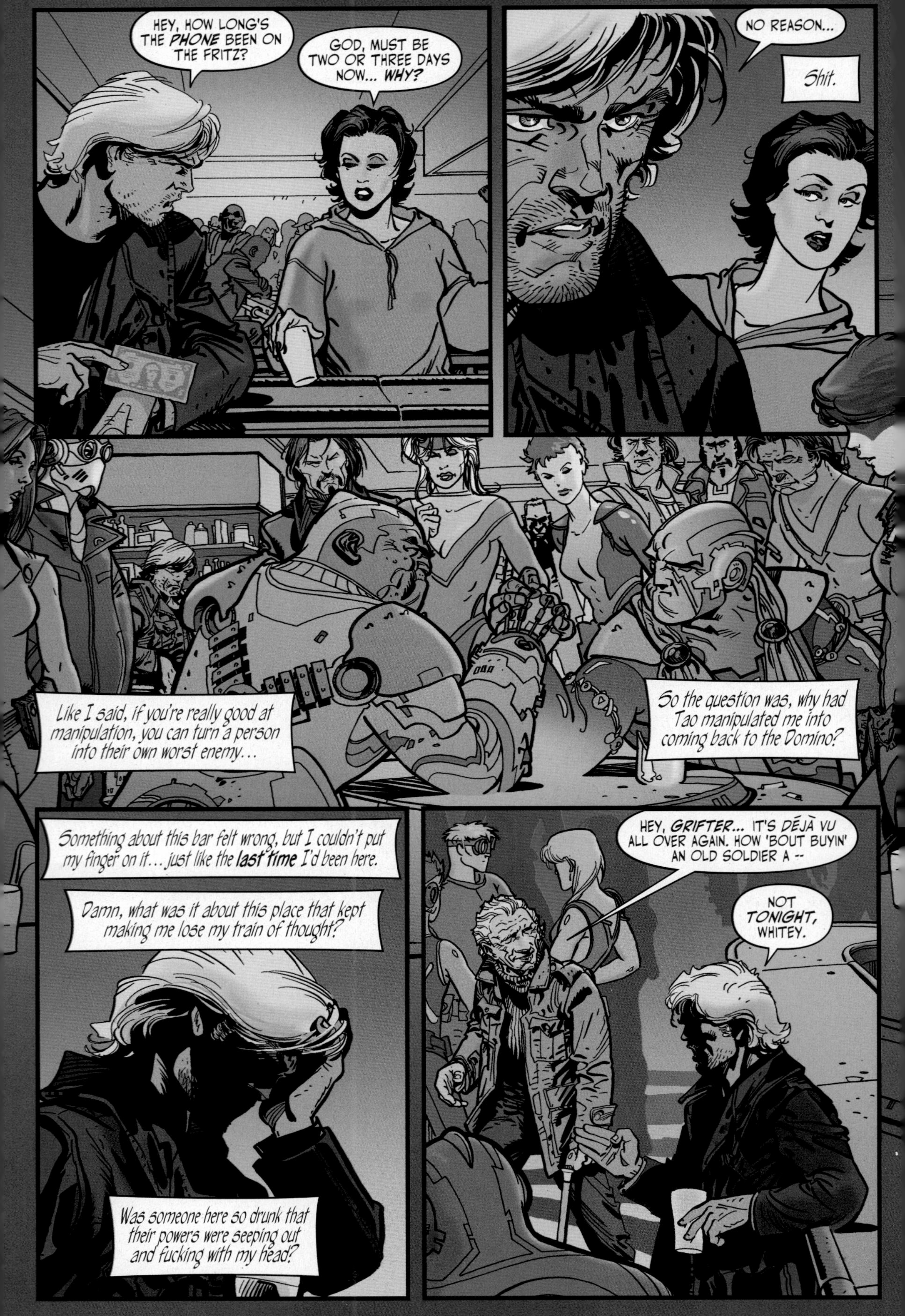
HEY, HOW LONG'S THE PHONE BEEN ON THE FRITZ?
GOD, MUST BE TWO OR THREE DAYS NOW... WHY?
NO REASON...
Shit.
Like I said, if you're really good at manipulation, you can turn a person into their own worst enemy...
So the question was, why had Tao manipulated me into coming back to the Domino?
Something about this bar felt wrong, but I couldn't put my finger on it... just like the last time I'd been here.
Damn, what was it about this place that kept making me lose my train of thought?
Was someone here so drunk that their powers were seeping out and fucking with my head?
HEY, GRIFTER... IT'S DÉJÀ VU ALL OVER AGAIN. HOW 'BOUT BUYIN' AN OLD SOLDIER A --
NOT TONIGHT, WHITEY.

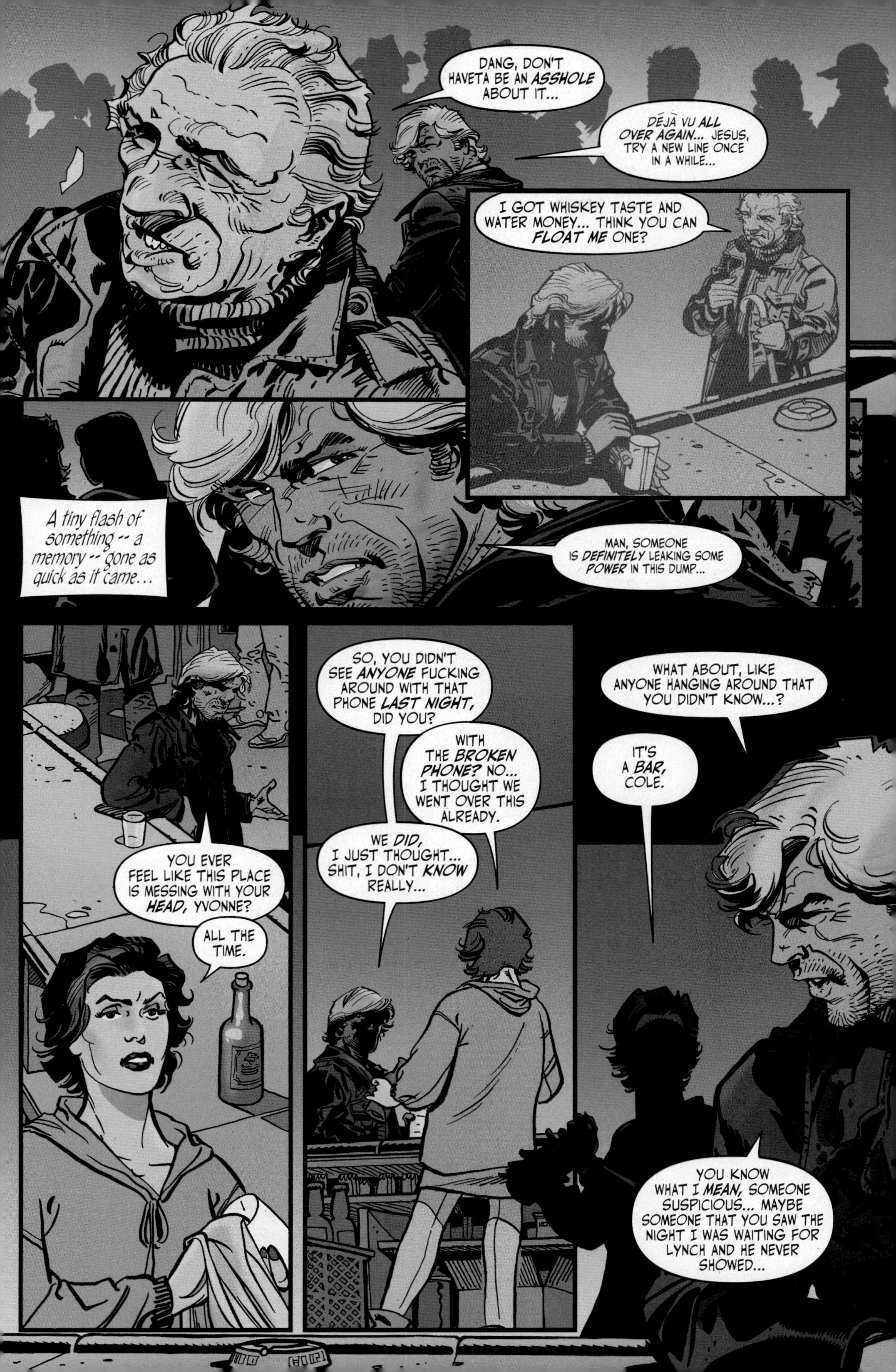
DANG, DON'T HAVETA BE AN *ASSHOLE* ABOUT IT...
DÉJÀ VU **ALL OVER AGAIN...** JESUS, TRY A NEW LINE ONCE IN A WHILE...
I GOT WHISKEY TASTE AND WATER MONEY... THINK YOU CAN *FLOAT ME* ONE?
A tiny flash of something -- a memory -- gone as quick as it came...
MAN, SOMEONE IS *DEFINITELY* LEAKING SOME *POWER* IN THIS DUMP...
YOU EVER FEEL LIKE THIS PLACE IS MESSING WITH YOUR *HEAD,* YVONNE?
ALL THE TIME.
SO, YOU DIDN'T SEE *ANYONE* FUCKING AROUND WITH THAT PHONE *LAST NIGHT,* DID YOU?
WITH THE *BROKEN PHONE?* NO... I THOUGHT WE WENT OVER THIS ALREADY.
WE *DID,* I JUST THOUGHT... SHIT, I DON'T *KNOW* REALLY...
WHAT ABOUT, LIKE ANYONE HANGING AROUND THAT YOU DIDN'T KNOW...?
IT'S A *BAR,* COLE.
YOU KNOW WHAT I *MEAN,* SOMEONE SUSPICIOUS... MAYBE SOMEONE THAT YOU SAW THE NIGHT I WAS WAITING FOR LYNCH AND HE NEVER SHOWED...

THAT NIGHT... YOU KNOW WHAT'S *REALLY* WEIRD ABOUT THAT NIGHT?

WHAT?

I COULD'VE SWORN LYNCH *DID* SHOW UP THAT NIGHT...

NO. I WAS SITTING *RIGHT HERE* ALL NIGHT, I'D HAVE SEEN HIM.

I *KNOW*. BUT I THINK HE CAME IN WHEN YOU WERE IN THE BATHROOM OR SOMETHING... I THINK.

HE WENT BACK THERE TO LOOK FOR YOU, AND I JUST *ASSUMED* YOU GUYS WENT OUT THE BACK DOOR... LYNCH WAS *ALWAYS* DUCKING OUT THE BACK, YOU KNOW.

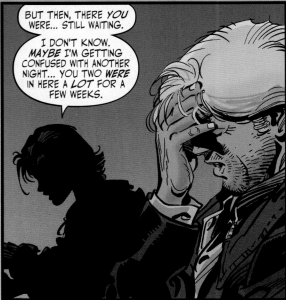

BUT THEN, THERE *YOU* WERE... STILL WAITING.

I DON'T KNOW. *MAYBE* I'M GETTING CONFUSED WITH ANOTHER NIGHT... YOU TWO *WERE* IN HERE A *LOT* FOR A FEW WEEKS.

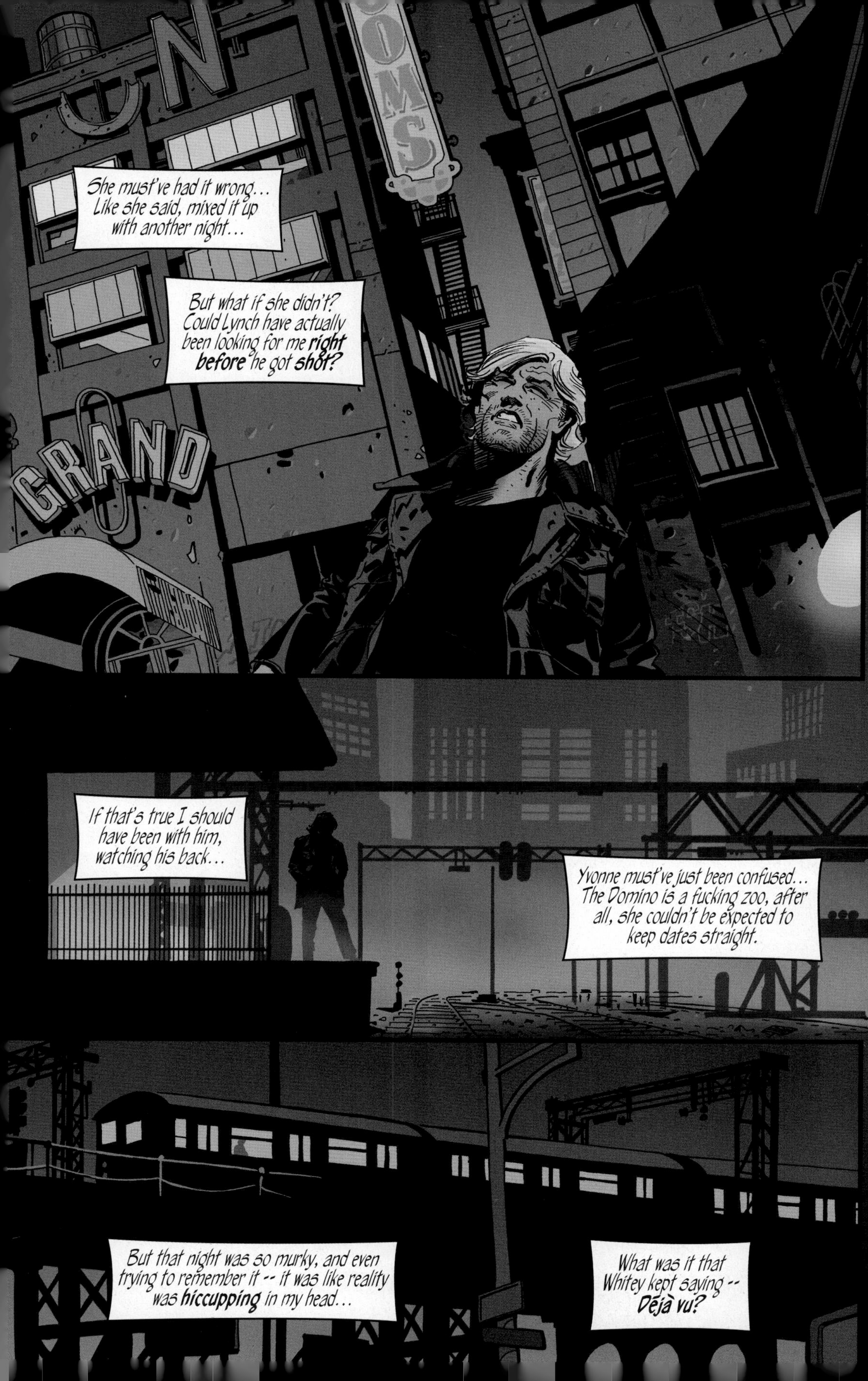

She must've had it wrong... Like she said, mixed it up with another night...
But what if she didn't? Could Lynch have actually been looking for me **right before** he got **shot?**
GRAND
If that's true I should have been with him, watching his back...
Yvonne must've just been confused... The Domino is a fucking zoo, after all, she couldn't be expected to keep dates straight.
But that night was so murky, and even trying to remember it -- it was like reality was **hiccupping** in my head...
What was it that Whitey kept saying -- **Déjà vu?**

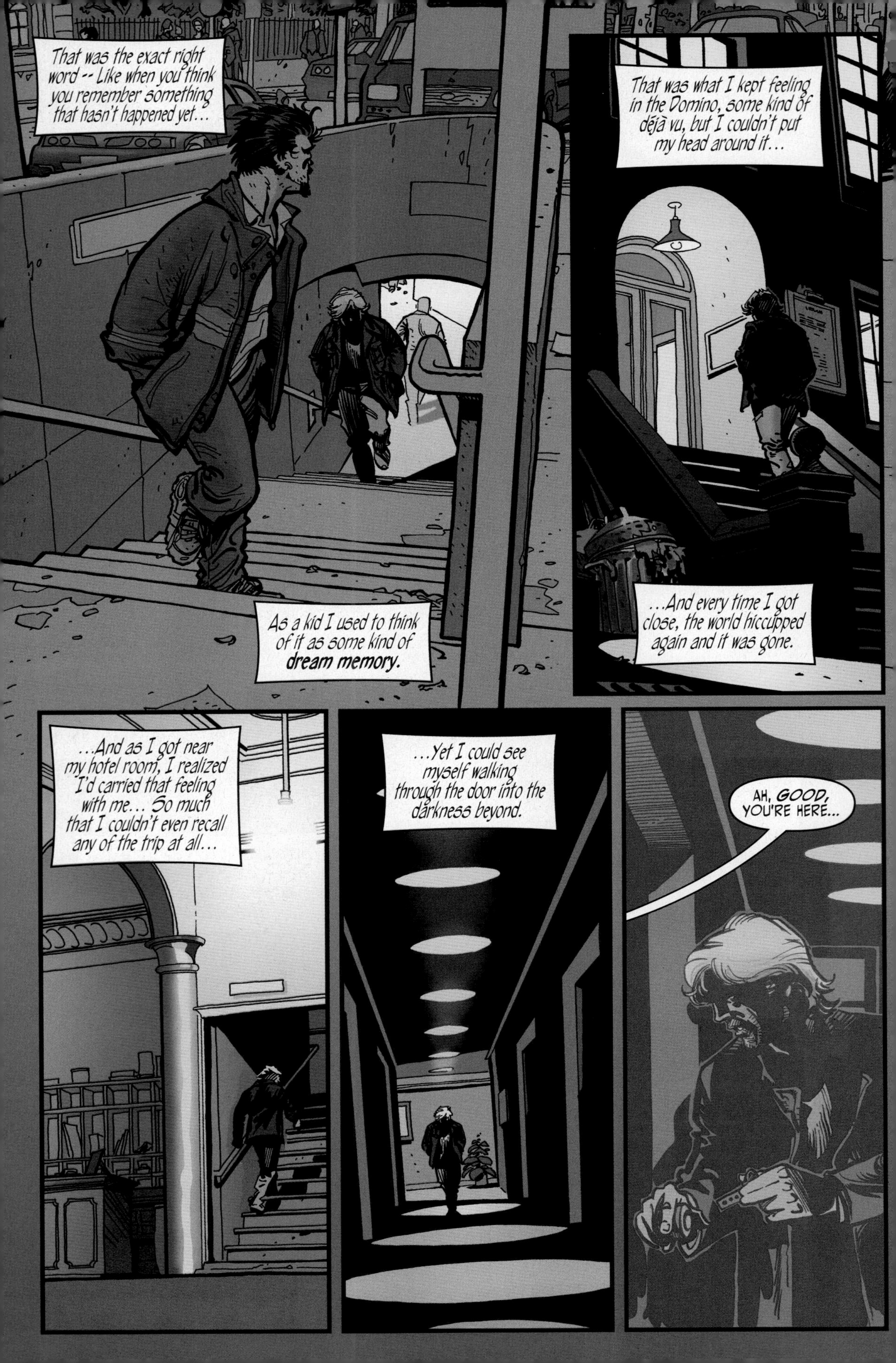

That was the exact right word -- Like when you think you remember something that hasn't happened yet...
That was what I kept feeling in the Domino, some kind of déjà vu, but I couldn't put my head around it...
As a kid I used to think of it as some kind of **dream memory.**
...And every time I got close, the world hiccupped again and it was gone.
...And as I got near my hotel room, I realized I'd carried that feeling with me... So much that I couldn't even recall any of the trip at all...
...Yet I could see myself walking through the door into the darkness beyond.
AH, GOOD, YOU'RE HERE...

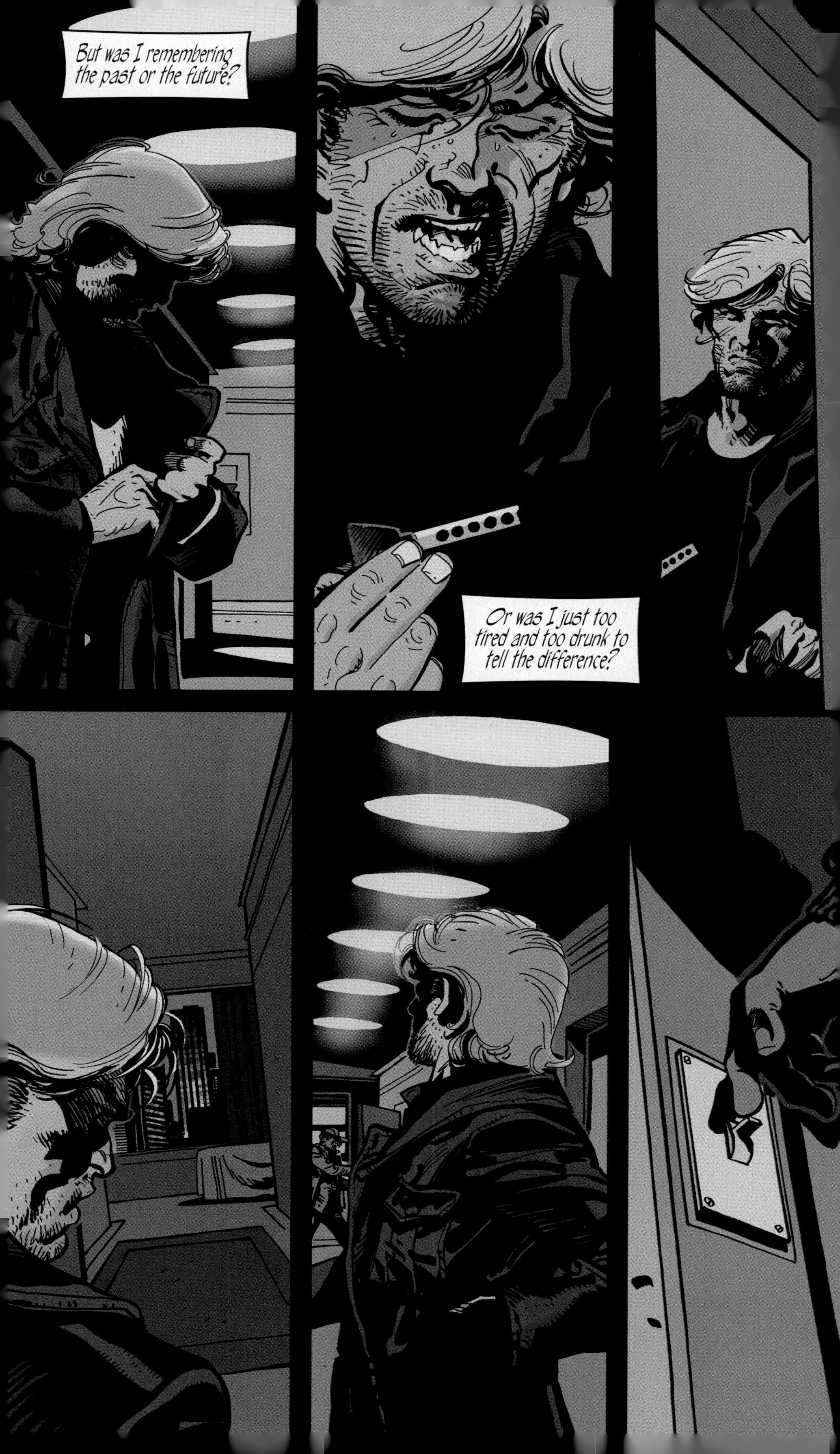

But was I remembering the past or the future?
Or was I just too tired and too drunk to tell the difference?

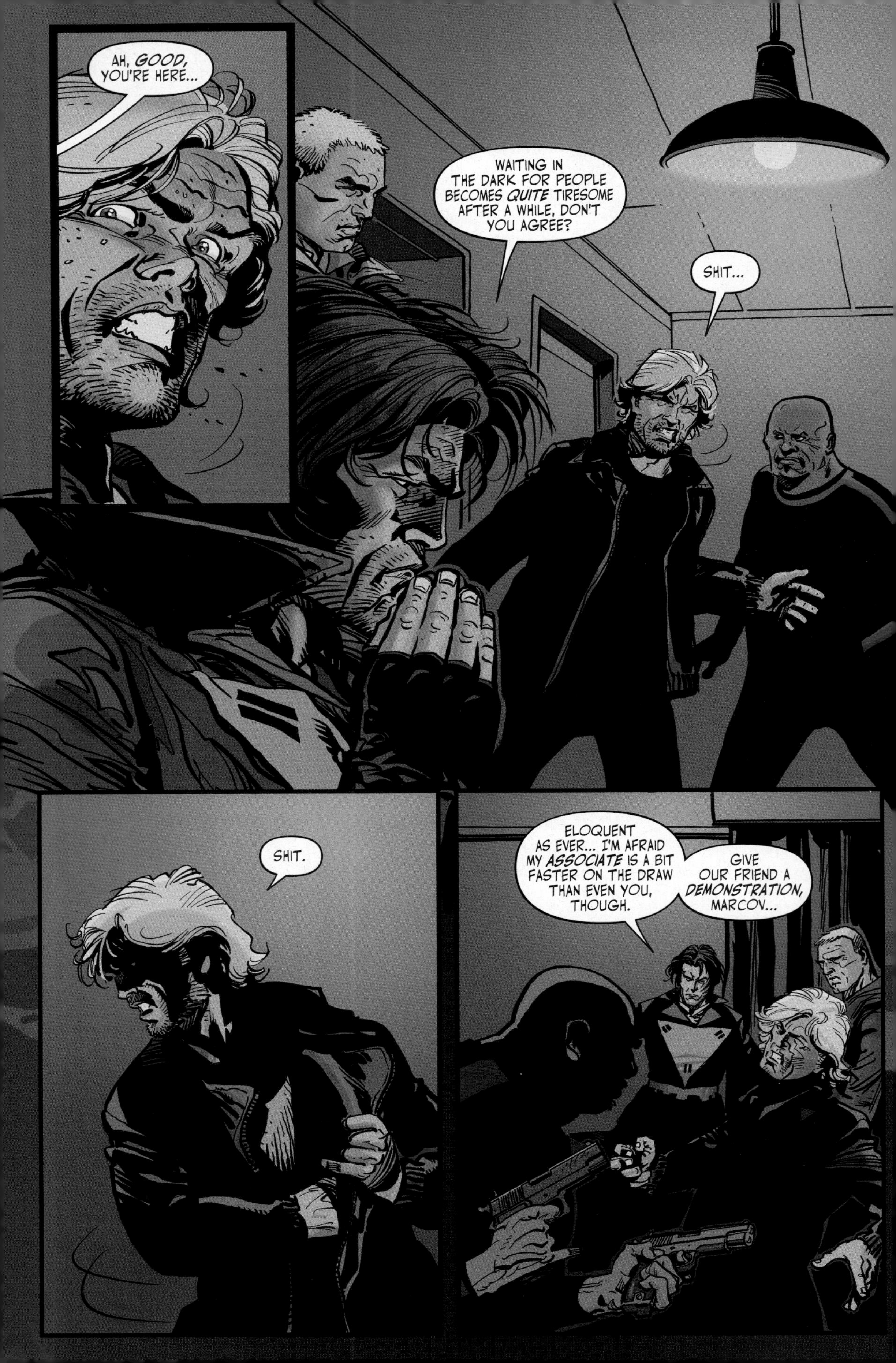

AH, GOOD, YOU'RE HERE...
WAITING IN THE DARK FOR PEOPLE BECOMES QUITE TIRESOME AFTER A WHILE, DON'T YOU AGREE?
SHIT...
SHIT.
ELOQUENT AS EVER... I'M AFRAID MY ASSOCIATE IS A BIT FASTER ON THE DRAW THAN EVEN YOU, THOUGH.
GIVE OUR FRIEND A DEMONSTRATION, MARCOV...

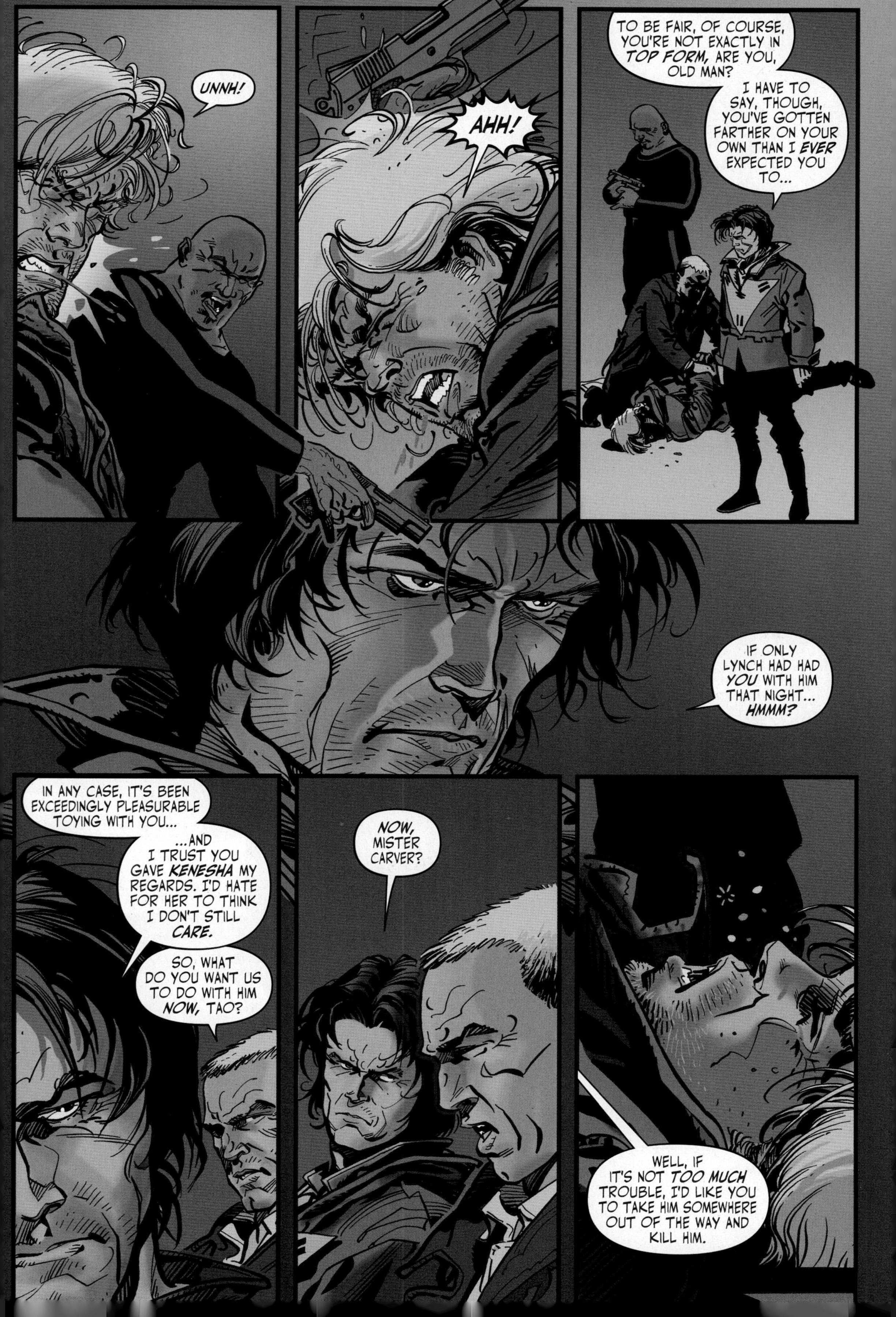
UNNH!
AHH!
TO BE FAIR, OF COURSE, YOU'RE NOT EXACTLY IN *TOP FORM,* ARE YOU, OLD MAN?
I HAVE TO SAY, THOUGH, YOU'VE GOTTEN FARTHER ON YOUR OWN THAN I *EVER* EXPECTED YOU TO...
IF ONLY LYNCH HAD HAD *YOU* WITH HIM THAT NIGHT... ***HMMM?***
IN ANY CASE, IT'S BEEN EXCEEDINGLY PLEASURABLE TOYING WITH YOU...
...AND I TRUST YOU GAVE ***KENESHA*** MY REGARDS. I'D HATE FOR HER TO THINK I DON'T STILL ***CARE.***
SO, WHAT DO YOU WANT US TO DO WITH HIM *NOW,* TAO?
NOW, MISTER CARVER?
WELL, IF IT'S NOT *TOO MUCH* TROUBLE, I'D LIKE YOU TO TAKE HIM SOMEWHERE OUT OF THE WAY AND KILL HIM.

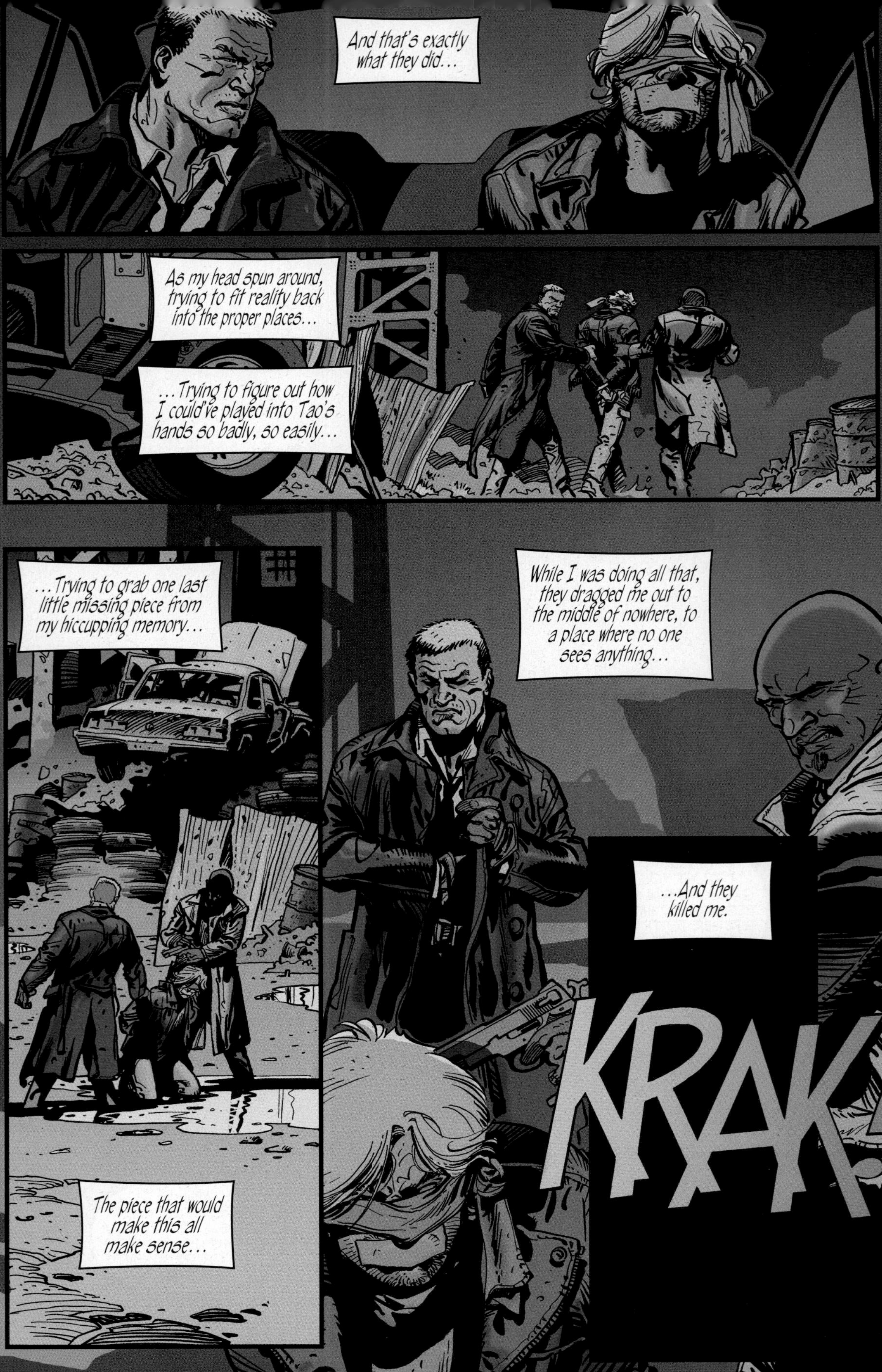
And that's exactly what they did...
As my head spun around, trying to fit reality back into the proper places...
...Trying to figure out how I could've played into Tao's hands so badly, so easily...
...Trying to grab one last little missing piece from my hiccupping memory...
The piece that would make this all make sense...
While I was doing all that, they dragged me out to the middle of nowhere, to a place where no one sees anything...
...And they killed me.
KRAK

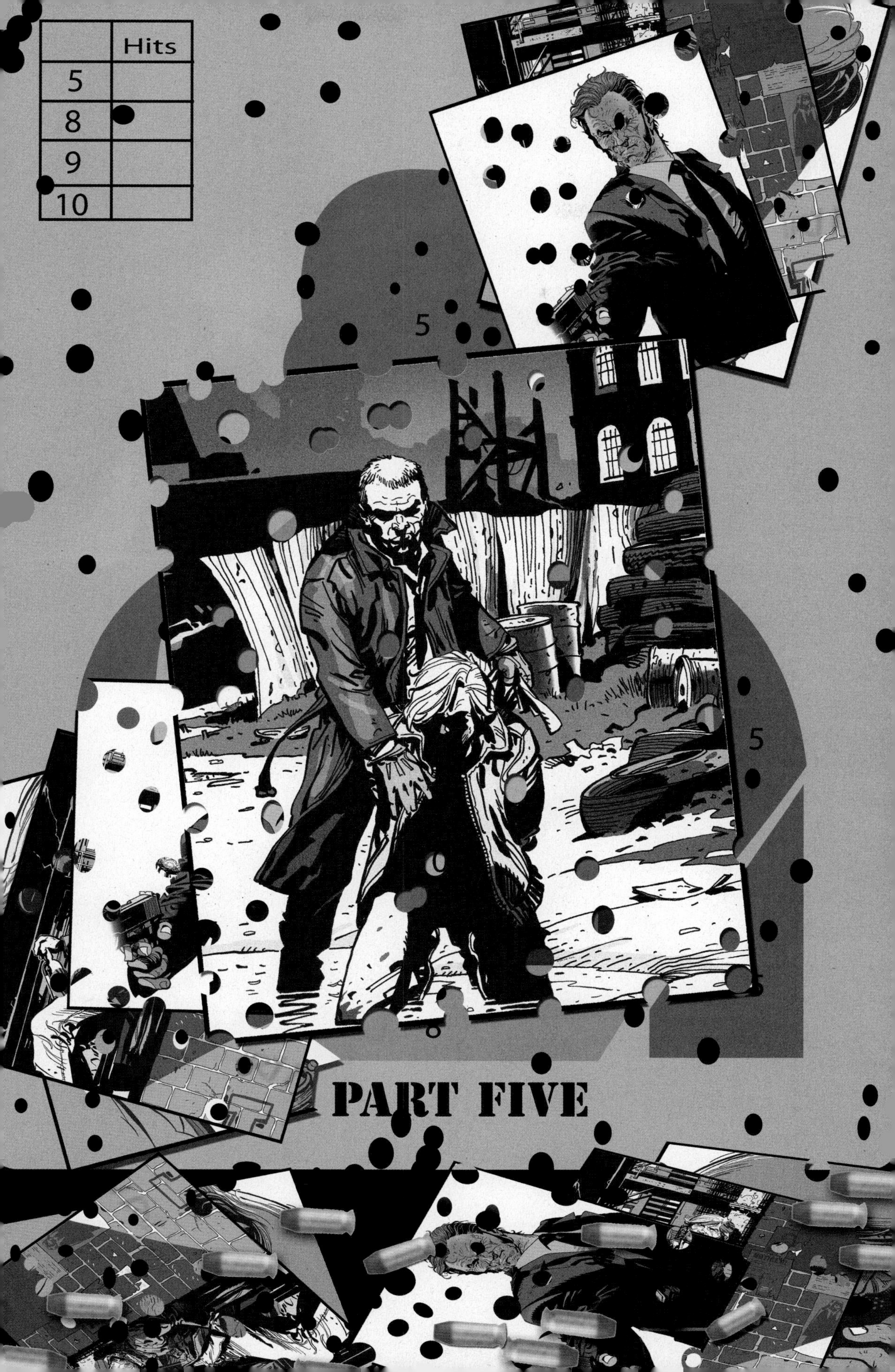
Hits
5
8
9
10
5
5

PART FIVE

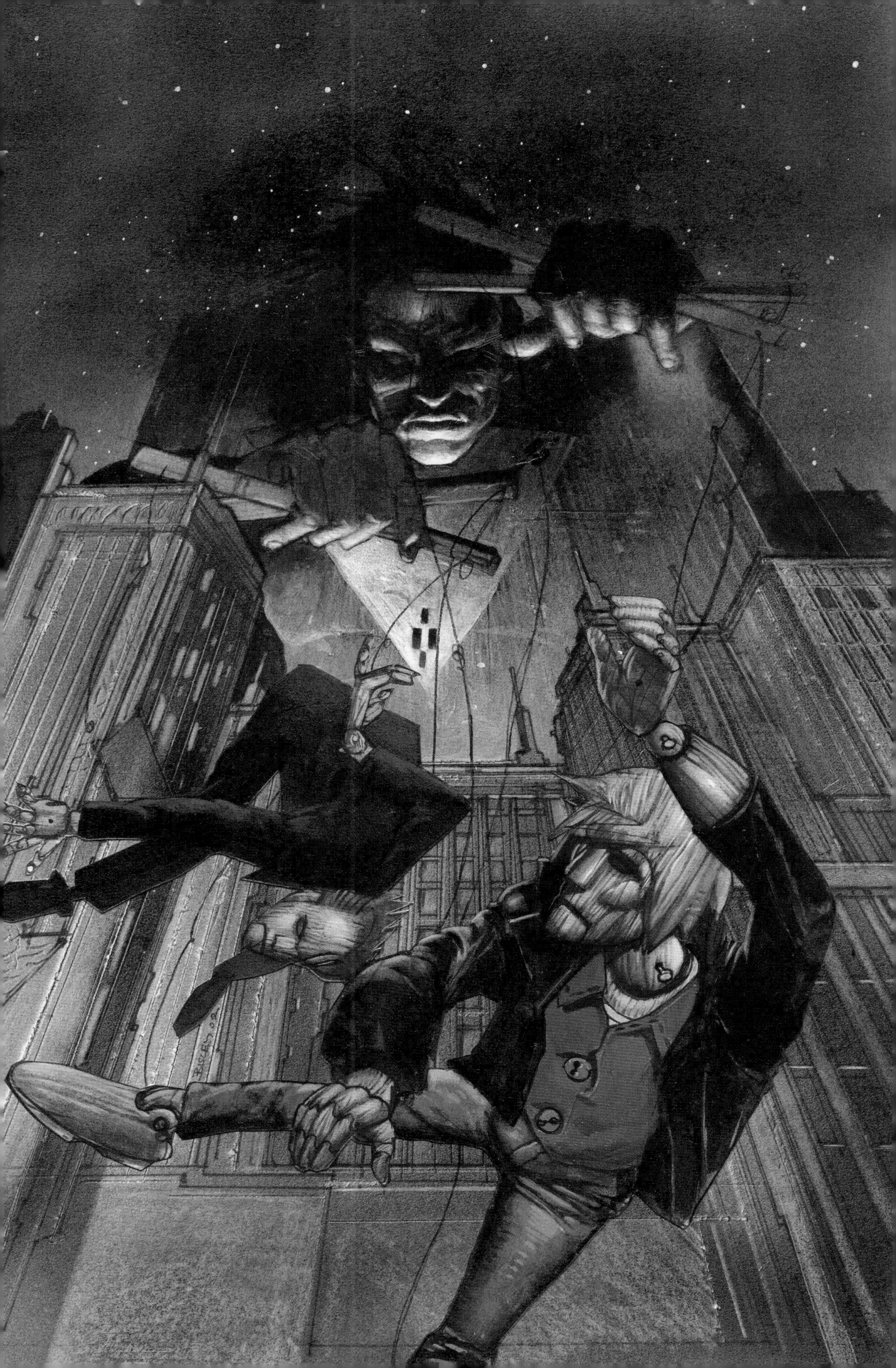

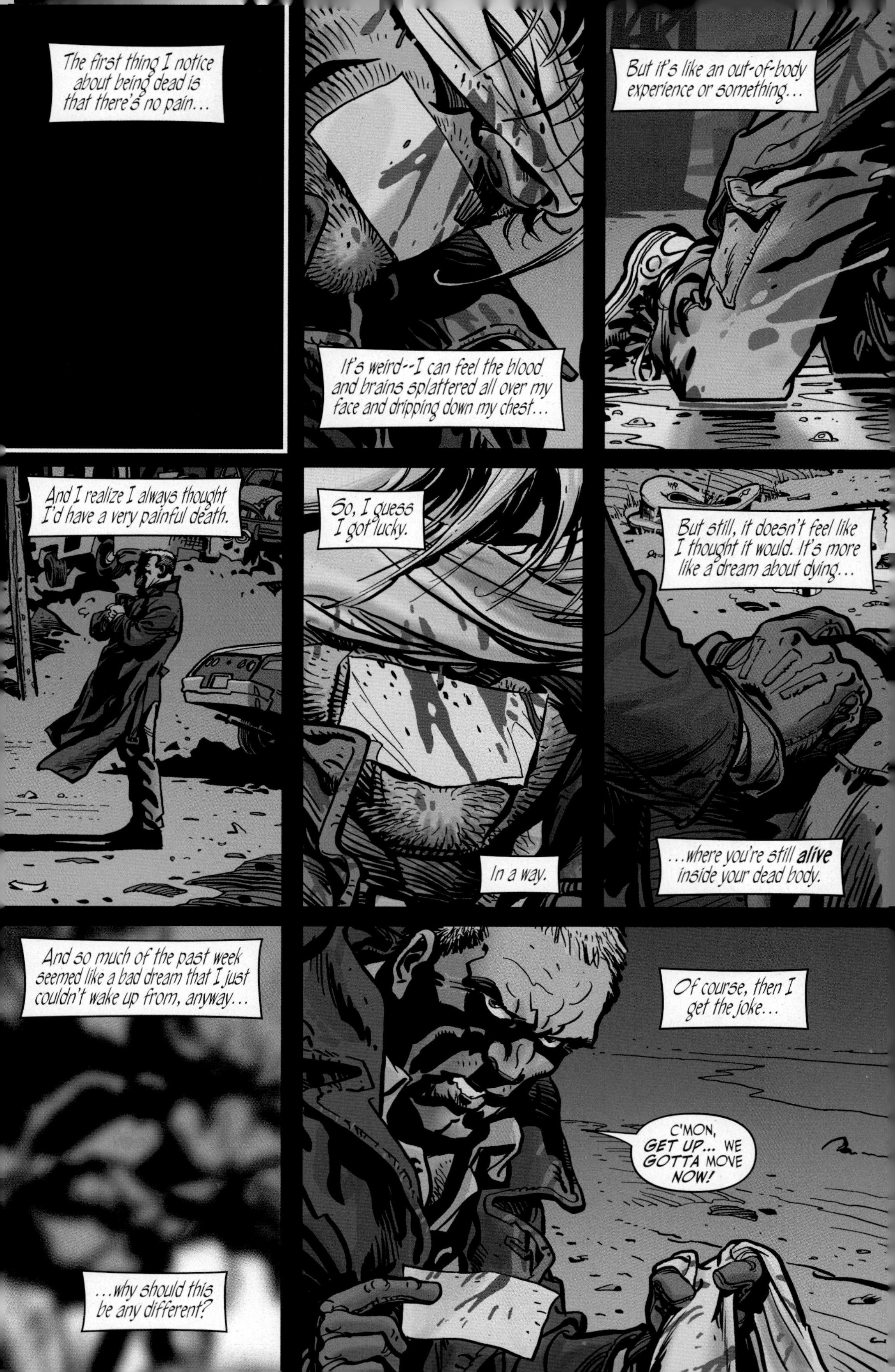
The first thing I notice about being dead is that there's no pain...
It's weird--I can feel the blood and brains splattered all over my face and dripping down my chest...
But it's like an out-of-body experience or something...
And I realize I always thought I'd have a very painful death.
So, I guess I got lucky.
In a way.
But still, it doesn't feel like I thought it would. It's more like a dream about dying...
...where you're still **alive** inside your dead body.
And so much of the past week seemed like a bad dream that I just couldn't wake up from, anyway...
...why should this be any different?
Of course, then I get the joke...
C'MON, **GET UP...** WE **GOTTA** MOVE **NOW!**

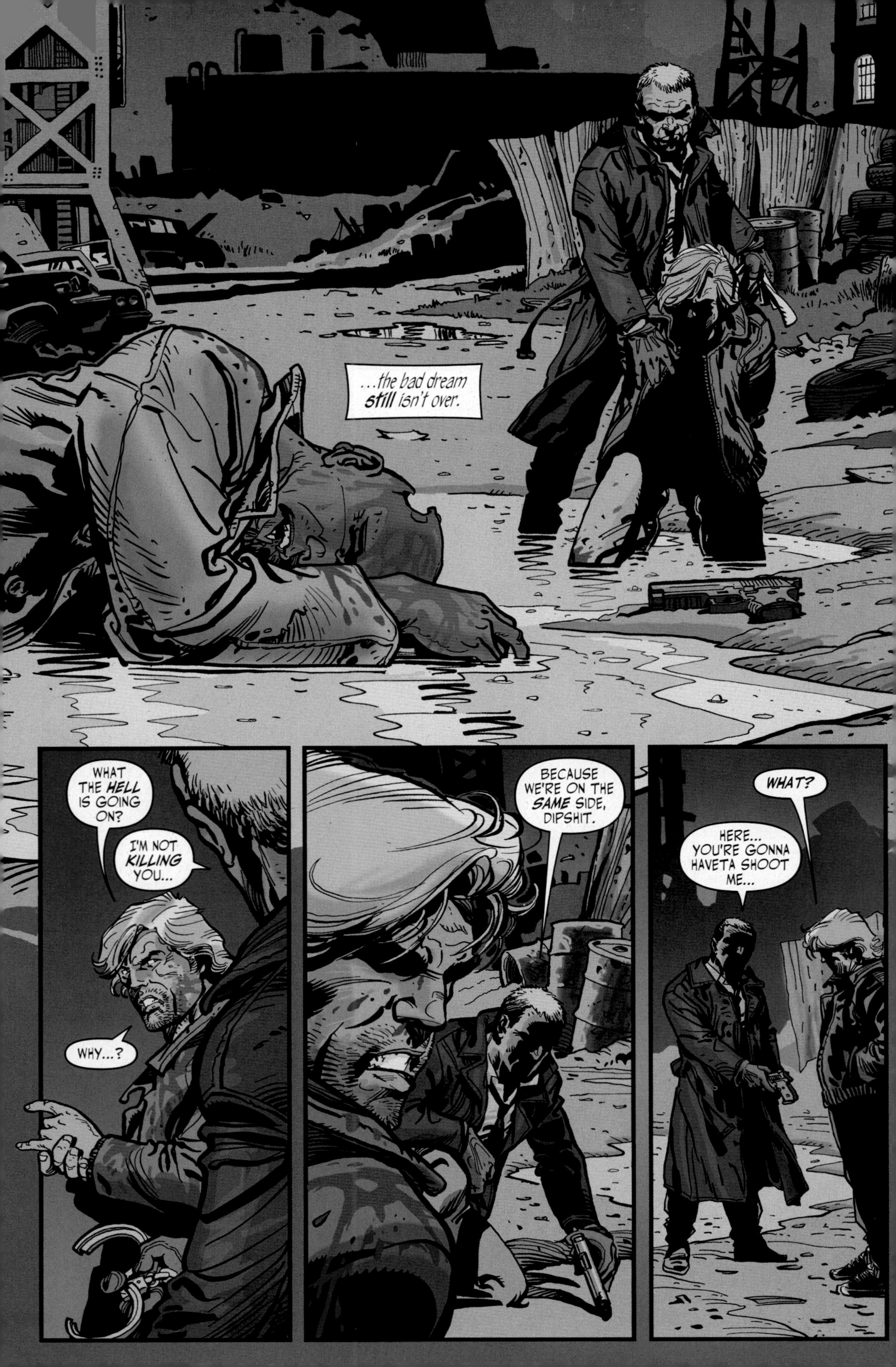
...the bad dream still isn't over.
WHAT THE HELL IS GOING ON?
I'M NOT KILLING YOU...
WHY...?
BECAUSE WE'RE ON THE SAME SIDE, DIPSHIT.
WHAT?
HERE... YOU'RE GONNA HAVETA SHOOT ME...

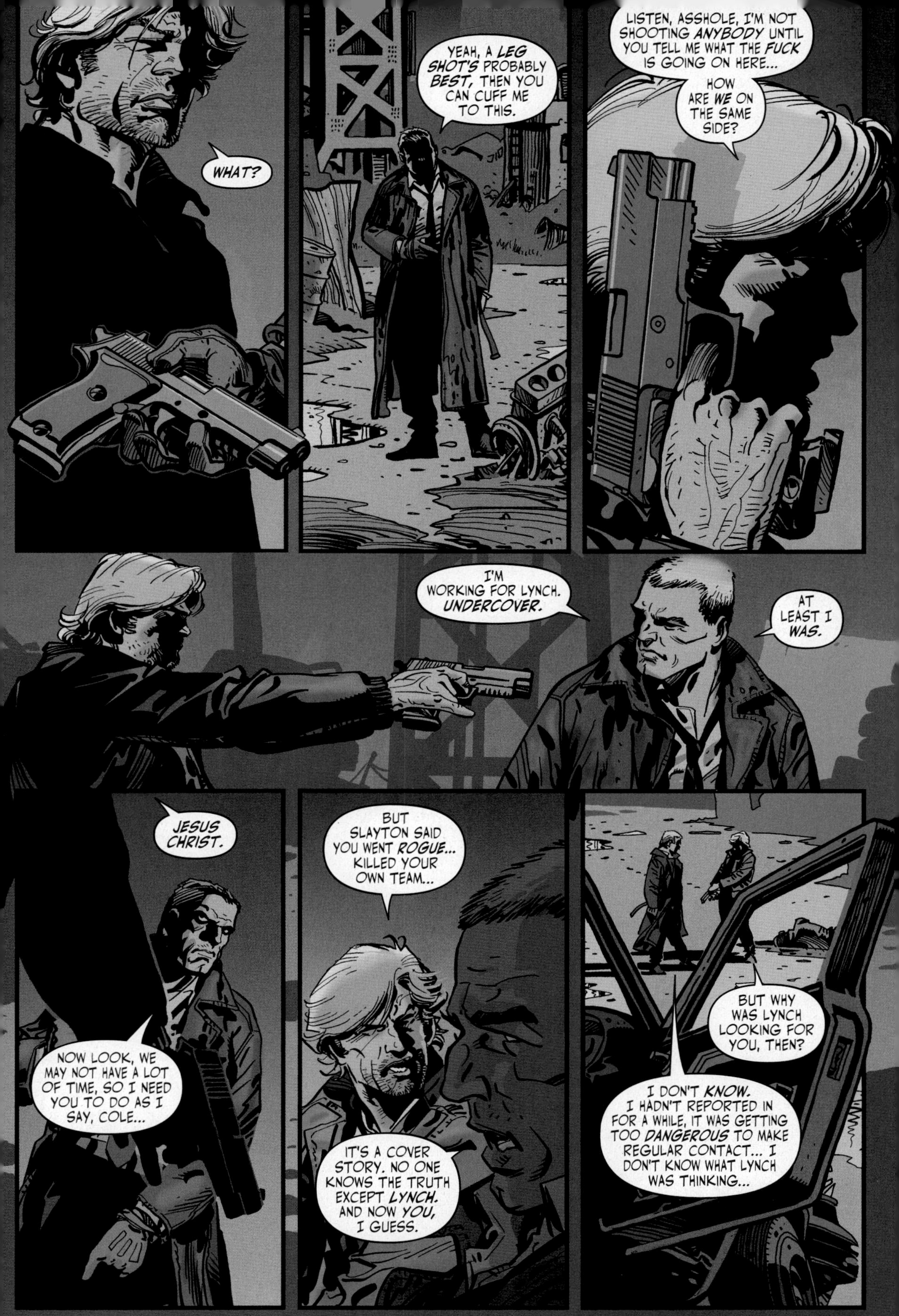
WHAT?
YEAH, A LEG SHOT'S PROBABLY BEST, THEN YOU CAN CUFF ME TO THIS.
LISTEN, ASSHOLE, I'M NOT SHOOTING ANYBODY UNTIL YOU TELL ME WHAT THE FUCK IS GOING ON HERE...
HOW ARE WE ON THE SAME SIDE?
I'M WORKING FOR LYNCH. UNDERCOVER.
AT LEAST I WAS.
JESUS CHRIST.
NOW LOOK, WE MAY NOT HAVE A LOT OF TIME, SO I NEED YOU TO DO AS I SAY, COLE...
BUT SLAYTON SAID YOU WENT ROGUE... KILLED YOUR OWN TEAM...
IT'S A COVER STORY. NO ONE KNOWS THE TRUTH EXCEPT LYNCH. AND NOW YOU, I GUESS.
BUT WHY WAS LYNCH LOOKING FOR YOU, THEN?
I DON'T KNOW. I HADN'T REPORTED IN FOR A WHILE, IT WAS GETTING TOO DANGEROUS TO MAKE REGULAR CONTACT... I DON'T KNOW WHAT LYNCH WAS THINKING...

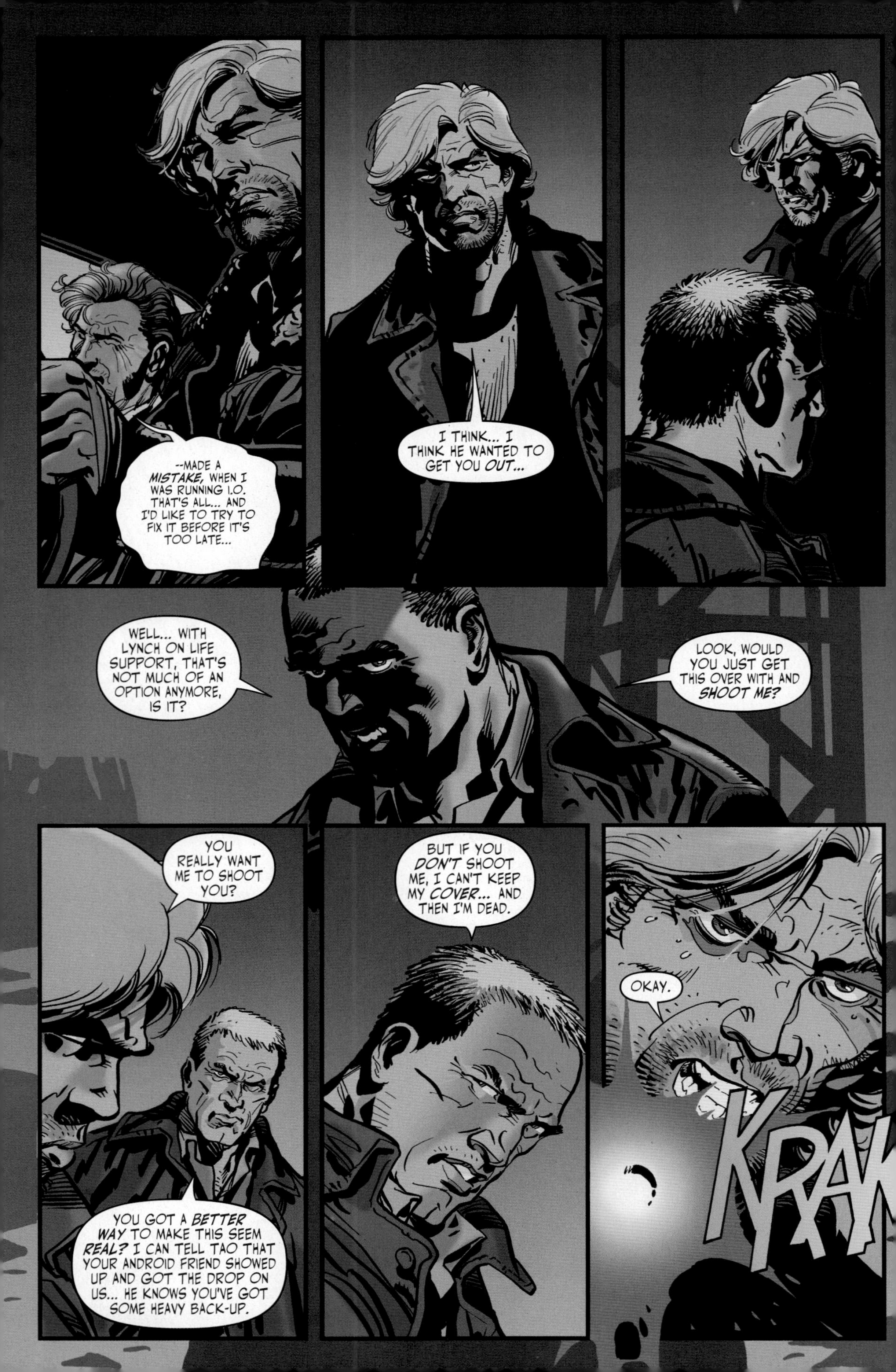
--MADE A MISTAKE, WHEN I WAS RUNNING I.O. THAT'S ALL... AND I'D LIKE TO TRY TO FIX IT BEFORE IT'S TOO LATE...
I THINK... I THINK HE WANTED TO GET YOU OUT...
WELL... WITH LYNCH ON LIFE SUPPORT, THAT'S NOT MUCH OF AN OPTION ANYMORE, IS IT?
LOOK, WOULD YOU JUST GET THIS OVER WITH AND SHOOT ME?
YOU REALLY WANT ME TO SHOOT YOU?
YOU GOT A BETTER WAY TO MAKE THIS SEEM REAL? I CAN TELL TAO THAT YOUR ANDROID FRIEND SHOWED UP AND GOT THE DROP ON US... HE KNOWS YOU'VE GOT SOME HEAVY BACK-UP.
BUT IF YOU DON'T SHOOT ME, I CAN'T KEEP MY COVER... AND THEN I'M DEAD.
OKAY.
KRAK

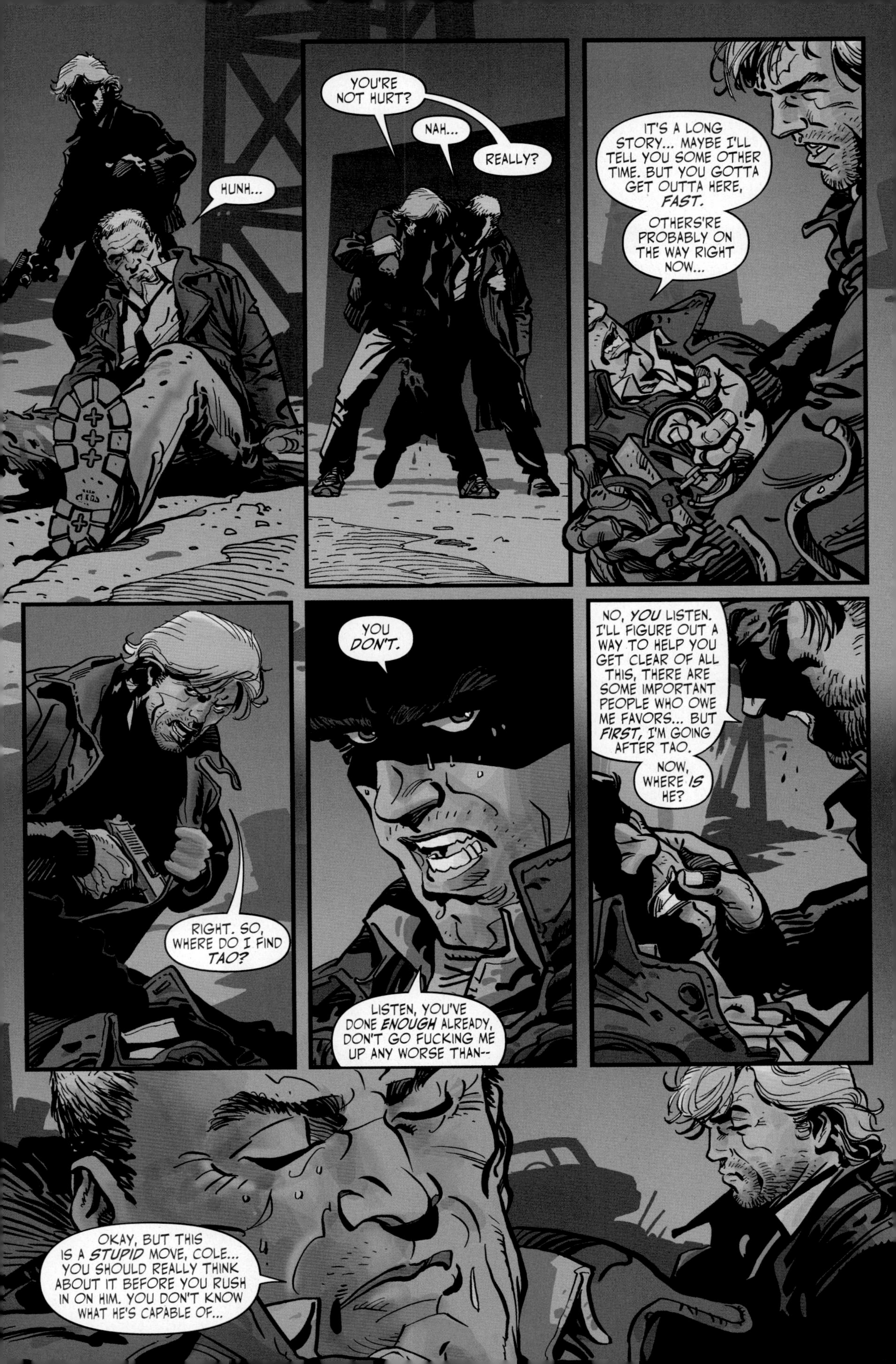
HUNH...
YOU'RE NOT HURT?
NAH...
REALLY?
IT'S A LONG STORY... MAYBE I'LL TELL YOU SOME OTHER TIME. BUT YOU GOTTA GET OUTTA HERE, FAST.
OTHERS'RE PROBABLY ON THE WAY RIGHT NOW...
RIGHT. SO, WHERE DO I FIND TAO?
YOU DON'T.
LISTEN, YOU'VE DONE ENOUGH ALREADY, DON'T GO FUCKING ME UP ANY WORSE THAN--
NO, YOU LISTEN. I'LL FIGURE OUT A WAY TO HELP YOU GET CLEAR OF ALL THIS, THERE ARE SOME IMPORTANT PEOPLE WHO OWE ME FAVORS... BUT FIRST, I'M GOING AFTER TAO.
NOW, WHERE IS HE?
OKAY, BUT THIS IS A STUPID MOVE, COLE... YOU SHOULD REALLY THINK ABOUT IT BEFORE YOU RUSH IN ON HIM. YOU DON'T KNOW WHAT HE'S CAPABLE OF...

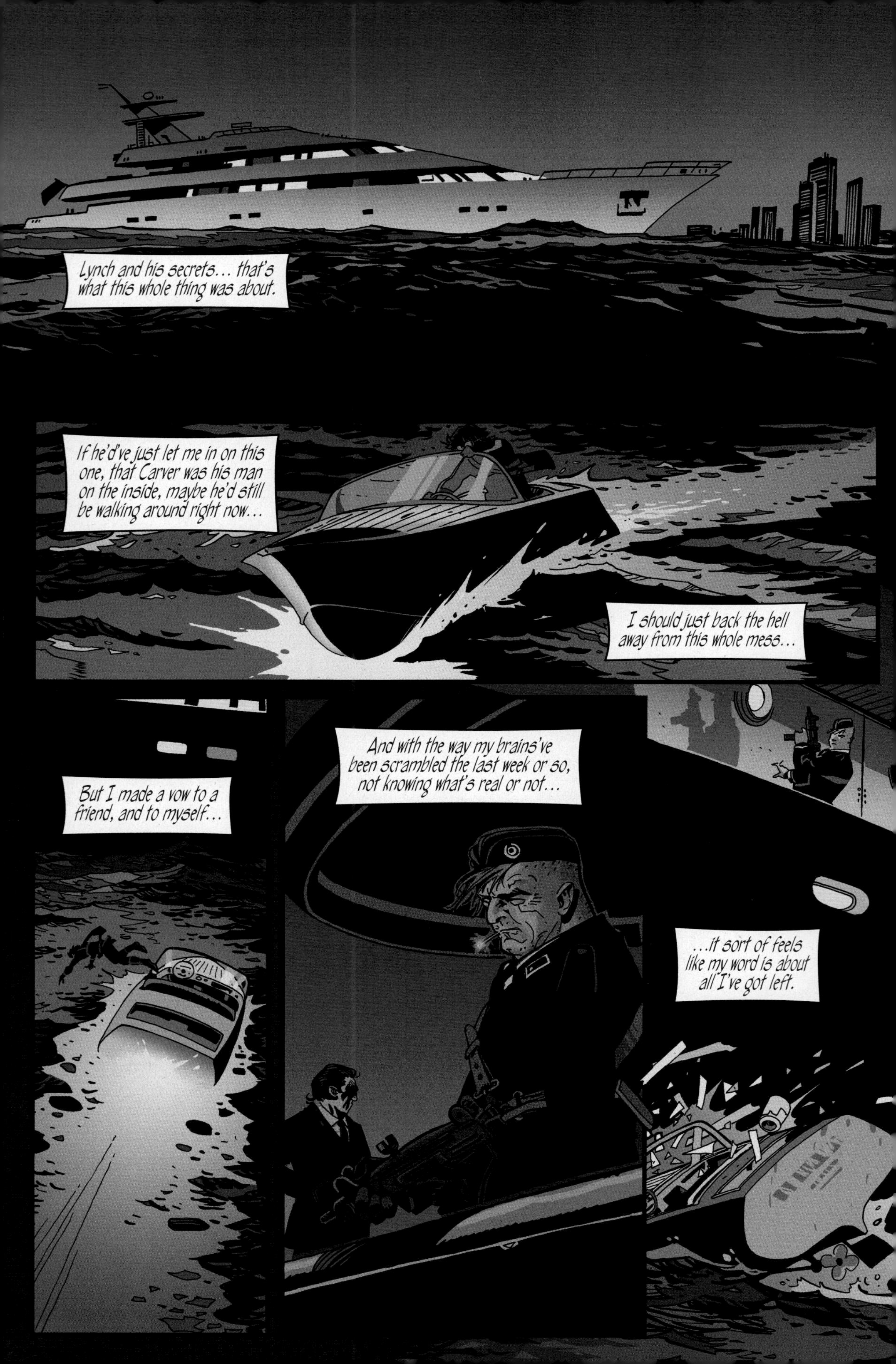
Lynch and his secrets... that's what this whole thing was about.
If he'd've just let me in on this one, that Carver was his man on the inside, maybe he'd still be walking around right now...
I should just back the hell away from this whole mess...
But I made a vow to a friend, and to myself...
And with the way my brains've been scrambled the last week or so, not knowing what's real or not...
...it sort of feels like my word is about all I've got left.

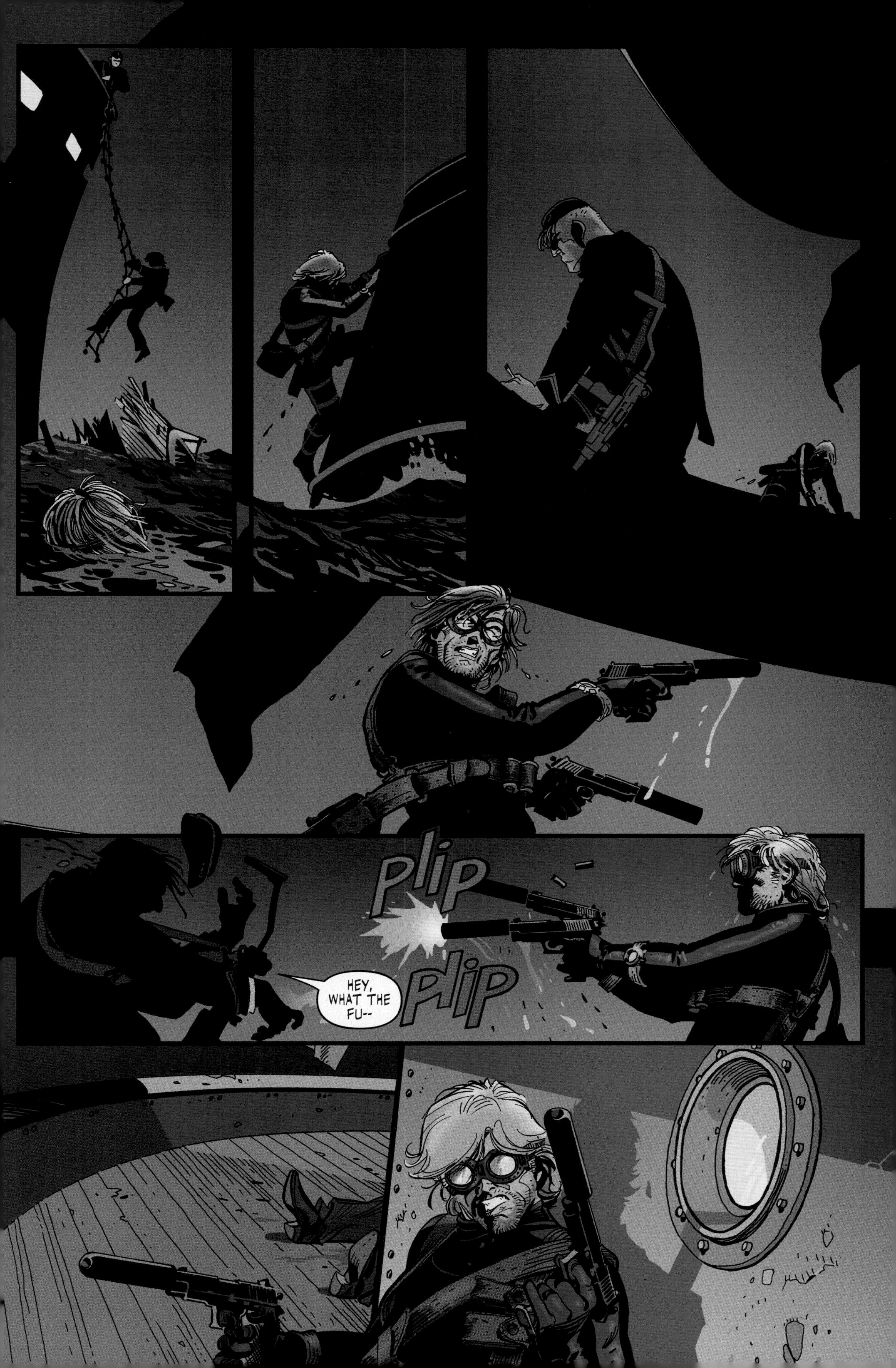
plip
HEY, WHAT THE FU--
plip

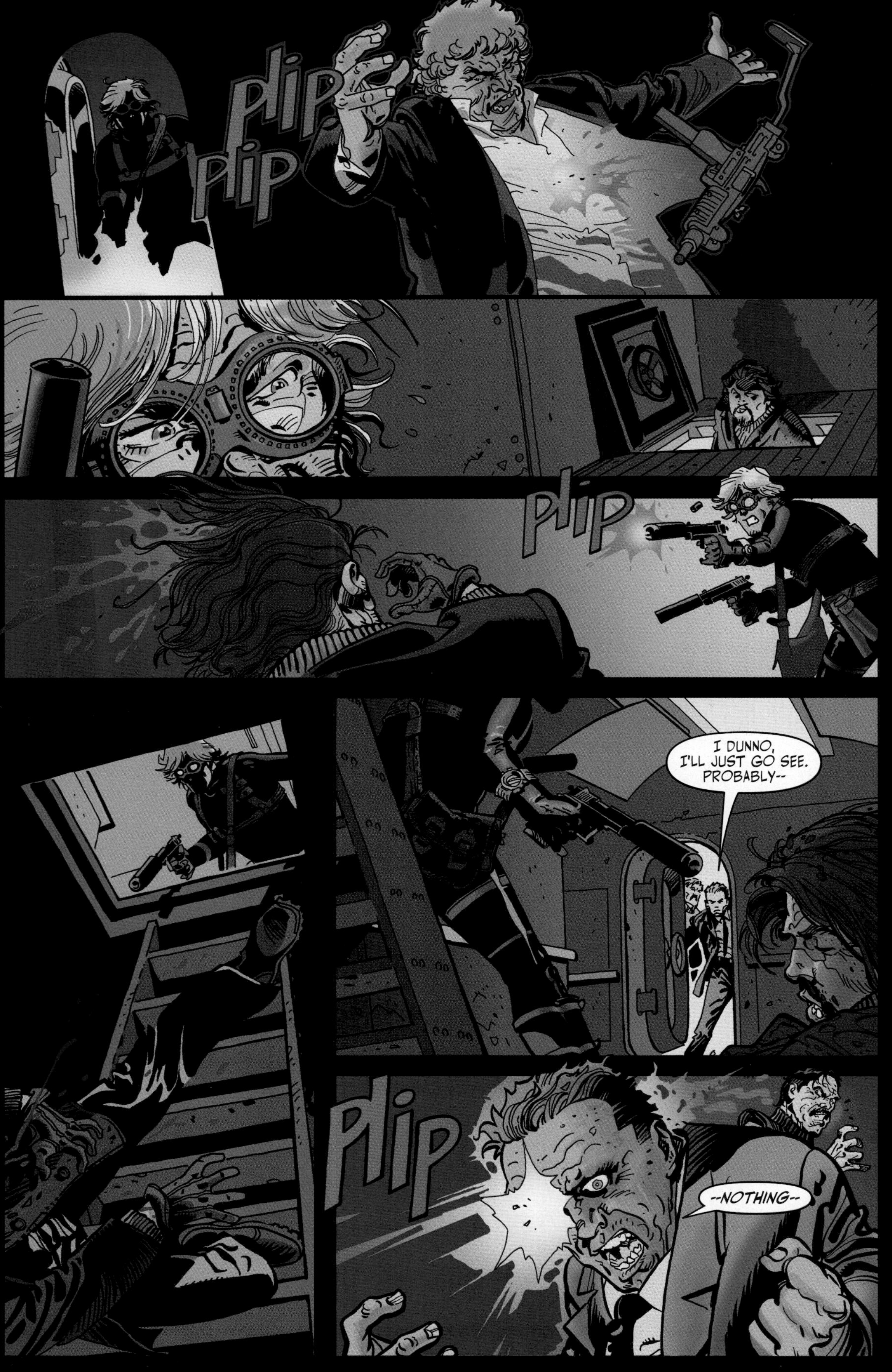
PLIP
PLIP
PLIP
I DUNNO, I'LL JUST GO SEE. PROBABLY--
PLIP
--NOTHING--

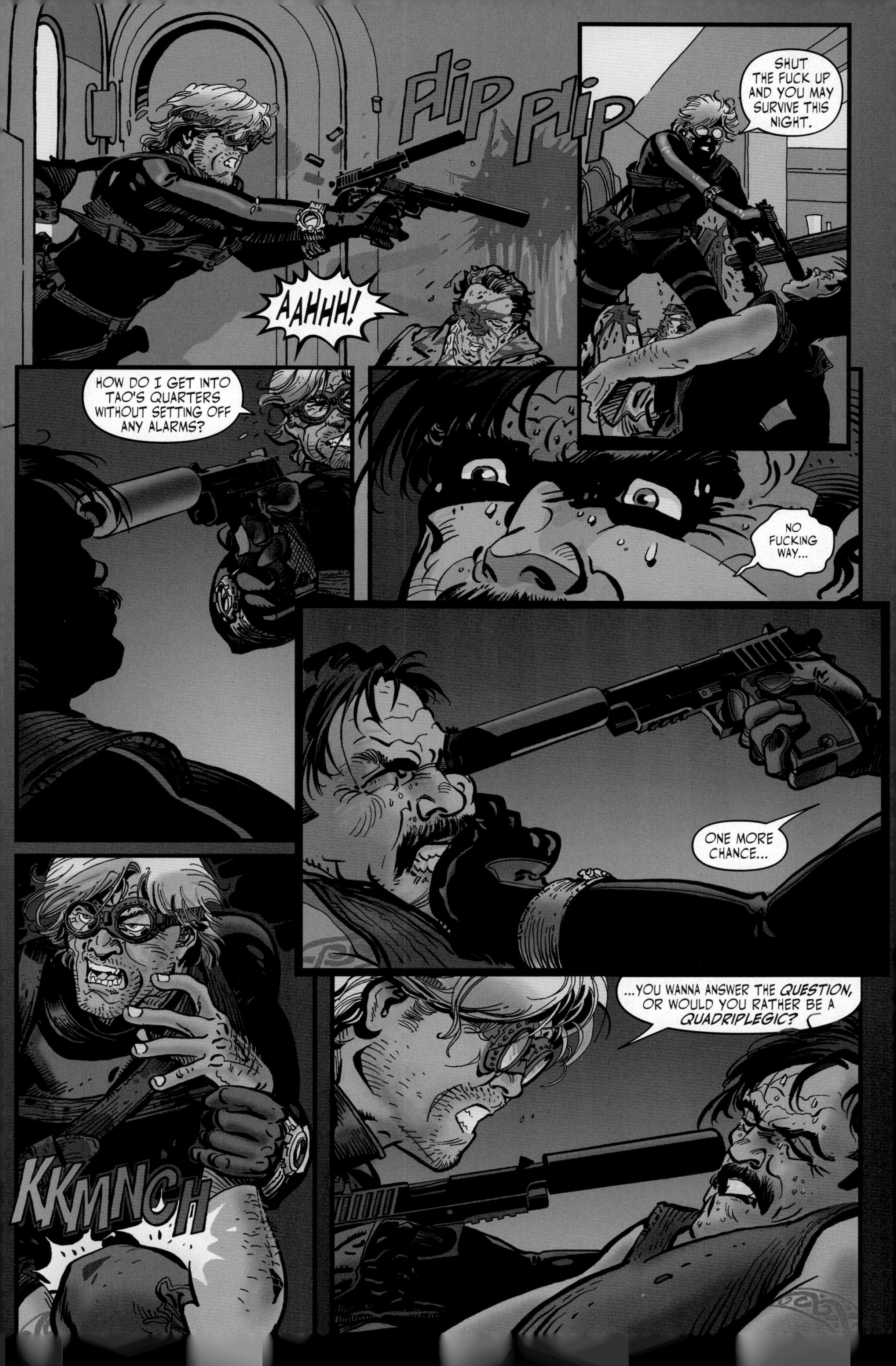
PLIP PLIP
AAHHH!
SHUT THE FUCK UP AND YOU MAY SURVIVE THIS NIGHT.
HOW DO I GET INTO TAO'S QUARTERS WITHOUT SETTING OFF ANY ALARMS?
NO FUCKING WAY...
ONE MORE CHANCE...
KKMNCH
...YOU WANNA ANSWER THE QUESTION, OR WOULD YOU RATHER BE A QUADRIPLEGIC?

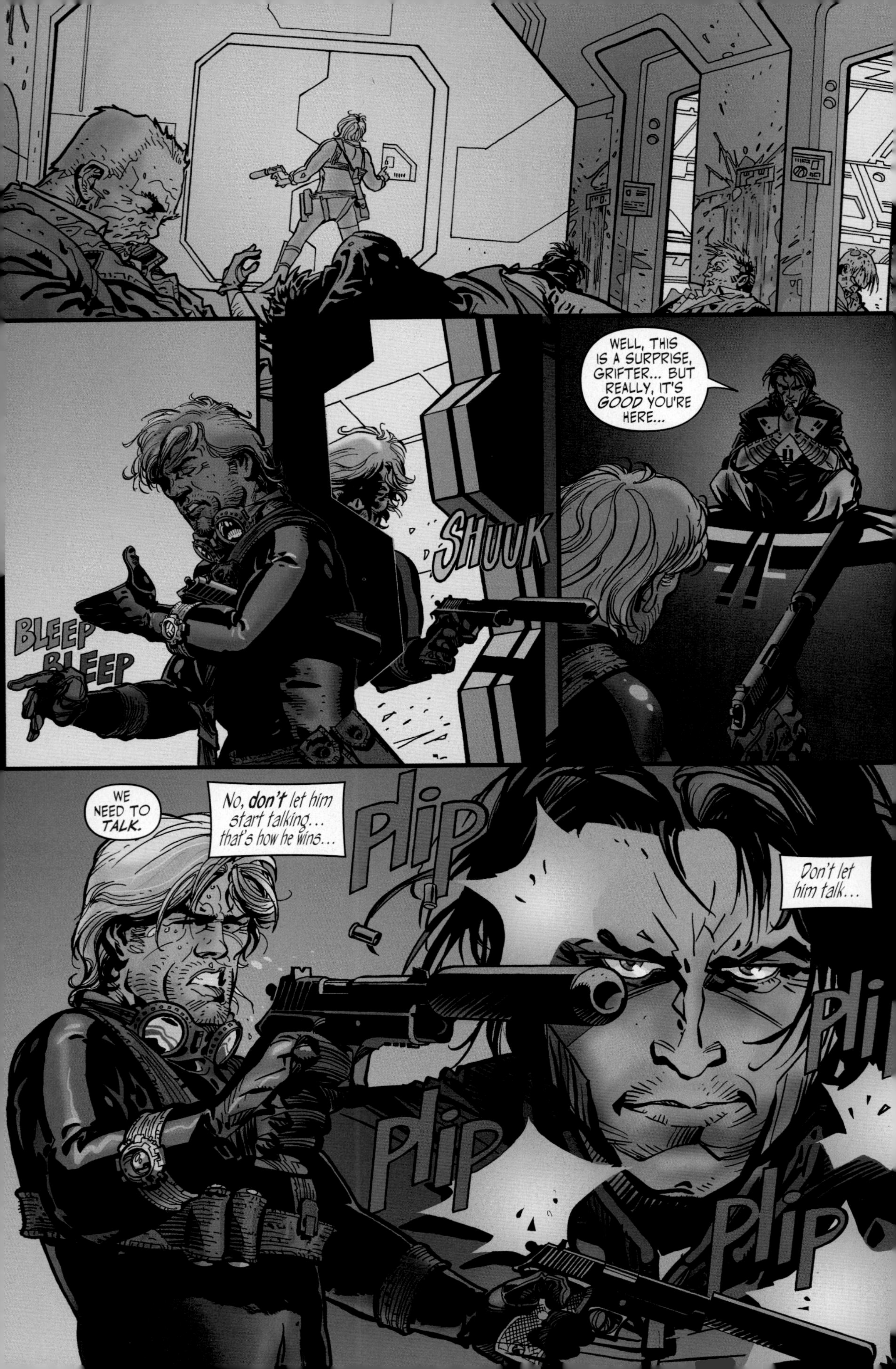

WELL, THIS IS A SURPRISE, GRIFTER... BUT REALLY, IT'S *GOOD* YOU'RE HERE...
SHUUK
BLEEP BLEEP
WE NEED TO *TALK.*
No, **don't** let him start talking... that's how he wins...
plip
Don't let him talk...
plip
plip

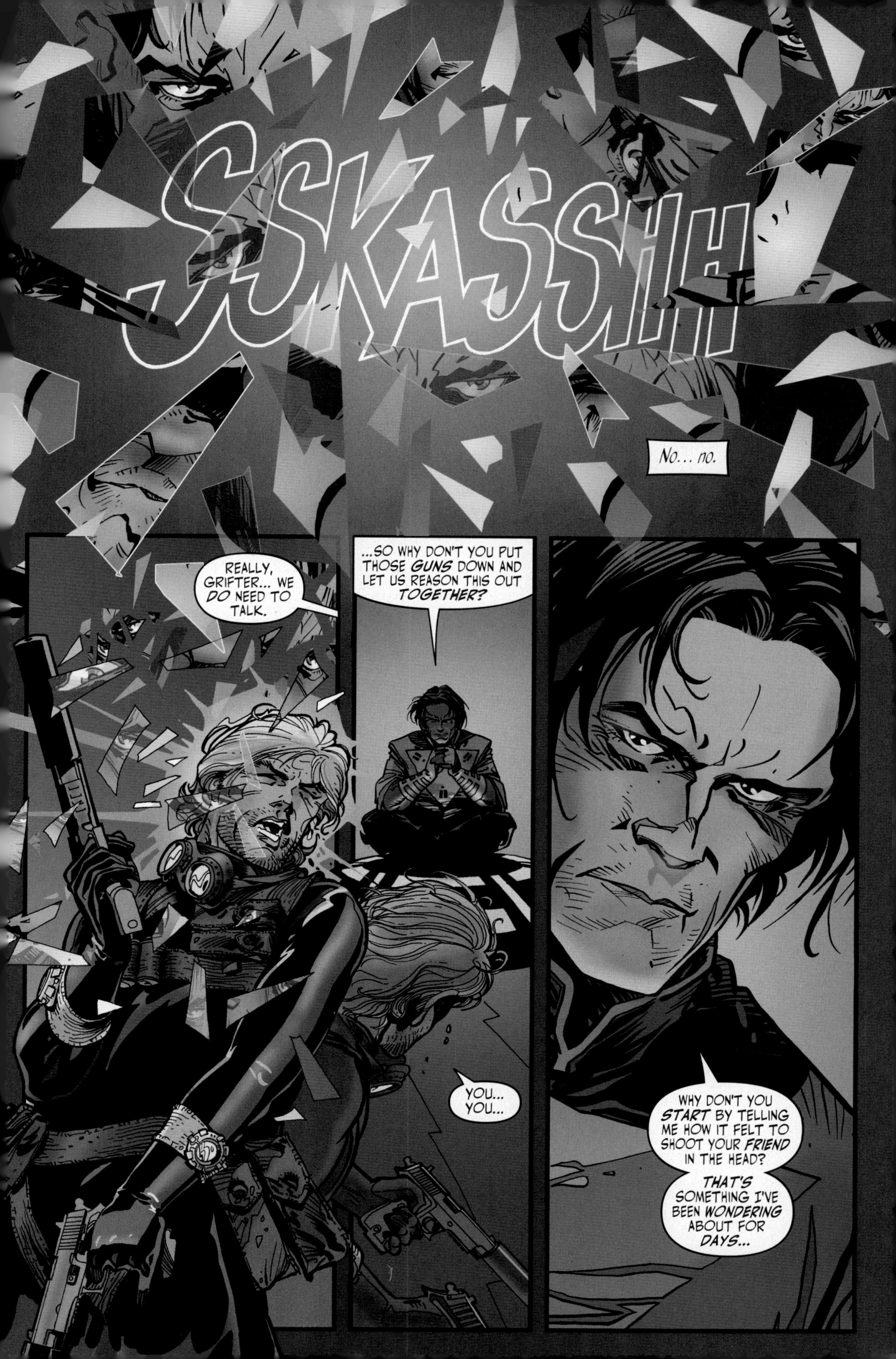
SSKASSHH
No... no.
REALLY, GRIFTER... WE DO NEED TO TALK.
...SO WHY DON'T YOU PUT THOSE GUNS DOWN AND LET US REASON THIS OUT TOGETHER?
YOU... YOU...
WHY DON'T YOU START BY TELLING ME HOW IT FELT TO SHOOT YOUR FRIEND IN THE HEAD?
THAT'S SOMETHING I'VE BEEN WONDERING ABOUT FOR DAYS...

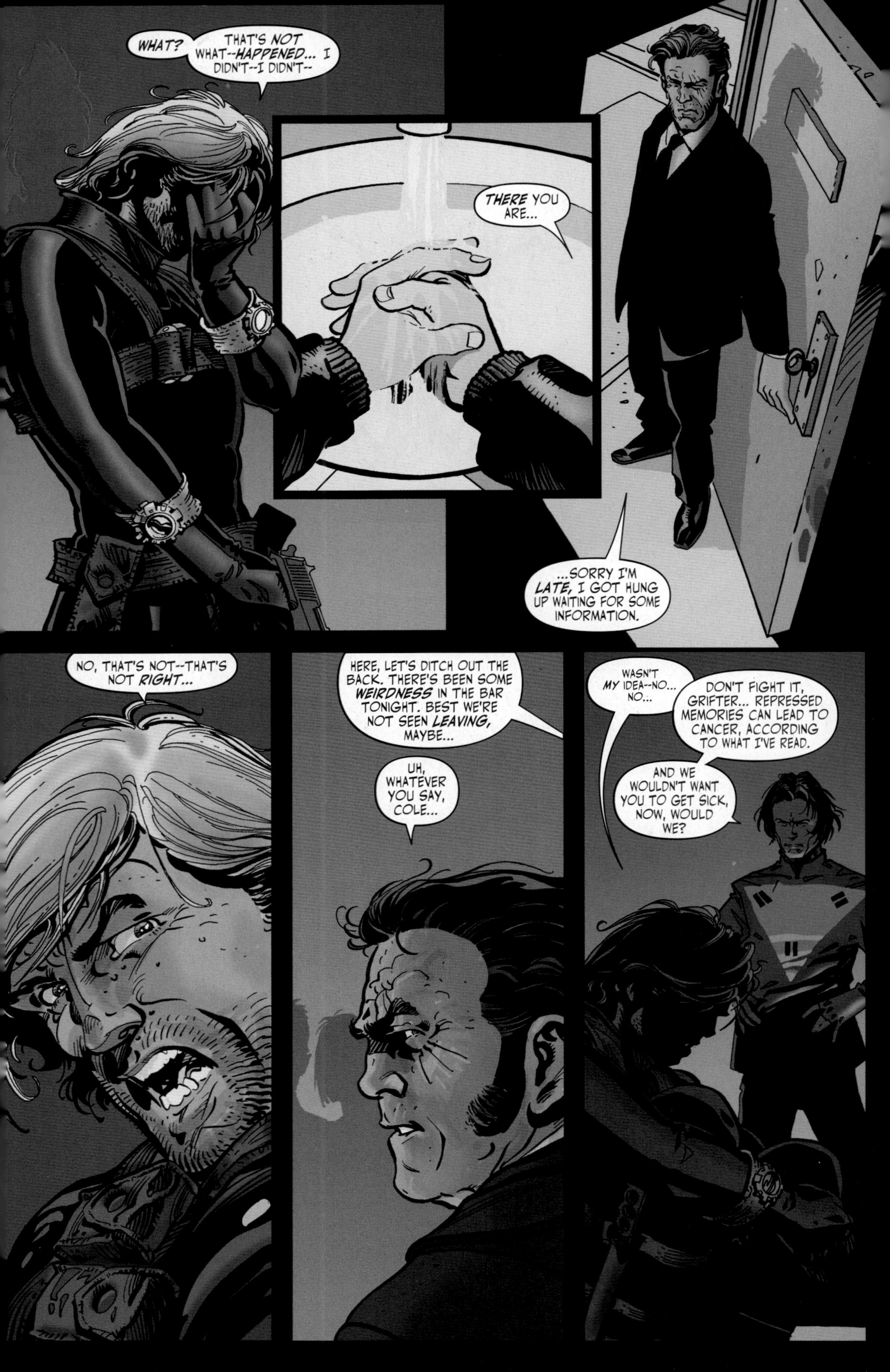
WHAT?
THAT'S NOT WHAT--HAPPENED... I DIDN'T--I DIDN'T--
THERE YOU ARE...
...SORRY I'M LATE, I GOT HUNG UP WAITING FOR SOME INFORMATION.
NO, THAT'S NOT--THAT'S NOT RIGHT...
HERE, LET'S DITCH OUT THE BACK. THERE'S BEEN SOME WEIRDNESS IN THE BAR TONIGHT. BEST WE'RE NOT SEEN LEAVING, MAYBE...
UH, WHATEVER YOU SAY, COLE...
WASN'T MY IDEA--NO... NO...
DON'T FIGHT IT, GRIFTER... REPRESSED MEMORIES CAN LEAD TO CANCER, ACCORDING TO WHAT I'VE READ.
AND WE WOULDN'T WANT YOU TO GET SICK, NOW, WOULD WE?

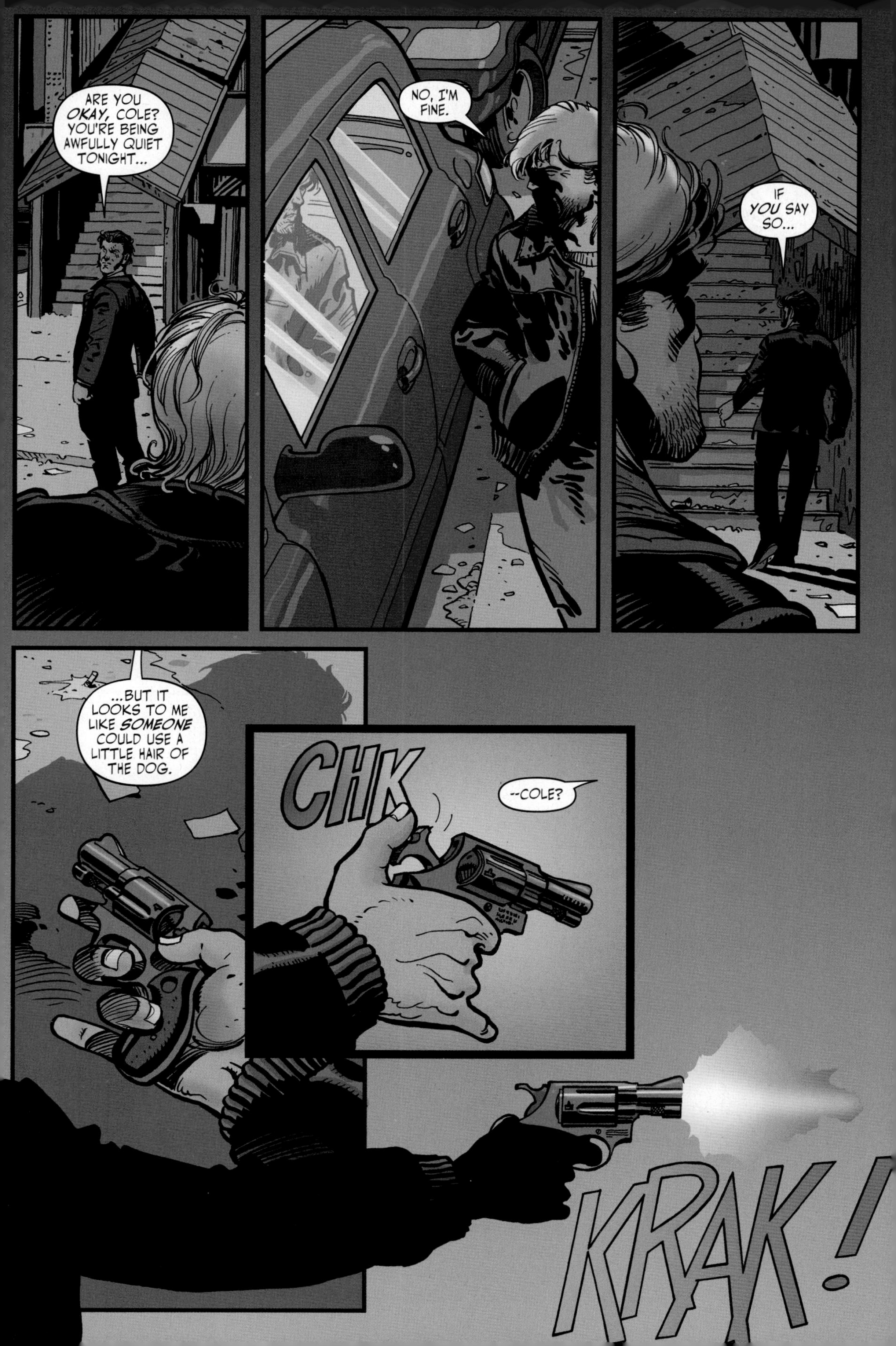
ARE YOU OKAY, COLE? YOU'RE BEING AWFULLY QUIET TONIGHT...
NO, I'M FINE.
IF YOU SAY SO...
...BUT IT LOOKS TO ME LIKE SOMEONE COULD USE A LITTLE HAIR OF THE DOG.
CHK
--COLE?
KRAK!

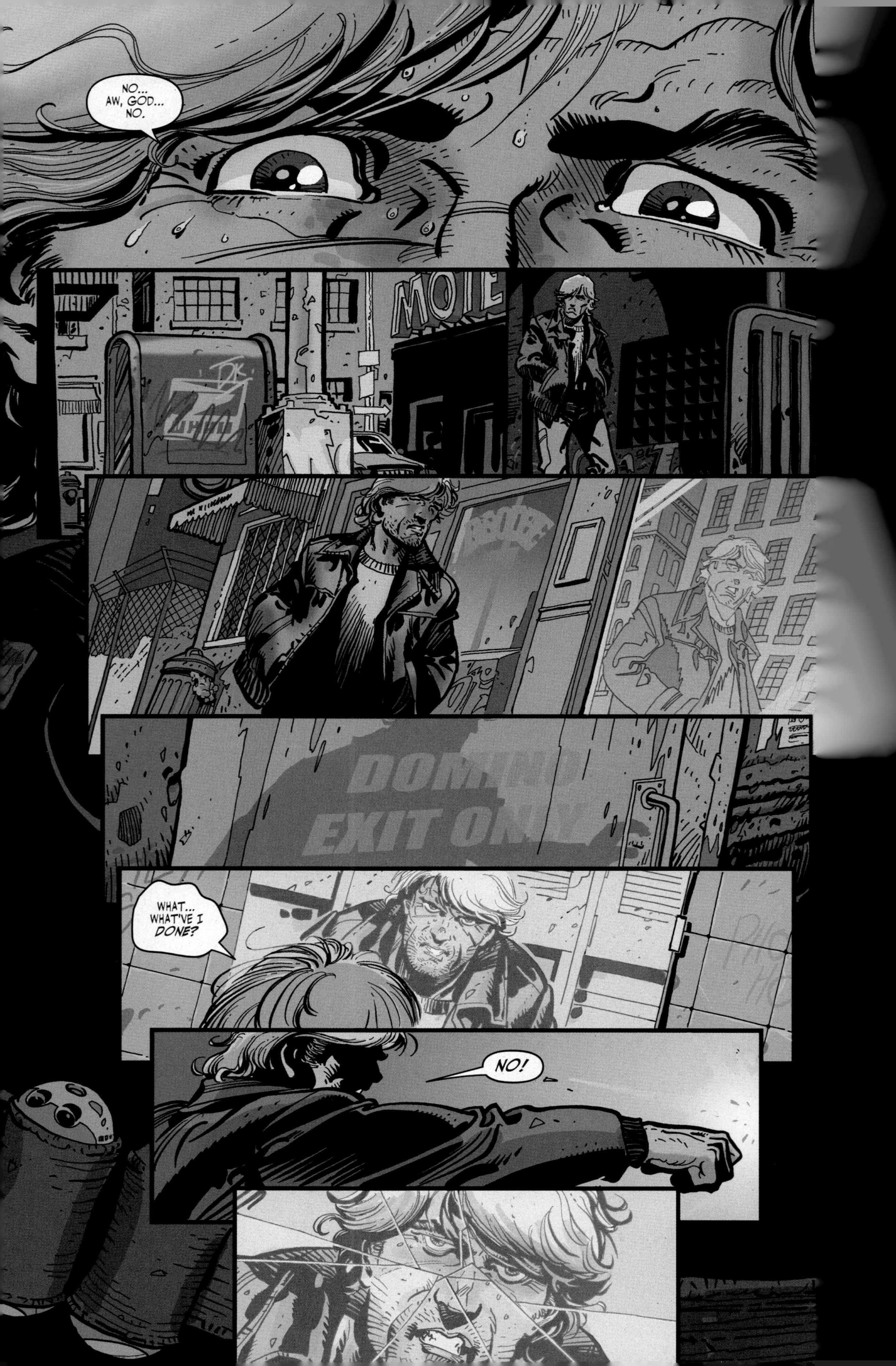
NO... AW, GOD... NO.
MOTE
DOMINO
EXIT ONLY
WHAT... WHAT'VE I *DONE?*
NO!

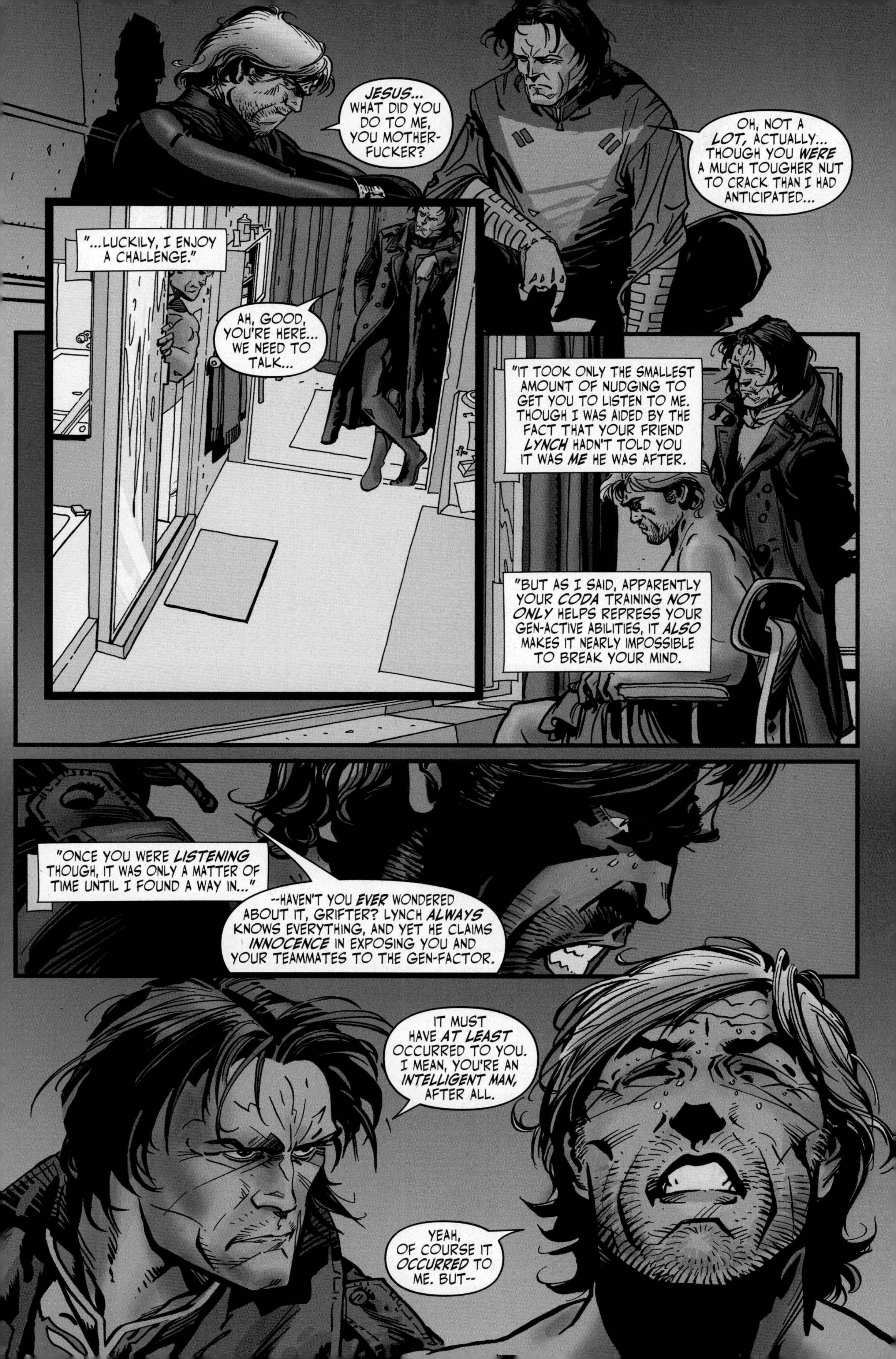
JESUS... WHAT DID YOU DO TO ME, YOU MOTHER-FUCKER?
OH, NOT A LOT, ACTUALLY... THOUGH YOU WERE A MUCH TOUGHER NUT TO CRACK THAN I HAD ANTICIPATED...
"...LUCKILY, I ENJOY A CHALLENGE."
AH, GOOD, YOU'RE HERE... WE NEED TO TALK...
"IT TOOK ONLY THE SMALLEST AMOUNT OF NUDGING TO GET YOU TO LISTEN TO ME. THOUGH I WAS AIDED BY THE FACT THAT YOUR FRIEND LYNCH HADN'T TOLD YOU IT WAS ME HE WAS AFTER.
"BUT AS I SAID, APPARENTLY YOUR CODA TRAINING NOT ONLY HELPS REPRESS YOUR GEN-ACTIVE ABILITIES, IT ALSO MAKES IT NEARLY IMPOSSIBLE TO BREAK YOUR MIND.
"ONCE YOU WERE LISTENING THOUGH, IT WAS ONLY A MATTER OF TIME UNTIL I FOUND A WAY IN..."
--HAVEN'T YOU EVER WONDERED ABOUT IT, GRIFTER? LYNCH ALWAYS KNOWS EVERYTHING, AND YET HE CLAIMS INNOCENCE IN EXPOSING YOU AND YOUR TEAMMATES TO THE GEN-FACTOR.
IT MUST HAVE AT LEAST OCCURRED TO YOU. I MEAN, YOU'RE AN INTELLIGENT MAN, AFTER ALL.
YEAH, OF COURSE IT OCCURRED TO ME. BUT--

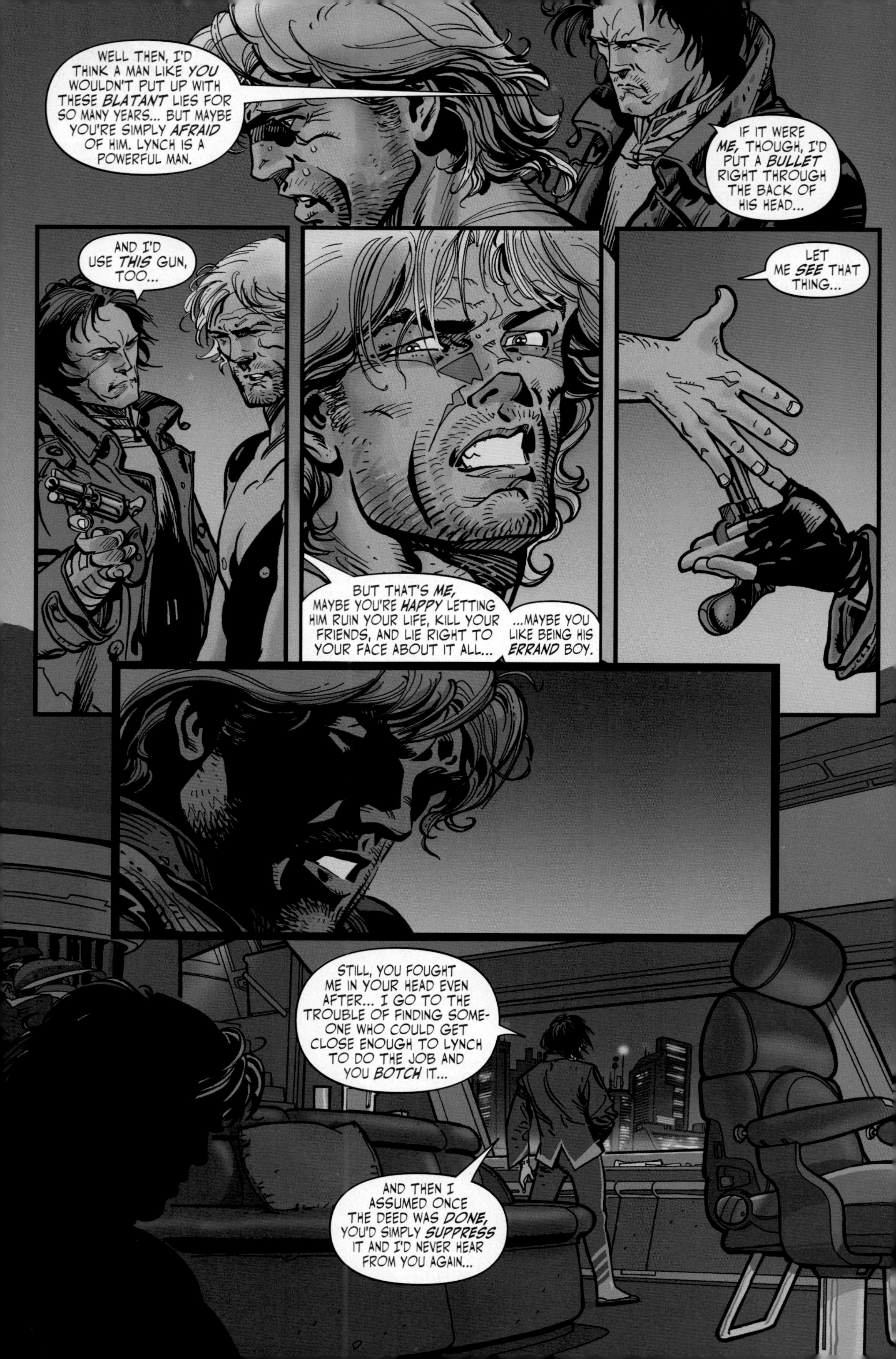
WELL THEN, I'D THINK A MAN LIKE YOU WOULDN'T PUT UP WITH THESE BLATANT LIES FOR SO MANY YEARS... BUT MAYBE YOU'RE SIMPLY AFRAID OF HIM. LYNCH IS A POWERFUL MAN.
IF IT WERE ME, THOUGH, I'D PUT A BULLET RIGHT THROUGH THE BACK OF HIS HEAD...
AND I'D USE THIS GUN, TOO...
BUT THAT'S ME, MAYBE YOU'RE HAPPY LETTING HIM RUIN YOUR LIFE, KILL YOUR FRIENDS, AND LIE RIGHT TO YOUR FACE ABOUT IT ALL...
...MAYBE YOU LIKE BEING HIS ERRAND BOY.
LET ME SEE THAT THING...
STILL, YOU FOUGHT ME IN YOUR HEAD EVEN AFTER... I GO TO THE TROUBLE OF FINDING SOME-ONE WHO COULD GET CLOSE ENOUGH TO LYNCH TO DO THE JOB AND YOU BOTCH IT...
AND THEN I ASSUMED ONCE THE DEED WAS DONE, YOU'D SIMPLY SUPPRESS IT AND I'D NEVER HEAR FROM YOU AGAIN...

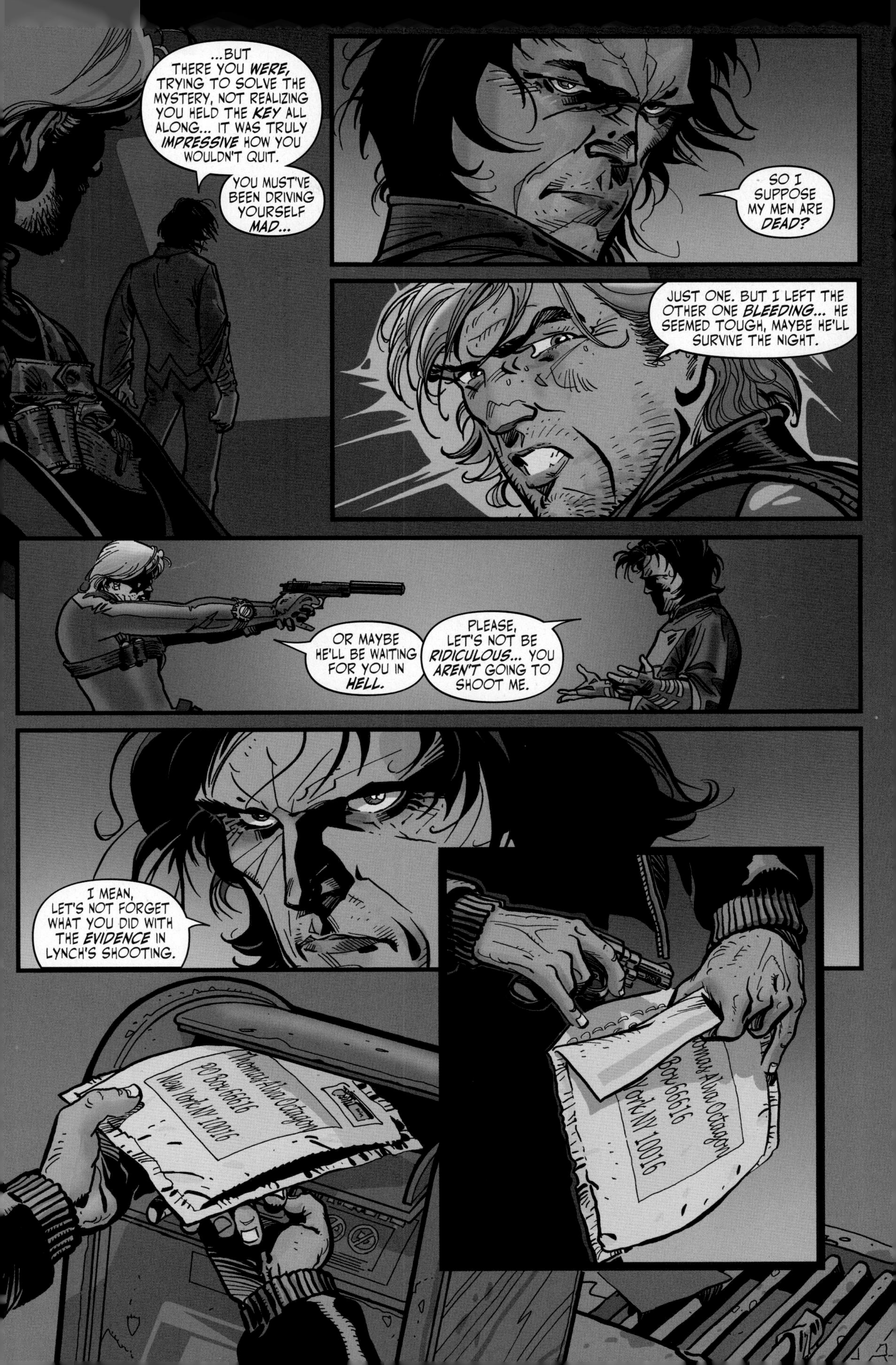

...BUT THERE YOU WERE, TRYING TO SOLVE THE MYSTERY, NOT REALIZING YOU HELD THE KEY ALL ALONG... IT WAS TRULY IMPRESSIVE HOW YOU WOULDN'T QUIT.
YOU MUST'VE BEEN DRIVING YOURSELF MAD...
SO I SUPPOSE MY MEN ARE DEAD?
JUST ONE. BUT I LEFT THE OTHER ONE BLEEDING... HE SEEMED TOUGH, MAYBE HE'LL SURVIVE THE NIGHT.
OR MAYBE HE'LL BE WAITING FOR YOU IN HELL.
PLEASE, LET'S NOT BE RIDICULOUS... YOU AREN'T GOING TO SHOOT ME.
I MEAN, LET'S NOT FORGET WHAT YOU DID WITH THE EVIDENCE IN LYNCH'S SHOOTING.
Thomas Alva Octagon
PO Box 66616
New York NY 10016

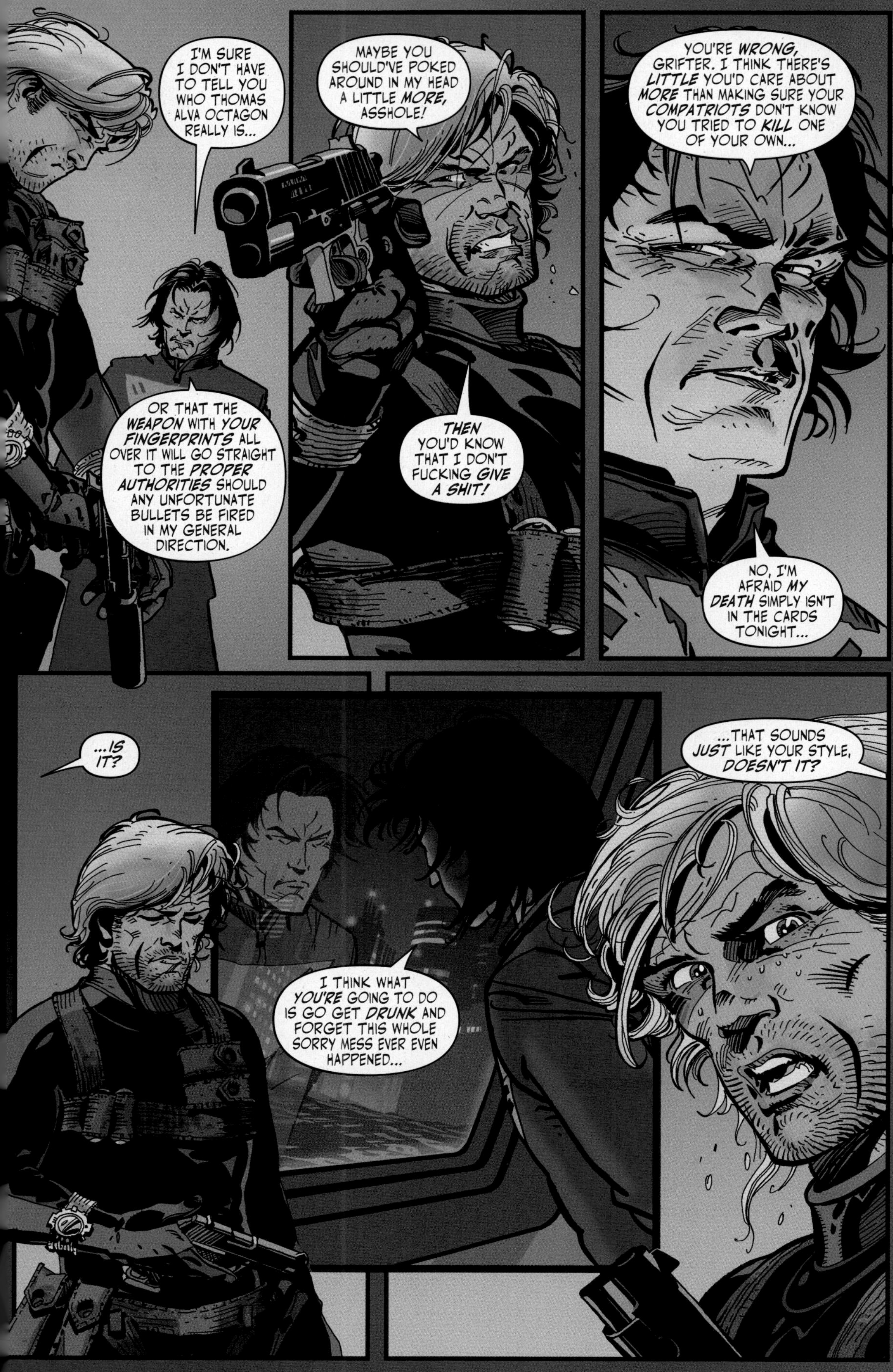
I'M SURE I DON'T HAVE TO TELL YOU WHO THOMAS ALVA OCTAGON REALLY IS...
OR THAT THE WEAPON WITH YOUR FINGERPRINTS ALL OVER IT WILL GO STRAIGHT TO THE PROPER AUTHORITIES SHOULD ANY UNFORTUNATE BULLETS BE FIRED IN MY GENERAL DIRECTION.
MAYBE YOU SHOULD'VE POKED AROUND IN MY HEAD A LITTLE MORE, ASSHOLE!
THEN YOU'D KNOW THAT I DON'T FUCKING GIVE A SHIT!
YOU'RE WRONG, GRIFTER. I THINK THERE'S LITTLE YOU'D CARE ABOUT MORE THAN MAKING SURE YOUR COMPATRIOTS DON'T KNOW YOU TRIED TO KILL ONE OF YOUR OWN...
NO, I'M AFRAID MY DEATH SIMPLY ISN'T IN THE CARDS TONIGHT...
...IS IT?
I THINK WHAT YOU'RE GOING TO DO IS GO GET DRUNK AND FORGET THIS WHOLE SORRY MESS EVER EVEN HAPPENED...
...THAT SOUNDS JUST LIKE YOUR STYLE, DOESN'T IT?

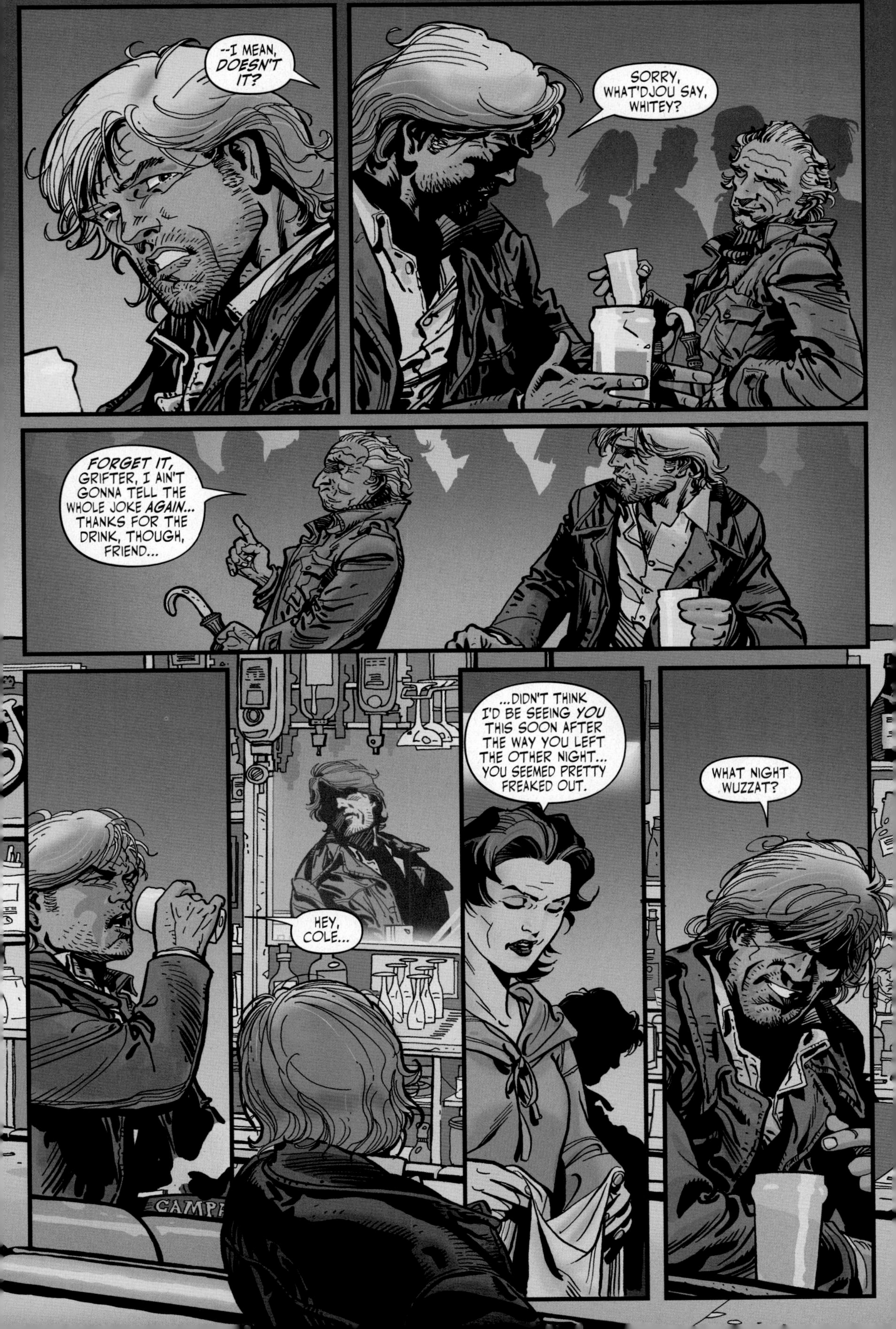
--I MEAN, DOESN'T IT?
SORRY, WHAT'DJOU SAY, WHITEY?
FORGET IT, GRIFTER, I AIN'T GONNA TELL THE WHOLE JOKE AGAIN... THANKS FOR THE DRINK, THOUGH, FRIEND...
HEY, COLE...
...DIDN'T THINK I'D BE SEEING YOU THIS SOON AFTER THE WAY YOU LEFT THE OTHER NIGHT... YOU SEEMED PRETTY FREAKED OUT.
WHAT NIGHT WUZZAT?

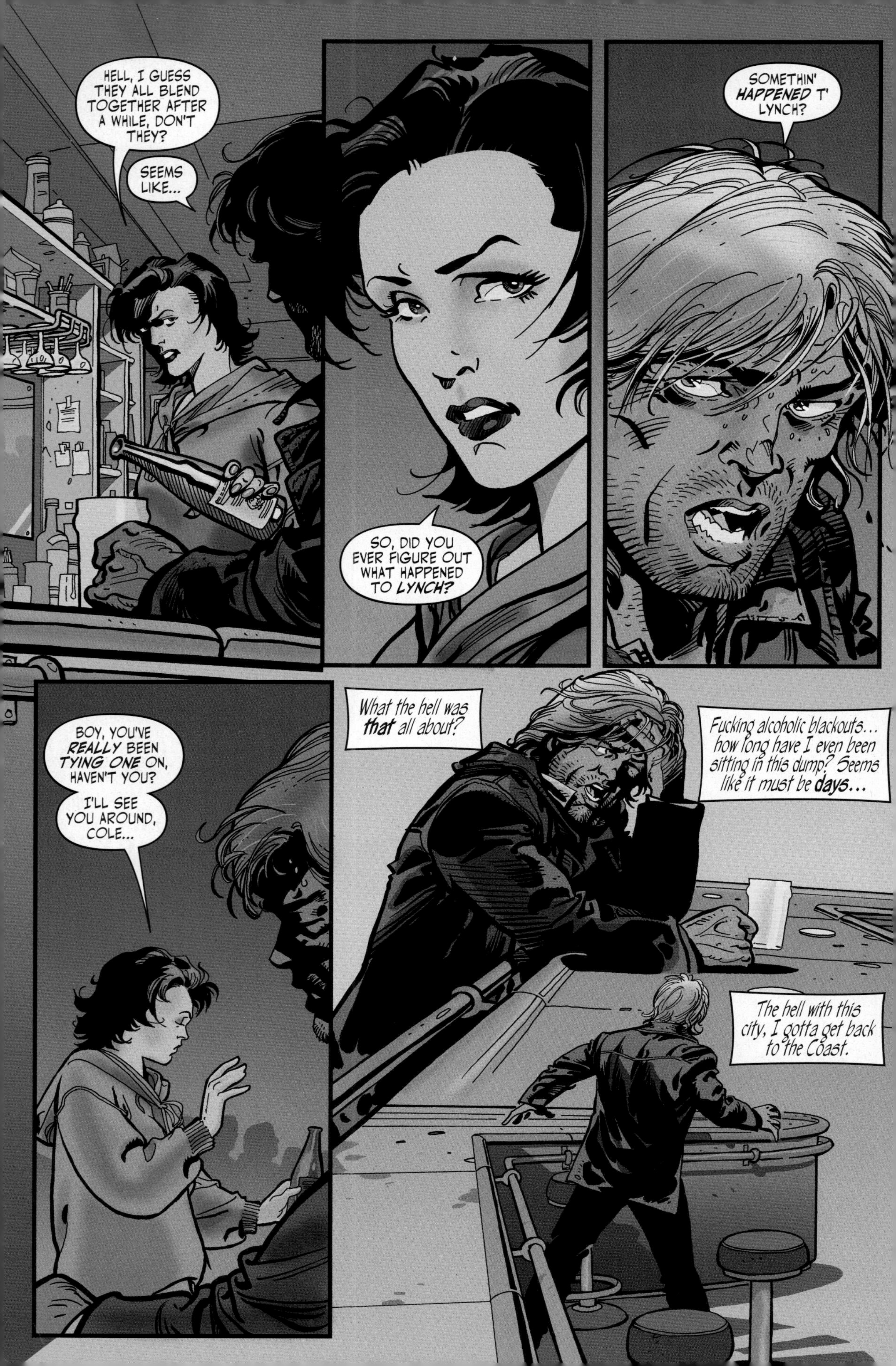
HELL, I GUESS THEY ALL BLEND TOGETHER AFTER A WHILE, DON'T THEY?
SEEMS LIKE...
SO, DID YOU EVER FIGURE OUT WHAT HAPPENED TO LYNCH?
SOMETHIN' HAPPENED T' LYNCH?
BOY, YOU'VE REALLY BEEN TYING ONE ON, HAVEN'T YOU?
I'LL SEE YOU AROUND, COLE...
What the hell was that all about?
Fucking alcoholic blackouts... how long have I even been sitting in this dump? Seems like it must be days...
The hell with this city, I gotta get back to the Coast.

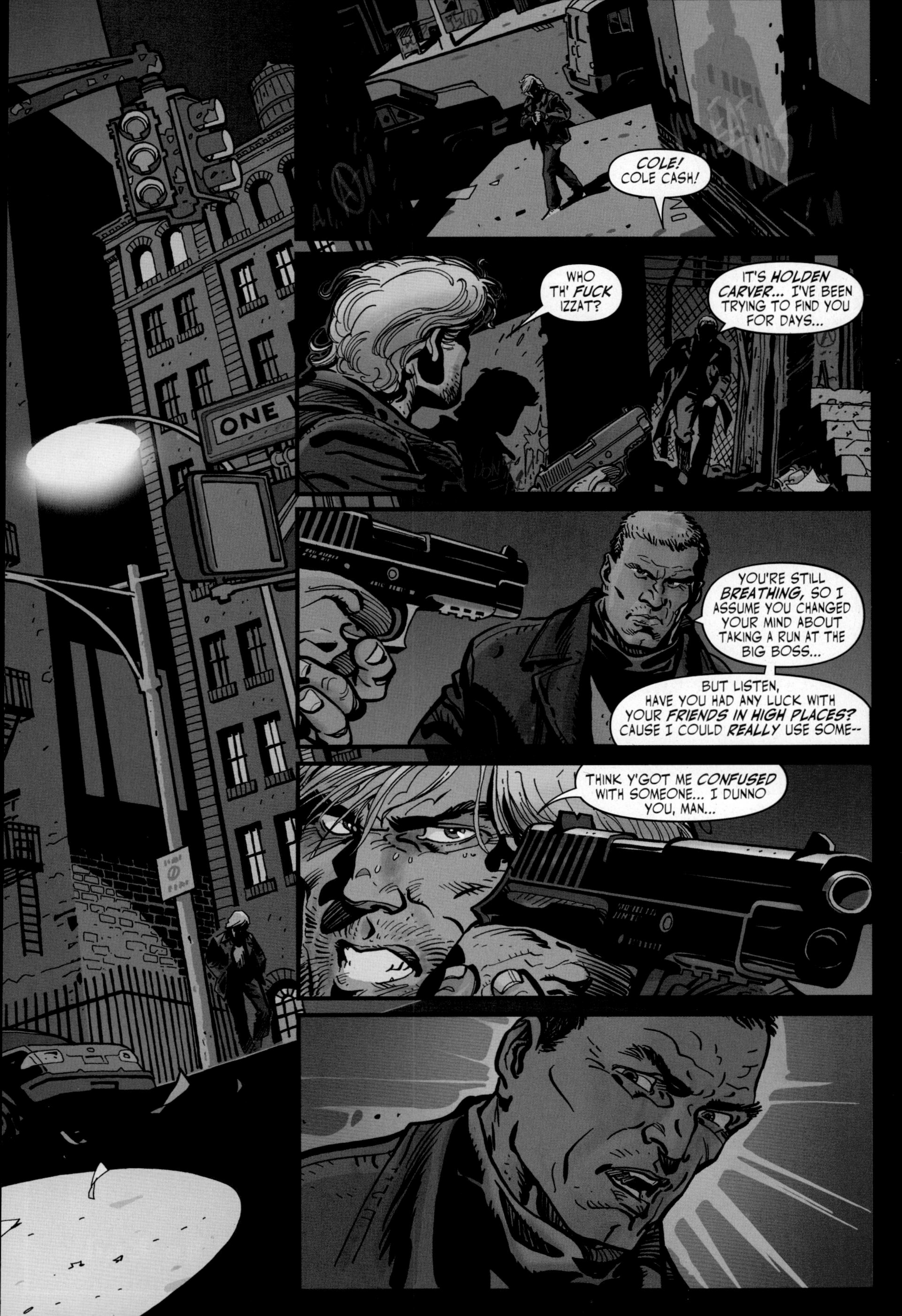
ONE WAY
COLE! COLE CASH!
WHO TH' FUCK IZZAT?
IT'S HOLDEN CARVER... I'VE BEEN TRYING TO FIND YOU FOR DAYS...
YOU'RE STILL BREATHING, SO I ASSUME YOU CHANGED YOUR MIND ABOUT TAKING A RUN AT THE BIG BOSS...
BUT LISTEN, HAVE YOU HAD ANY LUCK WITH YOUR FRIENDS IN HIGH PLACES? CAUSE I COULD REALLY USE SOME--
THINK Y'GOT ME CONFUSED WITH SOMEONE... I DUNNO YOU, MAN...

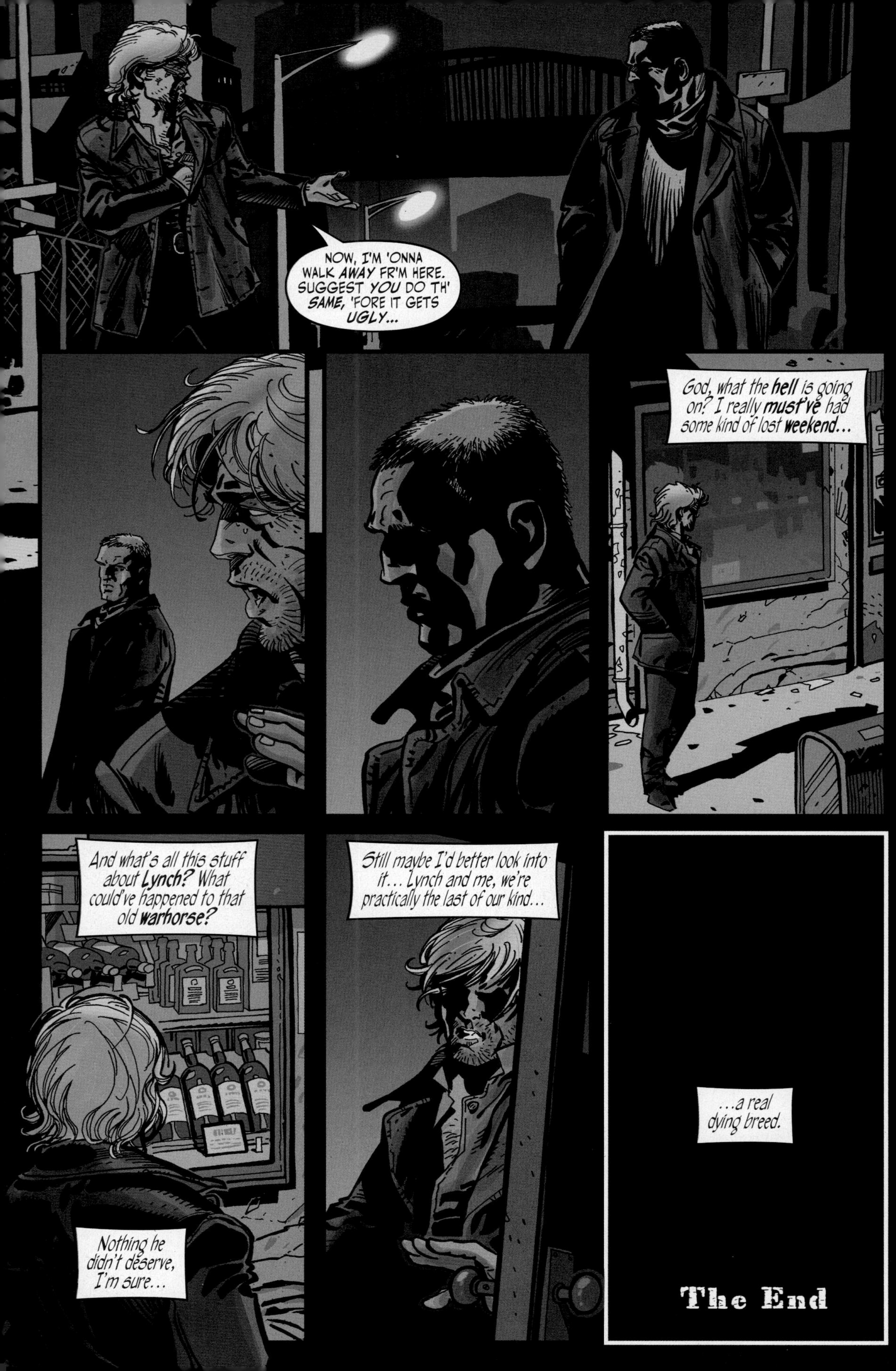
NOW, I'M 'ONNA WALK AWAY FR'M HERE. SUGGEST YOU DO TH' SAME, 'FORE IT GETS UGLY...
God, what the hell is going on? I really must've had some kind of lost weekend...
And what's all this stuff about Lynch? What could've happened to that old warhorse?
Nothing he didn't deserve, I'm sure...
Still maybe I'd better look into it... Lynch and me, we're practically the last of our kind...
...a real dying breed.
The End

AFTERWORD BY ED BRUBAKER

A violent little Möbius strip is what POINT BLANK was always intended to be. And I don't mean Moebius the cartoonist, but the thing he named himself after—a story that has no ending, that loops endlessly back onto itself. I always liked stories like that, when they were done well, and that's why the end of our story has Cole wondering if he should look into what happened to Lynch. Who knows how many times he'll go through the exact same experience? How many times will Tao mindfuck him? It could go on forever. Writers are at their best when they're being mean to their characters, I find.

There are a few things of note about the experience of creating this project. It went through many evolutions, for one thing, and it started with a phone call from Scott Dunbier one day asking me if I had any interest in writing a murder mystery that took place in the WildStorm Universe. I did, of course, because given my druthers, I'd almost always rather write a murder mystery. Of course, Lynch doesn't actually die, though. That was Jim Lee's idea. After thinking about it for a while, he just couldn't let us kill the old bastard, and thank god he didn't, because he's gone on to become one of my favorite characters to write, even though he's been in a coma for over a year now.

Another thing of note is the villain of our piece, TAO. Scott wanted me to use TAO, created by Alan Moore during his run on WildCATs, because Scott thought he was a great character that had never been utilized to his full potential after Alan left that book. I am a huge Alan Moore fan, and the opportunity to write characters he created was a thrill.

And inspired by the inclusion of TAO, and once the book became Mature Readers, things really opened up for me. I found myself asking what Mature Readers superhero comics should be. As you can see, I decided they should be really complicated. They should demand the reader's attention more than the average comic. They should assume intelligence on the part of the Mature Reader. Of course, assuming intelligence is not usually that commercial of a formula, though, is it? Still, I wanted a book that had the flavor of things like Watchmen or The Limey. I wanted scenes that cut quickly into other scenes, where the reader had to look back. I wanted a puzzle whose pieces had to be forced together.

Some readers got it immediately, and some did not. I think it benefits from being under one cover, though—I think the story works better, and it was really meant to be read in one sitting, so while you may have had to flip back, you didn't have to dig through last month's pile of comics and reread the past issue to make sense of it all. Also, I was trying to write an espionage story, where characters appeared and disappeared and all you needed to know about them was what was given to you on the page. It's obvious that Slayton and Cole have a history, and that Savant and Cole have more history, but we don't need to know what it is, more than what we see. The problem is that comics readers have a bizarre desire to know everything about any character if they've ever appeared elsewhere. And since part of this story was a tour of the WildStorm Universe, some readers felt compelled to know more than they needed to. But I'm telling you right now: everything you need to know is right here in this book.

When we were talking about it later, Scott pointed out that if Watchmen had actually featured the Charlton Comics characters instead of Alan Moore's and Dave Gibbons' new creations, a lot of readers would have complained that they couldn't understand the story because they didn't know enough about Charlton continuity. I think he might be right.

In any case, I had a lot of fun with this book. Cole Cash is a great noir character, and I was glad to have the chance to add to his guilty conscience, even if it's just on a subconscious level so far. And I had a great time working with Colin Wilson, who is a legend in the UK and Europe, but just getting known over here in the US. I learned early on that Colin, much like his friend Dave Gibbons, would draw anything you wrote in the panel description. That poor bastard. I ran him ragged after that.

And of course, after all the changes the project went through, from being a murder story, to an almost murder story, from a general audience book to a Mature Readers book, one day Scott called me up and asked if I had any ideas for an ongoing book to sort of spin out of POINT BLANK. I had none, but then thinking about Lynch in a coma, I suddenly came up with one, and the project changed one last time. Now Lynch's nebulous missions with Cole had more purpose. He had a deep-cover operative out there in the cold, and he was trying to bring him in.

So, what happens to a deep-cover operative when the only person who knows he's not a bad guy is in a coma ? That's what my current book with artist Sean Phillips— SLEEPER—is about. It's another gritty noir spy story with super-powered over-tones, except this time we focus on the villain's side of the story. If you enjoyed POINT BLANK, you'll want to check out SLEEPER: OUT IN THE COLD which is coming out hot on the heels of this collection.

ED BRUBAKER
2003

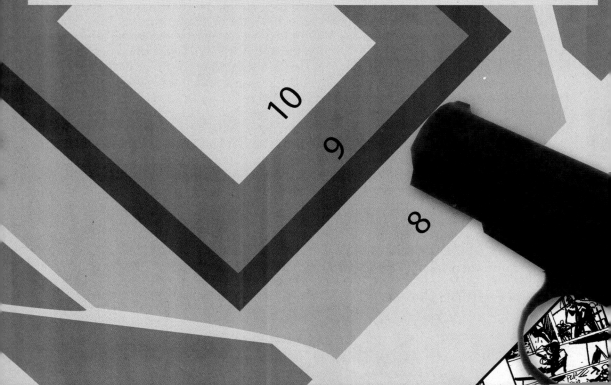

SKETCH PAGES BY
COLIN WILSON

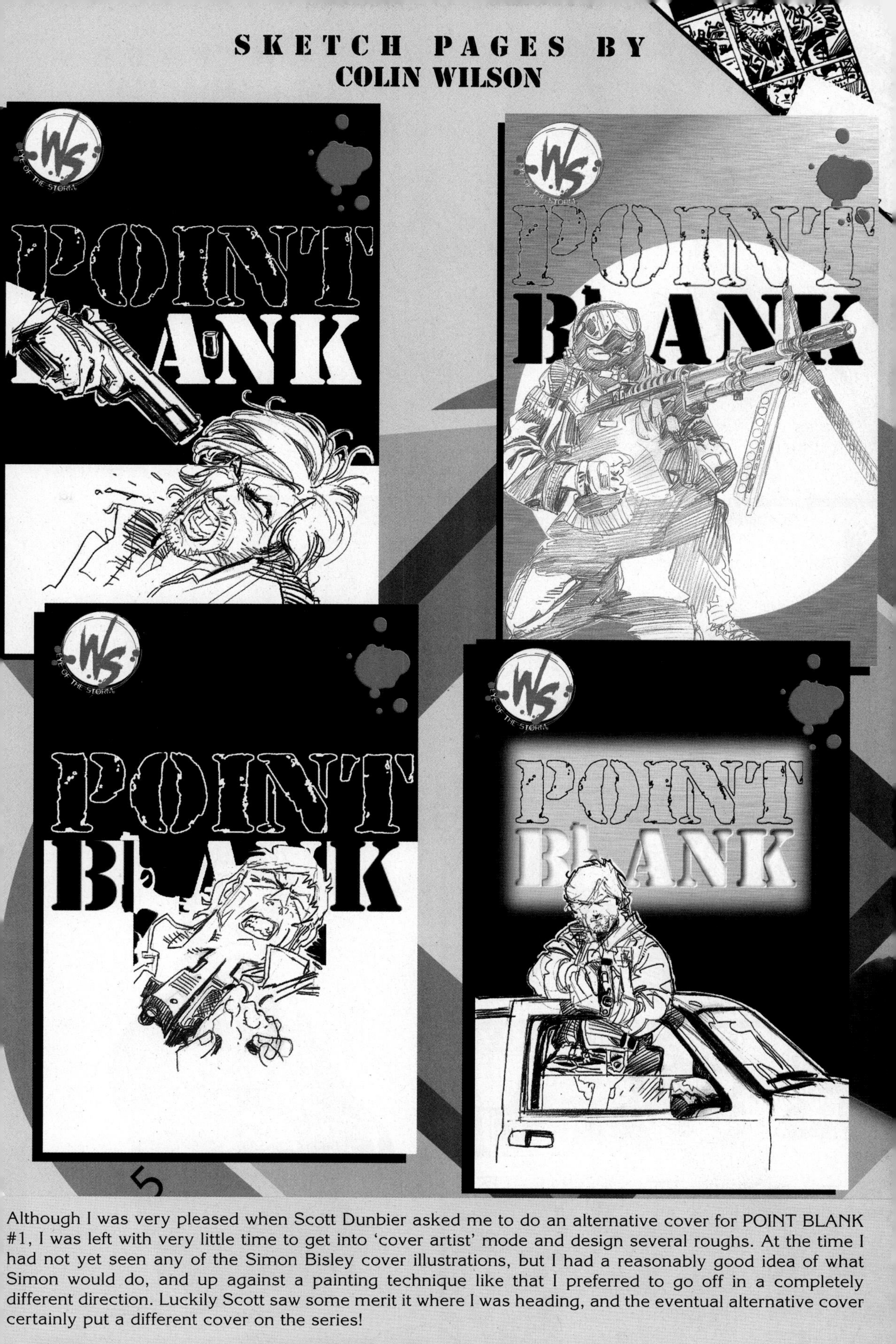
EYE OF THE STORM
POINT BLANK
EYE OF THE STORM
POINT BLANK
EYE OF THE STORM
POINT BLANK
EYE OF THE STORM
POINT BLANK

Although I was very pleased when Scott Dunbier asked me to do an alternative cover for POINT BLANK #1, I was left with very little time to get into 'cover artist' mode and design several roughs. At the time I had not yet seen any of the Simon Bisley cover illustrations, but I had a reasonably good idea of what Simon would do, and up against a painting technique like that I preferred to go off in a completely different direction. Luckily Scott saw some merit it where I was heading, and the eventual alternative cover certainly put a different cover on the series!

SKETCH PAGES
INITIAL CHARACTER SKETCHES/PENCILS

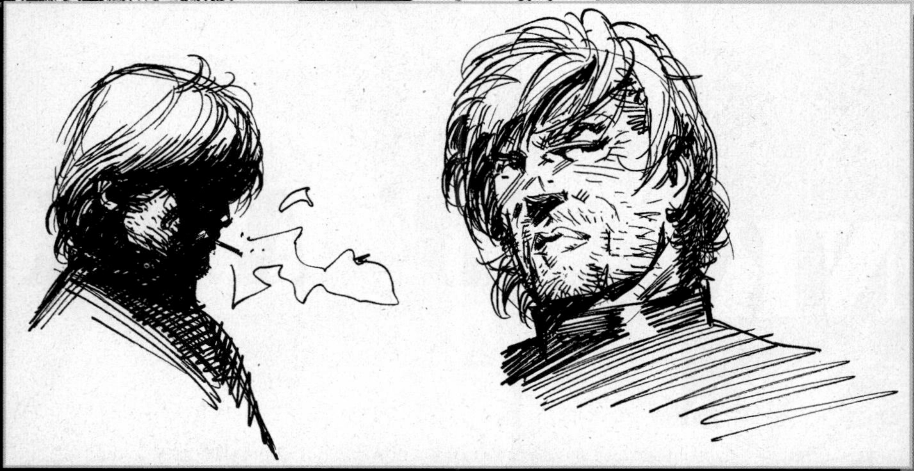

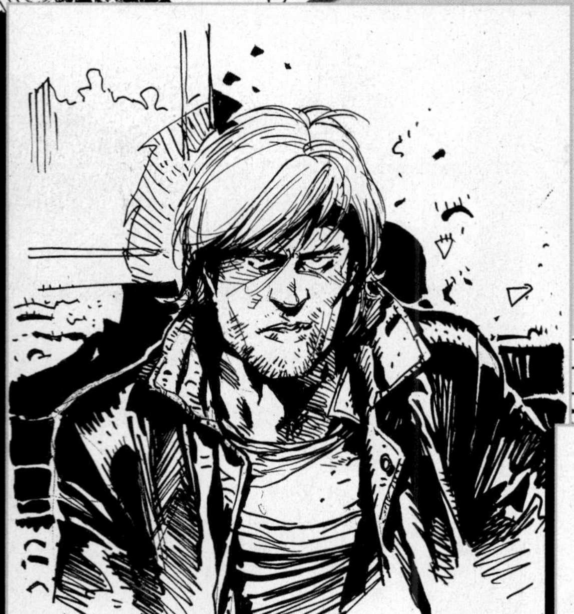
COLE

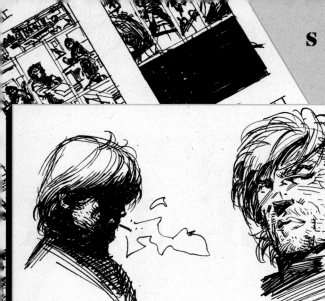

When WildStorm initially contacted me about working with Ed on POINT BLANK, I was on holiday with my family in France. I grabbed a bunch of WildC.A.T.s comics to study all the history I could find of the two main PB characters, and these were some of the first sample drawings I produced.

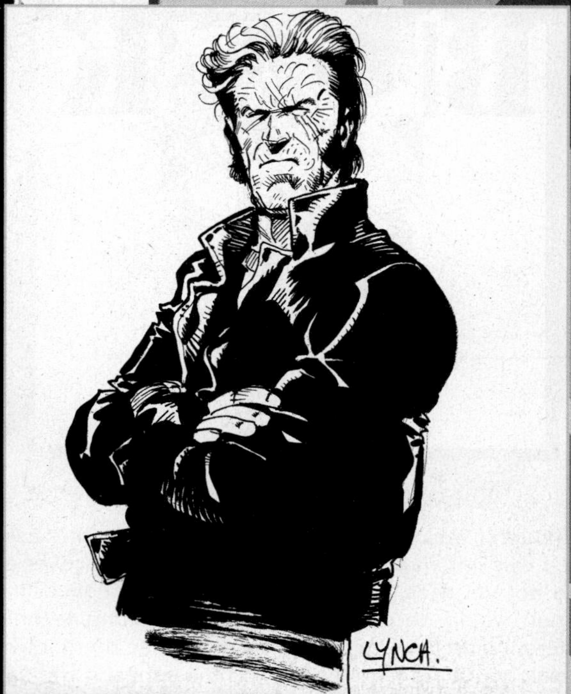
LYNCH.

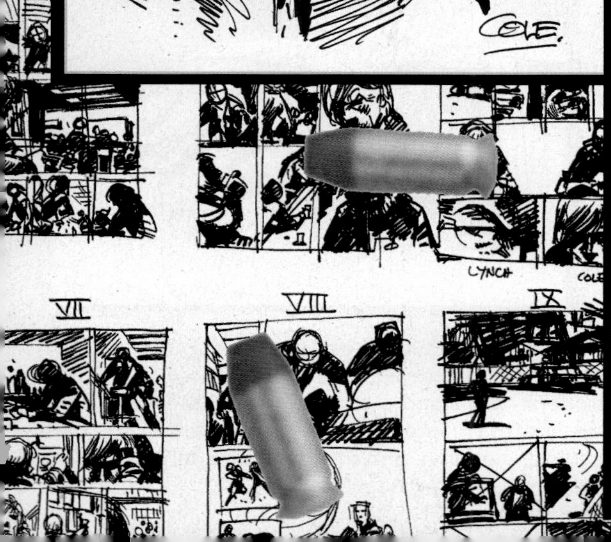
LYNCH
COLE
VII
VIII
IX

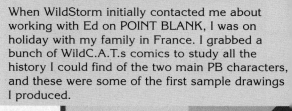

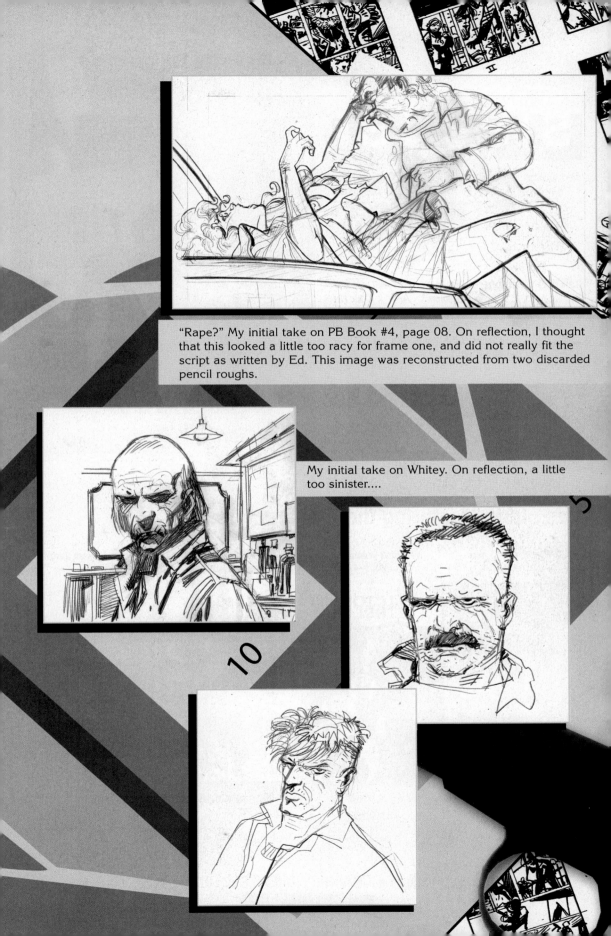

"Rape?" My initial take on PB Book #4, page 08. On reflection, I thought that this looked a little too racy for frame one, and did not really fit the script as written by Ed. This image was reconstructed from two discarded pencil roughs.

My initial take on Whitey. On reflection, a little too sinister....

10

5

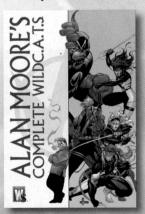